HOMEWORK HELPERS

Essays & Term Papers

By

Michelle McLean

CAREER
PRESS
Pompton Plains, NJ

HOMEWORK HELPERS: ESSAYS & TERM PAPERS
EDITED BY DIANA GHAZZAWI
TYPESET BY EILEEN MUNSON
Cover design by Lucia Rossman/Digi Dog Design
Printed in the U.S.A.

To order this title, please call toll-free 1-800-CAREER-1 (NJ and Canada: 201-848-0310) to order using VISA or MasterCard, or for further information on books from Career Press.

The Career Press, Inc.
220 West Parkway, Unit 12
Pompton Plains, NJ 07444
www.careerpress.com

Library of Congress Cataloging-in-Publication Data
McLean, Michelle (Michelle Marquis)
    Homework helpers : essays & term papers / by Michelle McLean.
        p. cm.
    Includes bibliographical references and index.
    ISBN 978-1-60163-140-4 -- ISBN 978-1-60163-687-4 (ebook)
        1. English language--Composition and exercises--Study and teaching. 2. Report writing--Study and teaching. 3. Essay--Authorship. 4. Homework. I. Title.
LB1576.M3985 2011
428.0071--dc22

                                                                        2010043709

For Shaun and Jeanette,
who were the first to ask me for help.
And for Mom and Dad,
who have always been
my loudest cheerleaders.

Acknowledgments

My heartfelt thanks go out to everyone who has made this book possible.

Krista Goering, my wonderful agent—it is a true pleasure to work with you.

Adam Schwartz, Michael Pye, and everyone at Career Press, for all their help and support. A special thanks to Kirsten Dalley and Diana Ghazzawi, for all your hard work in making this book the best it can be. I greatly appreciate all that you've done.

Christine Fonseca, author of *Emotional Intensity in Gifted Students*—you are the best critique partner and truest friend anyone could ask for. I don't know what I'd do without you. Thank you for everything.

Toni Kerr, Bethany Wiggins, Bonny Anderson, Cole Gibsen, Elana Johnson, and Kristal Shaff for always being there with your help and support. My life has been brighter with the six of you to light my days, and I thank my lucky stars for each and every one of you.

Patrick McDonald and the rest of my Querytracker.net family—this journey would never have happened without you. A special thank you to Carolyn Kaufman, for convincing me to send this book out into the world.

And last, but certainly never least, to Tom, my children, and the rest of my sweet family, for all their love and support.

Contents

Contents

Contents

Contents

Few tasks in our educational and post-educational careers can be as daunting and overwhelming as a writing assignment. Research papers and the assorted forms of essays often seem simple enough when discussed in a classroom or writing forum, but when faced with a blank page, many people simply don't know where to begin...or how to reach the conclusion.

In my experience, someone who is already frustrated will quickly become more so and give up altogether when presented with pages of formal, in-depth, textbook-like material. The last thing any confused student or writer wants to do is wade through hundreds of pages of technical material, trying to figure out how to do what he or she needs to do, especially when that material only serves to add to his or her stress.

Textbooks in particular tend to be long-winded and boring. The information is presented in such a complex way that, though it is accurate, it is too difficult for many students and beginning writers to follow. I've often wondered why someone didn't just write an easy, no-nonsense guide that told you exactly what you needed to do—and used examples. (I love examples! You could tell me how to do something a hundred times, and I'll just look at you like a cross-eyed monkey. But *show* me how to do it, and I can understand.)

I searched the bookstores for a guidebook that would teach students and writers how write essays, one that would explain the rules without using fancy language and hard-to-understand terms. And I couldn't find one. There were some that were okay. But they were either a little (or a lot) too technical or just plain boring. There was only one thing to do: I wrote my own book.

My goal in writing *Homework Helpers: Essays & Term Papers* was to give the confused and frustrated masses a quick, easy-to-read, narrative guide with simple, step-by-step processes and fun examples to follow. This book presents tips, steps, and information on research papers and several different types of essays, including the SAT essay, in a narrative manner simple enough for a junior high student to understand, yet thorough enough to assist a graduate student. It allows non-student users, such as freelance writers or bloggers, the opportunity to have thorough instruction without stepping foot in a language arts class. Additionally, *Homework Helpers: Essays & Term Papers* is written in a format that enables readers to quickly skim for the information they need without bogging them down in unnecessary pages of confusing material.

Let's face it, you're going to have to tackle writing assignments whether you want to or not. But there is no rule that says it has to be a miserable experience. Writing *can* be fun. I promise!

1

Before You Write

1
Before You Write

Lesson 1-1: Choosing a Topic

Before you can begin to write an essay or paper, you need something to write about. You will most likely be assigned a topic one of three ways:

1. Your teacher will give you a specific topic.
2. Your teacher will give you a list of topics from which to chose, or let you chose a topic within a set of guidelines.
3. You will be given the freedom to choose any topic you want.

No matter which of these is true for you, you will always have some choice in the topic of your paper. What do I mean by that? Well, regardless of your subject matter, you will need to find a certain aspect of that topic to *focus* on. Otherwise, you'd end up with a book instead of an essay.

Brainstorm

In most classes, your teacher will assign you a list of topics or let you choose a topic within a set of guidelines. Say, for example, you are reading *Romeo and Juliet* in your English class. You are asked to write about any topic that is related to the play. With such a rich text, it is impossible to discuss every idea, character, theme, or storyline presented in the play, so you must narrow your focus to just one of them. This isn't as hard as it might sound, even if you hate your subject. You just need to find something about the play that interests you. Do you like action and blood and danger? You could focus your paper on the conflicts between the two families and the numerous fights that erupt between them, or the deaths that occur as a result. Do you like romance or forbidden love? Focus your paper on the relationship between Romeo and Juliet. Do you like nature? Focus your paper on the plant imagery in the play and what it might symbolize. Politics? Focus on the political undertones in the play.

Maybe you need to write an essay on Napoleon Bonaparte for your history class. Find something about Napoleon that interests you. You can focus on his vast military campaigns, personal life, fashion sense, love life, political prowess, residences, or pets. How did his choice of clothing or favorite breed of dog influence French culture? How did France fare under his leadership? Why was his hand always shoved inside his vest?

Find something about your topic that won't bore you to tears and make that your focus.

Lesson 1-2: Make a List

Now, take your topic and make a list of everything you can think of that relates to that topic. You can include information you know, as well as information you want to find out. Let's say you have to write an essay on a country of your choice for your geography class. You chose Guatemala. Here is what your list may look like:

- ▶   It's in South America.
- ▶   Spanish is spoken there.
- ▶   It is mountainous.
- ▶   Climate?
- ▶   Tourist attractions?
- ▶   Economy?

▶ Government?

▶ Population?

This gives you a starting-off point. Instead of focusing on that five page essay or ten page paper, all you are focusing on is a simple list of items that you might want to discuss.

Lesson 1-3: Make Notes

Once you have a few items to look up, it's time to start researching. You'll need to make notes of the information you find. The better your notes, the easier it will be when it comes time to write. Gather a few sources (see Chapter 14 for tips on researching). When you find something that looks promising, you'll need to make a note of it.

You can write notes a few different ways, but using index cards seems to be the easiest. They are a very simple way to keep track of your info. However, if you don't want to use these, you can find your own way to keep track of your notes. Write them in a notebook, type them up in a document, or put them in a spreadsheet—whatever works for you. For now, we'll just assume that you are going to go the index-card route.

Other than actually writing the paper, this step will require the most work, but it can still be relatively painless. Grab one of the sources you chose, flip to the page or article where your information is located, and read. If it seems like something you can use, make a note on your index card. If you want the full quote, make sure you copy it exactly, with quotation marks, so you know it is a direct quote. If you just want the information but can put it in your own words, then paraphrase it. This is usually best, but you will still need to cite the source you found the information in, so the next step is *crucial*.

Only put one quote or paraphrase per card, and be sure to note the source! Copy exactly the source title, author, publisher, publication year, and page number the information was found on, and anything else you will need for your bibliography or works cited page. You do not want to accidentally plagiarize your material. Unless the information included in your paper is directly from your mind and no other, you need to cite your source, so be sure to get this information down. Writing down the source information also helps if you need to go back to that source for any reason, so you're not at a loss as to where it came from.

In addition to the actual information you will use for your paper and the source's information, you should make a note of what *kind* of information the card is listing. It is helpful if you have a general idea of the main points you'd like to discuss in your paper. If your paper about peanut butter will discuss the history of the food, techniques for making it, and its place in American culture, you'll want to make a note on the index card of which category the information falls under. Say you find a really good passage about how to make chunky peanut butter. On the card, paraphrase or quote the info, then note that this card will fall under the TECHNIQUES section of your paper.

So, each card should have the following information:

▶ Source title, author, publisher, publisher location, publication date, and page number (and URL and date accessed for online sources).

▶ Quoted or paraphrased information.

▶ Category or section in which the information belongs.

Peanut Butter: A History

by Thomas Jelly, Nutty Books, Inc. New York City, 2004, page 154.

"Hundreds of years ago, the Aztec mashed peanuts into paste similar to peanut butter."

Category: History of Peanut Butter

Lesson 1-4: Your Thesis Statement

A thesis statement is basically a sentence that will define the argument of your paper; it's the particular point you are trying to prove. It should make a specific claim that the rest of your paper will support. It tells your reader what your paper is about and, often, why she should care.

Your thesis statement should appear in the introduction to your essay or paper. That doesn't mean you have to come up with your thesis before you do any other work on the paper. In fact, before you can write your thesis statement, you need to have an idea of what your paper will discuss. For that, you first need to do a little research and get your information organized.

So don't worry if you aren't sure what your thesis statement will be right off the bat. As long as you know what the focus of your paper will be, you can start the preliminaries of researching and outlining, and perfect your thesis statement once you have all your information ready to go.

When crafting your thesis statement, there are a few questions you can ask yourself: who, what, when, where, why, how, and who cares? Though a couple of these may not be relevant for every topic, it's good to run through the list each time you write an essay. Be specific in answering them. Doing so will help you focus your ideas and shape your thesis.

Say you want to write a paper on why the local coffee shop should offer decaffeinated coffee. Ask:

- ▶ Who? Local coffee shop.
- ▶ What? Selling decaffeinated coffee.
- ▶ When? Not relevant.
- ▶ Where? The coffee shop.
- ▶ Why? It will increase sales.
- ▶ How? Not relevant.
- ▶ Who cares? Those who love coffee but not the caffeine it contains, and the owner, who would make a greater profit.

▶　Based on these answers, your thesis would be "Offering decaffeinated coffee at the local coffee shop would increase sales, consumer satisfaction, and the owner's profits."

Lesson 1-5: Make an Outline

Have you ever taken your Halloween candy and made an inventory of what you have? Once you've poured out your bag, you put all the chocolate items in one pile, all the gum in another pile, all the lollipops in another pile, and all the inedible items (like dimes and quarters) in another pile? Then maybe you broke those piles down even further. You grabbed the chocolate pile and broke them down into piles of plain chocolate (like Hershey's bars), candied chocolate (like M&M's), and candy bars (like Snickers). Well, this is basically what you are doing when you make an outline. You are taking your topic and breaking it down into smaller categories. Only instead of candy, you are categorizing the information that will go in your paper.

Start with your topic and break that into three main categories:

▶　Introduction.

▶　Body.

▶　Conclusion.

Then take each of those categories and break them down into subcategories:

▶　What goes in the introduction? Opening statements, thesis, summary points.

▶　What goes in the body? Main arguments, evidence, and outside sources.

▶　What goes in the conclusion? Restatement of thesis and main points.

Each category and subcategory is given a special number. The main categories are numbered with Roman numerals (I, II, III). The next subcategory is labeled with a capital letter (A, B, C), the subcategory after that with an Arabic number (1, 2, 3), and the category after that with a lowercase letter (a, b, c). The pattern repeats until all your information has been entered:

I. Main category (Introduction)

    A. Subcategory (Opening statements)

        1. Subcategory (Opening statement #1)

        2. Subcategory (Opening statement #2)

    B. Subcategory (Thesis statement)

    C. Subcategory (Summary of points that will be discussed)

II. Main category (Body)

    A. Subcategory (Point 1)

        1. Subcategory (Explanation)

           a. Subcategory (quotation)

    B. Subcategory (Point 2…and so on)

III. Main category (Conclusion)

As you can see, having your information on note cards will really be useful. You'll be able to take the information on those cards and plug them right into an outline. To do so, you'll want to:

1. Organize your cards into their categories. Many people do this as they go, either color-coding or keeping their cards in an index card file under the separate categories. As long as you've remembered to mark each card with the category it belongs to, this task should be reasonably painless.

2. Decide whether or not you will use each card (because you will probably, hopefully, have more information than you need) and put it with the others in that category (if you haven't previously done so). Once you have each card where it belongs, go through the cards and put them in the order in which you want to use them. When this has been decided, it's a good idea to number them so if you drop them, you can quickly put them back in order.

Say you've got a nice stack of note cards for the first section of your paper on the history of peanut butter. Go through them. What do you want to discuss first? Maybe you've got a card on how peanut butter became popular in the United States, one on what country peanut butter originated in, one on the first person to make peanut butter, and one with a quote from the first president to serve peanut butter in the White House. Organize them and number them in the order you want:

4 Quote from the first president to serve peanut butter in the White House.

3 How peanut butter became popular in the United States.

2 The first person to make peanut butter.

1 The country in which peanut butter originated.

Once you have all your cards organized, making a detailed, final outline is easy. Just go through the ordered cards and write the information down. Remember: All information that does not come directly from you must be cited. The quotes and paraphrases that you include should be used as evidence to support your own knowledge and opinions. So, your outline should now look like the one that follows, with each entry representing a note card:

I. Introduction
    A. Peanut butter has a rich and full history, there are several techniques for making this food, it is deeply rooted in American culture, and there are many interesting and popular recipes that include peanut butter as an ingredient.
    B. Thesis: Peanut butter, with its unique background and soaring popularity, is a food that is both common and yet unusual in its history and cultural significance.

II. History (Peanut butter has an interesting history....)
    A. Country of origin (Peanut butter was first made in....)
        1. Interesting fact #1 (with citation)
        2. Interesting fact #2 (with citation)
    B. First person to make peanut butter (Though peanuts have been eaten since ### BC, it wasn't until Mr. Smartypants tripped and pulverized his peanuts that modern peanut butter first made an appearance.)
        1. Quote from reliable source
        2. Interesting fact
    C. How peanut butter became popular in the United States. (Peanut butter was eaten by a few for some years, but didn't become popular throughout the United States until ####.)

1. Interesting fact #1 (with citation)
2. Interesting fact #2 (with citation)

D. Peanut butter in the White House (Though we wouldn't normally consider peanut butter to be found on the president's table....)
   1. Interesting fact #1 (with citation)
   2. Quote from President So-and-So

III. Techniques
   A. Making chunky peanut butter (Making chunky peanut butter is a little easier than making creamy.)
      1. Process detail #1
      2. Process detail #2
   B. Making creamy peanut butter (This process takes more time because.....)
      1. Process detail #1
      2. Process detail #2

IV. Popularity of peanut butter (Peanut butter is enjoyed throughout the United States....)
   A. How much peanut butter is consumed in the United States each year
      1. Percentage of the population that eats it
      2. Amount of peanut butter sales
   B. State it is most popular in (While the entire country consumes # pounds of peanut butter a year, there is one area of the United States that eats more than its fair share....)

V. Interesting recipes
   A. Number of recipes that use peanut butter
   B. Unusual recipes (Everyone knows about peanut butter and jelly sandwiches and peanut butter cookies, but there are a few recipes that are a little more unusual....)
      1. Example 1
      2. Example 2

VI. Conclusion
   A. Restate thesis
   B. Summarize arguments
   C. Strong closing statement

1

Before You Write

After you've made an outline, the hardest part of your job is done. The outline will make up most of your rough draft. All you need to do is write it in an essay format, adding a few sentences and explanations that connect or transition between your ideas. Then, proofread that rough draft and fix whatever errors you've made, and your paper is finished!

> For every type of essay or paper in this book, I'm going to tell you to do the same three things:
>
> ▶ Make a list.
> ▶ Make notes.
> ▶ Make an outline.
>
> Why? Because they take a huge, overwhelming project and break it down into small, manageable pieces. These three steps also help you to keep your ideas—and paper—well organized.

Exercise 1-1

Answer the following questions about getting started. (*Answers on page 309.*)

1. What should you record on a note card?

    _____

    _____

    _____

2. What is a thesis statement?

    _____

    _____

    _____

3. What are the three things you should do when writing any essay or paper?

    _____

    _____

    _____

2

Basic Essay

Lesson 2-1: What Is It?

The basic essay is the foundation for all other essays and papers. Luckily, it is fairly easy to learn. It consists of an introduction, which establishes your thesis and topic; the body, in which you will prove your point through well-thought-out ideas and well-researched evidence; and a conclusion, which sums up your arguments.

Lesson 2-2: Getting Started
Step 1: Choose a Topic

The first thing you need to do is choose a topic. Be sure to choose a topic that gives you plenty of information to discuss. Depending on your assignment, you might need outside sources to back up your statements, or it may be a purely opinion-based essay in which you discuss something with your own knowledge and views as arguments. Let's say you decide to write an essay on the history of sitcoms.

Step 2: Make a List

After you choose your topic, you'll need to decide what you want to include in your essay. Make a list of items you may want to discuss in

2 Basic Essay

your essay. If sitcoms are your main topic, what do you want to say about them? For a short, very basic essay, you might only need an introduction, three or four paragraphs discussing the main idea, and a conclusion. For a more in-depth or longer essay, you could really get into the subject, discussing how sitcoms got started, looking at sitcoms over the decades, and perhaps even spotlighting a few specific examples. In either case, you need to think of what information you want to include in your essay.

Brainstorm for a few minutes and write down everything you know (and want to know) about sitcoms. Your list might look something like this:

- What year did they start?
- Definition of sitcom.
- Recorded in front of an audience.
- Recorded in a studio.
- Average length of a sitcom?
- Radio and television sitcoms.
- Sitcoms in different countries.
- Award-winning sitcoms.
- What topics do sitcoms address?

Step 3: Research and Make Notes

Once you have your list, go through it and organize it a bit. Organize your ideas into a few main categories. Then decide which items you'd like to discuss in your essay. So, for our essay, our brainstorm items fall into a few main categories:

- The history of the sitcom.
- Characteristics of the sitcom.
- Examples of sitcoms.

This gives us a great starting place for research. As you gather information and note it down on your note cards, you can begin to form a thesis. The thesis of our sitcom essay is "Sitcoms have grown from obscurity to the most popular form of television programming."

Lesson 2-3: Elements of the Essay

The Introduction

The first part of your essay is the introduction. This section introduces your topic and your thesis. You can briefly state the ideas you will be discussing in the essay. It is also a good idea to start out with a sentence or two giving a little background on your topic, or with a question that will be answered in your essay. So, the basic outline for your introduction will look something like this:

> I. Introduction
>   A. Introductory statements and/or question
>   B. Thesis statement
>   C. Main ideas

The Body

The next section of the essay will contain all of your information and arguments. Get out your notes and plug your information into the outline. This portion of the basic outline for our sitcom essay will look something like this:

> II. Body
>   A. Characteristics
>   B. History
>   C. Examples

The Conclusion

Once you've presented all your information, you will need to conclude your essay. The conclusion typically contains a restatement of your thesis and a summary of the arguments you presented in the essay. Phrases such as "In conclusion," or "As you can see," are good, basic opening lines for your concluding paragraph. The basic outline for this section of the essay could look like this:

> III. Conclusion
>   A. Restate thesis
>   B. Summarize arguments

Basic Essay   2

Lesson 2-4: Putting It Together

Once you have all your information plugged into a detailed outline, all you'll need to do is put the ideas on paper. Just follow your outline straight through, adding a few transitional sentences (sentences that connect one thought to another, generally used between paragraphs to help your ideas flow smoothly from one to the next) to fill out your paragraphs, and you have a complete essay. You can see how a solid essay can take shape from this detailed outline:

I.   Introduction
    A. Introductory statement:
        There are many forms of television programming available today.
    B. Thesis statement:
        Sitcoms have grown from obscurity to the most popular form of television programming.
    C. Main Ideas
        1. Main characteristics
        2. An interesting history
        3. Examples of popular sitcoms from around the world

II. History
    A. Began as radio programming in 1926
    B. Sitcoms in the 1940s and '50s
    C. Sitcoms in the '60s
    D. Sitcoms in the '70s
    E. Sitcoms in the '80s
    F. Sitcoms in the '90s
    G. Present-day sitcoms

III. Main characteristics
    A. Definition of a sitcom
    B. Types of topics illustrated
    C. Live audience versus studio recording
    D. Average length, programming times, and other distinctive traits

IV. Examples of popular sitcoms around the world
    A. Most popular American sitcoms

B. Most popular British sitcoms

C. Other popular sitcoms

V. Conclusion

  A. Restate thesis:
    As you can see, the sitcom has undergone a unique and interesting transformation.

  B. Summarize arguments
    1. Sitcoms have many distinctive characteristics
    2. They have transformed from simple radio shows to the elaborate programs we see today.
    3. There are many wonderful examples of sitcoms worldwide.

Sample Essays

Look at the following essay that discusses how dinosaurs are classified according to their dict. This is a very simple essay that breaks dinosaurs into three categories: herbivores, carnivores, and omnivores. Each category is discussed in a paragraph, creating the basic five-paragraph essay.

Following is the detailed outline for the essay. Go through it, and then look at the rough draft to see how the essay falls into place. The parts of the essay are labeled in the rough draft with their corresponding numbers from the outline.

The Detailed Outline

I. Introduction

  A. Opening statements
    1. Dinosaurs lived on the Earth a long time ago.
    2. They looked different and lived in different places.
    3. They ate different things.

  B. Thesis: Dinosaurs are categorized into three different groups: herbivores, carnivores, and omnivores.

II. Herbivores

  A. Ate plants

  B. Teeth were flat and blunt.

C. Swallowed small stones for digestion

D. Believed to have lived in herds

E. Types of herbivores

    1. Brachiosaurus

    2. Argentinosaurus

    3. Diplodocus

III. Carnivores

A. Ate meat

B. Teeth were sharp and pointed.

C. Had claws and large jaws

D. Probably lived alone

E. Types of carnivores

    1. Tyrannosaurus Rex

    2. Velociraptor

    3. Allosaurus

IV. Omnivores

A. Ate both meat and plants

B. Some have teeth; some have a beak.

C. Much smaller than the other dinosaurs

D. Ate lizards, bugs, and plants

E. Types of omnivores

    1. Oviraptor

    2. Troodon

    3. Eoraptor

V. Conclusion

A. Restate thesis

B. Restate evidence

    1. Each type of dinosaur was built with the tools it needed.

    2. Carnivores had sharp claws and teeth.

    3. Herbivores had blunt teeth.

    4. Omnivores had characteristics of both carnivores and herbivores.

2 Basic Essay

Version 1: The Rough Draft

Dinosaur Diet

INTRODUCTION

(I A1) Dinosaurs were very large, lizard-like creatures that lived on the Earth millions of years ago. **(I A2)** They came in all shapes and sizes, and lived in all sorts of habitats. **(I A3)** Their diets consisted of a variety of foods. One of the ways dinosaurs can be classified is by the type of food they ate. **(I B)** Dinosaurs are categorized into three different groups: herbivores, carnivores, and omnivores.

BODY OF ESSAY

(II A) Herbivores are creatures that eat plants. **(II B)** Their teeth were flat teeth and also blunt so the plants and twigs and other vegetation they ate could be ground up. **(II C)** They swallowed small stones to help digest their food **(II D)** Many herbivore dinosaurs are believed to have lived in herds. **(II E1,2,3)** Brachiosaurus, argentinosaurus, and diplodocus were all herbivores.

(III A) Carnivores are creatures that eat meat. **(III B)** There teeth were sharp and pointed to help them tear into meat and bone. **(III C)** These dinosaurs usually had sharp claws and large jaws to help them catch pray. **(III D)** Carnivorous dinosaurs probably lived alone instead of with herds. **(III E1,2,3)** Tyrannosaurus rex, velociraptor, and allosaurus were all carnivores.

(IV A) Omnivores are creatures that eat both meat and plants. These creatures are a little more complex. **(IV B)** Some have sharp pointed teeth, and others have a toothless beak. **(IV C)** They are much smaller than the larger herbivore or carnivore dinosaurs. **(IV D)** Omnivores most likely ate lizards and other small reptiles, large insects, and small plants. **(IV E1,2,3)** Oviraptor, troodon, and eoraptor are thought to be omnivores.

CONCLUSION

(V A) As you can see, herbivores, carnivores, and omnivores all had very different diets. **(V B1)** Each type of dinosaur was built with the tools it needed too digest the food it ate. **(V B2)** Carnivores had sharp claws and teeth while plant eaters had more blunt teeth to chew leaves and trees. **(V B3)** Omnivores were a mix of the two.

2 Basic Essay

Resources

Igloo Books. *Dinosaurs*. Igloo Books Ltd.: Cottage Farm, Sywell, Northamptonshire, UK; 2009. Print.

Version 2: The Edited Draft

The second version of the essay is the edited copy of the rough draft. This version has comments and revision suggestions marked in red. When proofreading your essays, you want to look for technical mistakes, such as spelling and punctuation errors, incorrect grammar, missing words, and awkward sentence structures. You'll also want to look for areas where more extensive revision would be helpful. Maybe there is a statement that needs some additional information added, or a transition from one statement to another that could use a little beefing up. All of these things are part of the proofreading and editing process.

2 Basic Essay

Dinosaur Diet

Dinosaurs are very large, lizard-like creatures that lived on the Earth millions of years ago. They came in all shapes and sizes, and lived in all sorts of habitats. Their diets consisted of a variety of foods. One of the ways dinosaurs can be classified is by the type of food they ate. Dinosaurs are categorized into three different groups: herbivores, carnivores, and omnivores. *(The verb tense used must make logical sense. In this paper, both past and present tense are being used. Because dinosaurs are no longer alive, it makes sense to discuss them in the past tense. However, herbivores, carnivores, and omnivores still exist, so sentences that discuss these types of animals in general should be in the present tense.)*

Herbivores are creatures that eat plants. Their teeth were flat teeth and also blunt so the plants and twigs and other vegetation they ate could be ground up. *(This sentence is very wordy and a little awkward. Reword so it is more formal and understandable. Also, it's best to avoid ending sentences with prepositions when possible.)* They swallowed small stones to help digest their food *(Insert period)* Many herbivore dinosaurs are believed to have lived in herds. Brachiosaurus, argentinosaurus, and diplodocus were all herbivores. *(The names of the dinosaurs are proper nouns, so capitalize them.)*

Carnivores are creatures that eat meat. There *(should be "their")* teeth were sharp and pointed to help them tear into meat and bone. These dinosaurs usually had sharp claws and large jaws to help them catch pray *(should be "prey")*. Carnivorous dinosaurs probably lived alone instead of with herds. Tyrannosaurus rex, velociraptor, and allosaurus were all carnivores. *(Capitalize the dinosaur names.)*

Omnivores are creatures that eat both meat and plants. These creatures are a little more complex. Some have sharp *(insert comma)* pointed teeth, and others have a toothless beak. They are much smaller than the larger herbivore or carnivore dinosaurs. *(Redundant. You don't need to say they are "smaller than the larger" because one implies the other.)* Omnivores most likely ate lizards and other small reptiles, large insects, and small plants. Oviraptor, troodon, and eoraptor are thought to be omnivores. *(Again, watch the names!)*

As you can see, herbivores, carnivores, and omnivores all had very different diets. Each type of dinosaur was built with the tools it needed too *(should be to)* digest the food it ate. Carnivores had sharp claws and

2 Basic Essay

teeth while herbivoress had more blunt teeth to chew leaves and trees. Omnivores were a mix of the two. *(They aren't a "mix," but had characteristics of the other two.)*

Resources

Igloo Books. *Dinosaurs*. Igloo Books Ltd.: Cottage Farm, Sywell, Northamptonshire, UK; 2009. Print.

Version 3: The Final Draft

The third version of the essay is the final, revised copy so you can see how it has transformed from an outline, to a rough draft, to a polished essay ready to turn in.

Dinosaur Diet

Dinosaurs were very large, lizard-like creatures that lived on the Earth millions of years ago. They came in all shapes and sizes, and lived in all sorts of habitats. Their diets consisted of a variety of foods. Dinosaurs were herbivores, carnivores, or omnivores.

Herbivores are creatures that eat plants. Herbivorous dinosaurs generally had flat teeth, suitable for crushing plants and twigs. They swallowed small stones to help digest their food. Many believe herbivore dinosaurs lived in herds. The Brachiosaurus, Argentinosaurus, and Diplodocus were all herbivores.

Carnivores are creatures that eat meat. Carnivorous dinosaurs' teeth were sharp and pointed to help them tear into meat and bone. They usually had sharp claws and large jaws to help them catch prey. Carnivorous dinosaurs probably lived alone instead of in herds. Tyrannosaurus Rex, Velociraptor, and Allosaurus were all carnivores.

Omnivores are creatures that eat both meat and plants. Omnivorous dinosaurs were a little more complex. Some had sharp, pointed teeth, and others had a toothless beak. They were much smaller than the herbivorous or carnivorous dinosaurs. Omnivores most likely ate lizards and other small reptiles, large insects, and small plants. Oviraptor, Troodon, and Eoraptor are thought to have been omnivores.

As you can see, herbivorous, carnivorous, and omnivorous dinosaurs had very different diets. Each type of dinosaur was built with the tools it needed to digest the food it ate. Carnivores had sharp claws and teeth, while plant eaters had more blunt teeth to chew leaves and trees. Omnivores had characteristics of both herbivores and carnivores.

Resources

Igloo Books. *Dinosaurs*. Igloo Books Ltd.: Cottage Farm, Sywell, Northamptonshire, UK; 2009. Print.

2

Basic Essay

Exercise 2-1

Answer the following questions about the basic essay. (*Answers on page 309.*)

1. What are the three main components of a basic essay?

_____

_____

_____

_____

_____

_____

2. What should be included in the introduction?

_____

_____

_____

_____

_____

_____

3. What should be included in the conclusion?

_____

_____

_____

_____

_____

_____

2 Basic Essay

3

Argumentative/Persuasive Essay

Lesson 3-1: What Is It?

The argumentative essay does exactly what it says it does: it argues a specific point. This essay is also called a persuasive essay. The purpose of this type of essay is to convince your reader to agree with your point of view. For example, if your thesis is "Printed books are better than e-books," the body of your essay would focus on reasons to prove this point, backed up by solid sources and examples.

Part of writing an argumentative essay is presenting the opposing side's point of view and refuting it. For example, stating something like "There are those that would argue that large SUVs are better than small cars for such and such a reason. However, they are incorrect because of Reason One, Reason Two, and Reason Three."

You can convincingly argue for any side of any argument as long as you have valid points and facts to back up your arguments.

Lesson 3-2: Getting Started
Step 1: Choose a Topic

This may sound like a no-brainer, but you want to be sure to choose a topic for which you will be able to find information supporting both the pro and con positions of a topic. You might want to write on why vampires are better than wizards, but if you don't have enough hard, scholarly evidence to support your claims, it won't work. So pick something that will give you a lot of information to work with.

Step 2: Make a Pro and Con List

When brainstorming for a persuasive essay, you must think of reasons of why you are taking one side over another. Similarly, you must look at why a person would take the opposite position. Remember: Part of writing an argumentative essay involves presenting opposing ideas and refuting them.

You need to be sure you will have enough material to satisfy the length requirement of your assignment, so be sure to brainstorm enough ideas. You will probably need at least a paragraph or two for each argument. You also need to be sure you have enough evidence to support your arguments. Unfortunately, you can't just say "This is my opinion, and that is that." You must have solid, factual evidence to support your statements.

For our example, let's say you are going to write an essay arguing why printed books are better than e-books. First, brainstorm a pro and con list. It might look something like the list shown on this page.

Why Printed Books Are Better Than E-Books	
Pros **(Arguments for your position)**	**Cons** **(Arguments against your position)**
► Not all books come in e-form. ► E-readers are expensive. ► You don't need an Internet connection to read a printed book. ► E-readers can break and lose the book.	► E-books are cheaper. ► You can carry many books all on one reader. ► E-books are eco-friendly.

Now you have a starting point for your research.

Step 3: Research and Make Notes

Once you know what you need to look for, it's time to gather your evidence. Find at least one (two or more would be even better) solid, scholarly, citable sources for each of your arguments.

So, you could find facts such as:

▶ A university or national survey showing how many readers had access to the Internet or Websites that sold e-books.

▶ A quotation from an article on how vulnerable e-readers were to breaking, electronic bugs, or other problems that could erase stored information.

▶ A few statistics on how many printed books are available opposed to how many e-books are available.

▶ A price comparison for a few different stores on the price of printed versus e-books would be great to support the price argument for the con position.

You also need to know which opposing statements you will be using and find evidence to refute those arguments. For the opposing arguments we have listed, you could find:

▶ An article or national study on Americans' traveling habits.

▶ An advertisement on how many books an e-reader can store.

▶ An article on the ecological benefits of e-readers.

As you do your research, remember to record all your information and its sources.

Lesson 3-3: Elements of the Essay

There are four main components in this essay.

▶ **Thesis Statement**

A strong statement informing your readers of the position you will be taking is essential to an argumentative essay.

▶ **Supporting Arguments and Evidence**

Once you've stated your position, you need strong evidence to back up your case. For a longer and more complex assignment, you may need extensive evidence.

▶ **Opposing Arguments and Refuting Evidence**

Choose one or two statements that oppose the position you are taking, then state why these arguments are untrue or unreliable. Use outside sources to back up your reasoning. The purpose of this is to show you are aware of all sides of the argument and to further prove the strength of your position by explaining why the opposing side is wrong, or at least not as right as your side.

▶ **Conclusion**

Wrap it up by restating your thesis and giving a brief recap of the arguments you used to prove your point.

Lesson 3-4: Putting It Together

Once you have your information, arguments, and evidence ready, you just need to put it together. Let's take a look at the parts of the essay. I have listed them in outline form, the way they would be presented. Your outline would end up looking something like this:

I. Introduction
  A. Thesis: Evidence shows that printed books continue to be more popular than e-books.
  B. Summary of arguments: Printed books are not subject to an e-reader's issues, printed books are readily available anywhere, and they are affordable for everyone.

II. Body of Essay
  A. Supporting statement 1: Not all books come in e-form.
    1. Cite source of supporting statistics
  B. Supporting statement 2: E-readers can break and lose all the information/books stored on them.
    1. Cite article of supporting quote
  C. Supporting statement 3: Not everyone has the Internet or means to download e-books.
    1. Cite national survey supporting this statement

D. Opposing statement 1: E-books are cheaper.
1. Refute this statement (Some may argue that ebooks are cheaper, however, when the price of the e-readers is factored in, electronic books become unaffordable to many readers.)

III. Conclusion
A. Summarize arguments
B. Restate position

With a few convincing arguments, a little research, and some evidence to back up your statements, you've got yourself a nice, well-documented argumentative essay.

Sample Essays

Look at the following essay, which argues that primates are able to communicate with human beings. The essay cites the many experiments that have shown primates communicating through the use of American Sign Language, using the experiences of two particular chimps as supporting evidence. The essay also mentions the opposing side's argument that primates might mimic signs, but that doesn't mean they understand what they are doing. An example describing an instance with the chimp Washoe is used to refute the opposing argument. It concludes that primates do, indeed, communicate with humans. This essay cites its sources using MLA style.

Here is the detailed outline for the essay. Go through it, and then look at the rough draft to see how the essay falls into place. The parts of the essay are labeled in the rough draft with their corresponding numbers from the outline.

The Detailed Outline

I. Introduction
A. Opening statement: There's been a lot of debate on whether monkeys, etc. can communicate with humans.
B. Introduce supporting evidence: A lot of experiments have been done.

3 Argumentative / Persuasive Essay

    C.   Thesis: It's been proven through many experiments that primates can communicate with humans.

    D.   Introduce opposing argument: Many scientists don't believe primates know what they're doing.

II.   Supporting evidence 1

    A.   Griffin quote in Walker, page 356

    B.   Chimp learned 10 words, Walker, page 357

    C.   What scientists learned, Awareness quote, page 17

III. Supporting evidence 2

    A.   Washoe

    B.   Learned 150 signs

    C.   Similar to a 2-year-old

    D.   Quote from Ember, page 52

IV. Opposing Argument

    A.   Quote from Walker, page 356

    B.   Refuting evidence

        1.   Washoe using the word dirt, paraphrase from Ember page 63

V.   Conclusion

    A.   Recap evidence

    B.   Restate thesis

Version 1: The Rough Draft

Monkey See, Monkey Do

> INTRODUCTION

(**I A**) There's been a lot of debate as to whether or not monkeys, apes, etc. can really communicate with us. (**I B**) A lot experiments have been conducted to see if these animals, especially chimps, can learn to communicate with other species. (**I C**) It's been proven threw many experiments that primates can communicate with humans. (**I D**) While some scientists think the the monkeys and apes and other primates don't really know what there doing, they really do.

> BODY OF ESSAY

(**II A**) Donald R. Griffin relates one such experiment that involved a chimp that was born and raised in a human home "hearing English as well as seeing ASL gestures" (Walker 356). (**II B**) The chimp learned 10 words (spoon, foot, curtain, water, banana, shocker, raisin, nut, leaf, and pillow) and could fetch these objects if verbally told (Walker 357) (**II C**) From this, scientists learned that chimps can "learn to identify objects and pictures on hearing the names in spoken English"

(**III A**) One of the most well-known chimps is Washoe. Her trainers, Allen and Beatrice Gardener, taught her ASL. (**III B**) Washoe succeeded in learning 150 signs. (**III C**) While Washoe learned to communicate, the order that she organized her words and signs in very similar to a two-year-old's vocabulary. (**III D**) Once on an island with other chimps, Washoe saw some people across the water drinking iced tea.

> She kept signing, "Roger ride come gimme sweet eat please hurry hurry you come please gimme sweet you hurry you come ride Roger come give Washoe fruit drink hurry hurry fruit drink please." ...A plane flew over just then, and Washoe mentioned that, too. She signed, "You me ride in plane" (qtd in Ember 62).

(**IV A**) Scientists do not disagree "so much about whether chimpanzees learn to associate particular gestures with particular objects, and particular actions," but whether or not "they achieve the higher levels of mental organization" that mean they understand the "relationship between words" (Walker 356). However, there have been many primates that prove they understand the relationship between, and meaning of, the words they are using.

3 Argumentative / Persuasive Essay

(IV B) Some primates have shown the ability to learn words and to use them, in some cases, in ways that she was not taught. **(IV B1)** For instance, Washoe was taught the sign for dirty, to refer to waste products and other dirty things like soil. But she began to use it as an insult. Whenever her trainer, Roger Fouts, did something that Washoe didn't like, or refuse to give her something that she wanted, Washoe would sign "dirty Roger" (Ember 63).

CONCLUSION

(V A) Whether or not humans accept these results, the facts are there. The tests and experiments have almost all shown that monkeys and apes possess an intelligence that we had previously not thought possible. The primates involved haven't merely mimicked what their trainers do. They have actually communicated with their trainers and keepers, using a form of human language, sign language, as a way to describe how they feel and think. **(V B)** These animals are capable of communication with humans.

Works Cited

Bright, Michael. *Animal Language*. London: Cornell University Press, 1985. Print.

Ember, Carol R. and Melvin Ember. *Cultural Anthropology*. Englewood Cliffs, NJ: Prentice Hall, 1993. Print.

Griffin, Donald R. *Animal Thinking*. Cambridge, Mass: Harvard University Press, 1984. Print.

———. *The Question of Animal Awareness*. New York, Rockefeller University Press, 1976. Print.

Hoage, R.J. and Larry Goldman, ed. *Animal Intelligence*. Washington D.C.: Smithsonian Institution Press, 1986. Print.

Walker, Stephen F. *Animal Thought*. Boston: Routledge and K. Paul, 1983. Print.

Argumentative / Persuasive Essay 3

Version 2: The Edited Draft

The second version of the essay is the edited copy of the rough draft. This version has comments and revision suggestions marked in red. When proofreading your essays, you want to look for technical mistakes, such as spelling and punctuation errors, incorrect grammar, missing words, and awkward sentence structures. But you'll also want to look for areas where more extensive revision would be helpful. Maybe there is a statement that needs some additional information added, or a transition from one statement to another that could use a little beefing up. All of these things are part of the proofreading and editing process.

Monkey See, Monkey Do

There's *(Get rid of the contraction.)* been a lot of debate as to whether or not monkeys, apes, ~~etc.~~*(Don't use "etc.")* can really communicate with us. A lot *(Replace with "Many" to make it sound more formal.)* experiments have been conducted to see if these animals, especially chimps, can learn to communicate with other species. It's *(Get rid of contraction.)* been proven threw *(Change to "through.")* many experiments that primates can communicate with humans. While some scientists think the the *(Delete the second "the.")* monkeys and apes and other primates don't really know what there doing, they really do. *(This sentence is awkward, wordy, and confusing. The end makes it sound like the scientists don't know what they are doing when it is referring to the primates.)*

Donald R. Griffin *(Add a brief explanation about who this is.)* relates one such experiment that involved a chimp that was born and raised in a human home "hearing English as well as seeing ASL gestures" (Walker 356). The chimp learned 10 words (spoon, foot, curtain, water, banana, shocker, raisin, nut, leaf, and pillow) and could fetch these objects if verbally told (Walker 357) *(Because these quotes are from the same source, just a page apart, you can list the citation at the end of the second one, listing both page numbers.)* From this, scientists learned that chimps can "learn to identify objects and pictures on hearing the names in spoken English" *(citation?)*.

One of the most well-known chimps is Washoe. Her trainers, Allen and Beatrice Gardener, taught her ASL. Washoe succeeded in learning 150 signs. While Washoe learned to communicate, the order that she organized her words and signs in *(improper grammar—reword)* were *(Change "were" to "was" because "the order" is singular.)* very similar to a two-year-old's vocabulary. Once on an island with other chimps, Washoe saw some people across the water drinking iced tea.

> She kept signing, "Roger ride come gimme sweet eat please hurry hurry you come please gimme sweet you hurry you come ride Roger come give Washoe fruit drink hurry hurry fruit drink please." ...A plane flew over just then, and Washoe mentioned that, too. She signed, "You me ride in plane" (qtd in Ember 62).

Scientists do not disagree "so much about whether chimpanzees learn to associate particular gestures with particular objects, and particular actions," but whether or not "they achieve the higher levels of mental organization" that mean they understand the "relationship between words" (Walker 356). *(You could paraphrase this instead of using direct quotes.)* However, there have been many primates that prove they understand the relationship between, and meaning of, the words they are using.

Some primates have shown the ability to learn words and to use them, in some cases, in ways that she was not taught. For instance, Washoe was taught the sign for dirty, to refer to waste products and other dirty things like soil. But *(This is technically okay, but "however" would be better.)* she began to use it as an insult. Whenever her trainer, Roger Fouts, did something that Washoe didn't like, or refuse *(should be "refused")* to give her something that she wanted, Washoe would sign "dirty Roger" (Ember 63).

Whether or not humans accept these results, the facts are there. The tests and experiments have almost all shown *(wordy and weakens the argument—reword)* that monkeys and apes possess an intelligence that we *(Who is we? Maybe reword to make the statement more general.)* had previously not thought possible. The primates involved haven't merely mimicked what their trainers do. They have actually communicated with their trainers and keepers, using a form of human language, ~~sign language~~ *(This is technically okay, but not really necessary as we already know this is the language to which you are referring.)* as a way to describe how they feel and think. These animals are capable of communication with humans.

Works Cited

Bright, Michael. *Animal Language*. London: Cornell University Press, 1985. Print.

Ember, Carol R. and Melvin Ember. *Cultural Anthropology*. Englewood Cliffs, NJ: Prentice Hall, 1993. Print.

Griffin, Donald R. *Animal Thinking*. Cambridge, Mass: Harvard University Press, 1984. Print.

———. *The Question of Animal Awareness*. New York, Rockefeller University Press, 1976. Print.

Hoage, R.J. and Larry Goldman, ed. *Animal Intelligence*. Washington D.C.: Smithsonian Institution Press, 1986. Print.

Walker, Stephen F. *Animal Thought*. Boston: Routledge and K. Paul, 1983. Print.

Version 3: The Final Draft

The third version of the essay is the final, revised copy so you can see how it has transformed from an outline, to a rough draft, to a polished essay ready to turn in.

Monkey See, Monkey Do

There has been a lot of debate as to whether or not monkeys and apes can really communicate with us. Many experiments have been conducted to see if these animals, especially chimps, can learn to communicate with other species. It has been proven through many experiments that primates can communicate with humans. Though some scientists argue that the primates may not understand the signs they are using, the experiments prove otherwise.

Donald R. Griffin, an associate of the Museum of Comparative Zoology at Harvard and the creator of the field of cognitive ethology, relates one such experiment that involved a chimp that was born and raised in a human home "hearing English as well as seeing ASL gestures." The chimp learned 10 words (spoon, foot, curtain, water, banana, shocker, raisin, nut, leaf, and pillow) and could fetch these objects if verbally told (Walker 356–7). From this, scientists learned that chimps can "learn to identify objects and pictures on hearing the names in spoken English" (*Awareness* 17).

One of the most well known chimps is Washoe. Her trainers, Allen and Beatrice Gardener, taught her ASL. Washoe succeeded in learning 150 signs. While Washoe learned to communicate, the order in which she organized her words and signs were very similar to a two-year-old's vocabulary. Once on an island with other chimps, Washoe saw some people across the water drinking iced tea.

> She kept signing, "Roger ride come gimme sweet eat please hurry hurry you come please gimme sweet you hurry you come ride Roger come give Washoe fruit drink hurry hurry fruit drink please." …A plane flew over just then, and Washoe mentioned that, too. She signed, "You me ride in plane" (quoted in Ember 62).

Scientists do not disagree "so much about whether chimpanzees learn to associate particular gestures with particular objects, and particular actions," but whether or not "they achieve the higher levels of mental organization" that mean they understand the "relationship between words" (Walker 356). However, there have been many primates that prove they understand the relationship between, and meaning of, the words they are using.

Washoe, for instance, showed the ability to learn words and to use them, in some cases, in ways that she was not taught. For example,

3
Argumentative /
Persuasive Essay

Washoe was taught the sign for dirty, to refer to waste products and other dirty things like soil. However, she began to use it as an insult. Whenever her trainer, Roger Fouts, did something that Washoe didn't like, or refused to give her something that she wanted, Washoe would sign "dirty Roger" (Ember 63).

Whether or not humans accept these results, the facts are there. The tests and experiments have shown that monkeys and apes possess an intelligence that some researchers had previously not thought possible. The primates involved haven't merely mimicked what their trainers do. They have actually communicated with their trainers and keepers, using a form of human language, as a way to describe how they feel and think. These animals are capable of communication with humans.

Works Cited

Bright, Michael. *Animal Language*. London: Cornell University Press, 1985. Print.

Ember, Carol R. and Melvin Ember. *Cultural Anthropology*. Englewood Cliffs, NJ: Prentice Hall, 1993. Print.

Griffin, Donald R. *Animal Thinking*. Cambridge, Mass: Harvard University Press, 1984. Print.

———. *The Question of Animal Awareness*. New York, Rockefeller University Press, 1976. Print.

Hoage, R.J. and Larry Goldman, ed. *Animal Intelligence*. Washington D.C.: Smithsonian Institution Press, 1986. Print.

Walker, Stephen F. *Animal Thought*. Boston: Routledge and K. Paul, 1983. Print.

Exercise 3-1

Answer the following questions about the argumentative/persuasive essay. (*Answers on page 309.*)

1. What are the first three steps you should complete when starting your essay?

    _____

    _____

    _____

    _____

    _____

    _____

2. What are the four main elements of this essay?

    _____

    _____

    _____

    _____

    _____

    _____

3. What is the point of this essay?

    _____

    _____

    _____

    _____

    _____

    _____

3 Argumentative / Persuasive Essay

4

Cause and Effect Essay

Lesson 4-1: What Is It?

The cause and effect essay analyzes a topic in terms of a) what caused it and b) what happened as a result. A simple essay will most likely have just one or two effects. For example, if you forget to take the dog out before you go to work (the cause) you will probably come home to a little surprise on your kitchen floor (the effect). You may also come home to a frantic dog clawing at the door (another effect). A more complex essay will generally deal with multiple effects.

You may also have an essay that explores several causes that all lead to the same effect. For example, you may write an essay that discusses the economic collapse of a small, once-prosperous town (the effect). The causes leading to that effect might be the factory that provided most of the jobs in town going out of business, a horrific natural disaster, and the collapse of the bridge that connected the town to the main highway. Your essay will explore the relationship between the causes and effects of your given topic.

Cause and effect essays can be used to persuade your audience to your way of thinking. For example, if you believe that the use of too much sunscreen

4
Cause and Effect Essay

actually causes sunburns, rather than prevents them, you could use this type of essay to show how you arrived at that line of thinking. Or, you could use this essay to inform your audience of an already-proven fact by walking your readers through the causes to the known effect.

Chain Reactions

Cause and effect essays can be a lot of fun and very interesting, especially when exploring incidents that seem to have no relation, as in instances when the effect is caused by a chain reaction. For example, maybe the end result (the effect) is that your dog is given to another family. The beginning cause of this is the fact that you accidentally planted pumpkin seeds instead of tomato seeds.

At first glance, these events don't seem to be related at all. How can planting the wrong seeds result in your dog being given away? The relationship between these incidents is something a cause and effect essay can discover by going through each effect of the underlying cause. For instance, as a result of planting pumpkin seeds instead of tomato, your garden is thrown off balance, you have no tomatoes come harvest time, you can't make your prize-winning salsa, Grandma now refuses to speak to you because you can't keep her supplied with salsa, so she doesn't give you the message that the animal shelter found your dog (all effects of the original cause). The end result: Your dog is given to another family.

Lesson 4-2: Getting Started
Step 1: Choose a Topic

You may be assigned a topic, but if not, you'll need to choose one. Your choice of topic will be influenced by how complex and in-depth your assignment is, and what your specific requirements are. For instance, if your assignment is to write a two-page essay, you won't need a topic with many of causes or effects. You could choose a subject with one cause and one effect. If you are required to write a seven-page essay, you might want to find a richer topic.

Step 2: Make a Cause and Effect List

Once you've chosen your topic, you need to narrow the focus of your essay into a few specific causes and effects. A good way to do this is by making a list. If we look at the example of the town that is experiencing an economic collapse, you could list several possible causes and even brainstorm what other effects those causes may have. Our list might look like this:

Causes	Effects
Factory out of business	Economic collapse of town
Natural disaster	Many businesses destroyed
Bridge collapse	Town deserted

For our essay, we want to focus on the economic collapse of the town. But it is good to know what other effects the causes we are discussing may have, especially if you are trying to write a more complex paper.

One of the purposes of this type of essay is often to persuade your audience to your point of view. In this case, there could be other sources that claim that the economic collapse of the town was caused by something else—perhaps the poor quality of education that the inhabitants received. It is your job to persuade your audience to believe as you do: that the town's economy collapsed because of the closing of the factory, a natural disaster, and the collapse of the bridge. Focus on the effects that will best persuade your readers to your point of view and back those examples up with factual evidence.

Step 3: Research and Make Notes

With most assignments, you'll need to find some outside sources to back up your claims and examples. Even essays that are entirely personal (for example, an essay on how going to the beach led to the worst sunburn of your life) can use an outside source. If you are exploring your sunburn, you could look up statistics on how hot the sun is or what time of the day a person is most likely to get burned. Complex topics will need more research to back up the information you are presenting.

Find as much as you can on your chosen topic. It is always better to have too much information, rather than too little. As always, record your notes and your source information. You'll need these when you write your outline.

Lesson 4-3: Elements of the Essay
The Introduction

For this section, you'll need to introduce your topic and your thesis. You could start off with a few lines about how seemingly unrelated issues could actually be interconnected, or you could just jump right into your topic. Your thesis needs to be stated firmly and decisively. If you are going to discuss how many causes create an effect, you might say something like "This paper will discuss the many causes of the economic collapse of the town." Or if you are discussing a particular cause, you can say "Sunburns are caused by the harmful rays of the sun."

If you are discussing how certain effects were created by a particular cause, you could say something like "The closing of the Dairy Queen will create many adverse effects."

If you are discussing both the causes and effects, you could say "This paper will explore the many causes of cancer and the effects this disease has on a society." Whichever way your essay is geared, you need to be clear and up-front about what you will be discussing.

The Body

This is where you will present all of your arguments, ideas, proof, and the outside sources that back them up.

A good way to keep your statements organized is to arrange them according to when the events occurred (the chronology), in order of importance (in our tomato seed fiasco resulting in the family dog disappearing example, maybe the fact that Grandma withheld the message is more important than you planting the wrong seeds), or by specific categories (all planting related information discussed first, all human related activity discussed second, all canine related activity discussed third). Generally speaking, discussing events in the order they happened is a good way to keep everything organized and easy to follow.

The Conclusion

This section is where you will restate your thesis and make a final, conclusive statement along the lines of "As you can see, my actions the day I planted the wrong seeds caused my dog to be given away." Then you can briefly summarize your arguments ("My actions 1, 2, and 3 started the chain reaction that led to the unfortunate result").

Lesson 4-4: Putting It Together

Outlines are always a good idea, but an outline is especially helpful if you have several causes or effects or if you are exploring a chain reaction. Putting your information into outline form keeps it organized, and, when it comes time to write the essay, most of your work will already be done. Once you've gone through and filled in the details of your outline, you are ready to write your essay. You should have a detailed outline that looks something like this:

I. Introduction
   A. Opening remarks
      1. Many events in life appear unrelated when in fact, they are intricately connected.
   B. Thesis: This essay will prove that my mistake in planting the wrong seeds caused my dog to be given away.
   C. Brief rundown of upcoming arguments
      1. Planted wrong seeds
      2. Led to Grandma being angry
      3. Resulted in dog being given away
II. Planted wrong seeds
   A. Evidence: Empty packet of pumpkin seeds found
   B. Evidence: Confession
III. Garden is thrown off balance
   A. Evidence: Eyewitness accounts of garden

IV. No tomatoes come harvest time
   A. Evidence: Report of bare vegetable drawer in the fridge

V. Can't make your prize-winning salsa
   A. Evidence: Witness testimonies of empty salsa jars
   B. Evidence: Police report of excess bags of chips going to waste

VI. Grandma now refuses to speak to me because I can't keep her supplied with salsa through the winter.
   A. Evidence: Confession of Grandma
   B. Evidence: Phone records showing lack of calls

VII. She doesn't give me the message that the animal shelter found the dog.
   A. Evidence: Phone records from shelter
   B. Evidence: Testimony of shelter workers
   C. Evidence: Grandma's confession

VIII. Conclusion
   A. Restate thesis: As you can see, these events led to end result of my dog being given away.
   B. Summarize arguments
      1. These events were all causes of the end effect.
   C. Ending statement
      1. Hopefully this story will serve as a warning to forgetful planters everywhere.

Sample Essays

The following essay explores the effects of a non-native species being introduced into an established environment. It discusses the various ways a foreign species could be detrimental to the native species and its habitat, and uses quotations from environmental reports to back up the information included. The essay concludes that the introduction of a foreign species into an established ecosystem could be devastating for the native species and environment. This essay uses the MLA style of citations.

Following is the detailed outline for the essay. Go through it, and then look at the rough draft to see how the essay falls into place. The parts of the essay are labeled in the rough draft with their corresponding numbers from the outline.

Cause and Effect Essay

4

The Detailed Outline

I. Introduction

    A. Opening statements

        1. Nature has a delicate balance.

        2. Everything has its place.

        3. Anything that disrupts that could be devastating.

    B. Thesis: For instance, the effects of a non-native species being introduced into a new environment would catastrophically change the balance of its ecosystem.

    C. Summary points

        1. Lack of predators

        2. Breeding

        3. Increased competition for resources and habitat

II. Lack of predators

    A. A new species might not have predators in their new home.

    B. Would become an unchecked predator themselves

        1. Lake Superior sea lamprey example (Lake Superior Work Group)

III. Breeding

    A. They'd breed with each other.

        1. A lack of predators would lead to a high birth rate.

            a. Eco-Pros quote: "When there are no established natural controls, such as predators to keep the non-native harmful species in check, there can be a population explosion of the invasive non-native species causing an ecological catastrophe."

    B. They'd interbreed.

        1. "Hybridize with native species and decrease biodiversity by crowding out native species." (Lake Superior Work Group)

    C. Result: They'd outbreed the native species.

IV. Increased competition for resources and habitat

    A. More of them means less of everything else for the other species.

        1. Eco-Pros quote: "When natural habitat or food supply is destroyed, by alien species or from other circumstances, animals have to leave to find shelter and food in an ecosystem which will sustain them. Some native animals cannot leave. Without proper habitat and food supplies, they die."

4 Cause and Effect Essay

IV. Conclusion
    A.   Restate thesis
    B.   Restate main points
        1.   Lack of predators
        2.   Breeding habits
        3.   Increased competition for resources

Once you have your outline complete, your essay is pretty much done. All you need to do is plug the information you have in the outline into the essay format. And you're done!

Version 1: The Rough Draft

Foreign Invasion

INTRODUCTION

(I A1) There is a delicate balance to nature. **(I A2)** Everything has its place on the food chain and in the habitat in which it lives. **(I A3)** So when something comes along that disrupts that balance, the effects can be devastating. **(I B)** For instance, the effects of a non-native species being introduced into an environment would be catastrophic. **(I C1)** The foreign species might have a lack of predators in the new habitat **(I C2)** and they could outbreed the existing species, **(I C3)** which would result in increased competition for resources and habitat.

BODY OF ESSAY

(II A) Though a certain species may have several predators in their natural habitat, they may not have any at all in a foreign environment. **(II B)** Without predators to keep the foreign species in check, they could decimate the native population. This situation is shown in a report with the example of the sea lamprey in Lake Superior. **(II B1)** "Due to its successful predatory behavior—only one out of every seven fish attacked survive—the sea lamprey continues to have adverse effects on large fish species in the Great Lakes" (Lake Superior 6).

(III A) Another contributing issue would be the breeding habits of the foreign species. **(III A1)** When a species has "no established natural controls, such as predators to keep [it] in check, there can be a population explosion of the invasive non-native species causing an ecological catastrophe" (Eco-Pros). **(III B1)** In addition, the foreign species could interbreed "with native species and decrease biodiversity by crowding out native species" (Lake Superior 6). **(III C)**

(IV) These circumstances would greatly increase the competition for resources and habitat within the environment. **(IV A)** To put it simply, more of the foreign species means less food and living space for everything else. **(IV A1)** The native species would be pushed out of their natural environment and would either have to change or leave to find new living spaces and food sources. However, "some native animals cannot leave. Without proper habitat and food supplies, they die" (Eco-Pros).

4 Cause and Effect Essay

CONCLUSION

(V A) As you can see, the introduction of a foreign species into an established environment could have devastating effects. **(V B1)** Without predators to keep the invasive species in check, **(V B2)** especially if the species has the ability to interbreed with native species, the non-native species would quickly become the leading population in the habitat. **(V B3)** The resulting increase in population would create an increased competition for resources and could lead to the evacuation or death of many native species.

Works Cited

Eco-Pros. *Invasive Non-native Species.* Environmental Education on the Web. 20 May 2006.

Web. 12 September 2010. <http://www.eco-pros.com/invasive_non-native_species.htm>

The Lake Superior Work Group. *Lake Superior Aquatic Invasive Species Complete Prevention*

Plan. 2009. Web. 12 September 2010. <http://www.epa.gov/glnpo/lakesuperior/lakesuperior_ais_draft.pdf>

Version 2: The Edited Draft

The second version of the essay is the edited copy of the rough draft. This version has comments and revision suggestions marked in red. When proofreading your essays, you want to look for technical mistakes, such as spelling and punctuation errors, incorrect grammar, missing words, and awkward sentence structures. But you'll also want to look for areas where more extensive revision would be helpful. Maybe there is a statement that needs some additional information added, or a transition from one statement to another that could use a little beefing up. All of these things are part of the proofreading and editing process.

Foreign Invasion

There's *(Spell out instead of using a contraction.)* a delicate balance to nature. Everything has it's *(Delete apostrophe.)* place on the food chain and in the habitat that it lives in. *(Change to "in which it lives.")* So when something comes along that disrupts that balance, the effects can be devastating. For instance, the effects of a non-native species being introduced into an environment would be catastrophic *(Reword slightly to "the effects of introducing a non-native species...." Also, strengthen this a bit. Who or what would this be catastrophic for?)* The foreign species might not have any predators in the new habitat *(Insert comma.)* and they could outbreed the existing species, which would result in a lot more *(Use "increased" instead of "a lot more.")* competition for resources and habitat.

Though a certain species may have several predators in their *(Don't use a singular "their," because species is singular in this case. Use "its.")* natural habitat, they *(Again, "a certain species" means one species, so use "it" not "they.")* may not have any at all in a foreign environment. Without predators to keep the foreign species in check, they *(it)* could total *(Try "decimate" or "destroy" instead of the informal "total.")* the native population. This situation is shown in a report with the example of the sea lamprey in Lake Superior. *(Be a little more specific. What report? Who wrote it? If you introduce the information here, you'll only need to list the page number after the quote.)* "Due to its successful predatory behavior—only one out of every seven fish attacked survive—the sea lamprey continues to have adverse effects on large fish species in the Great Lakes" (Lake Superior 6). *(Great quote, but try to preface it or paraphrase a little more so the entire sentence isn't a quote. It isn't against the rules to do this, but it's better to put it in your own words as much as possible. If you do, don't forget to cite the source!)*

Another contributing issue would be the breeding habits of the foreign species. When a species has "no established natural controls, such as predators to keep [it] in check, there can be a population explosion of the invasive non-native species causing an ecological catastrophe" (Eco-Pros). In addition, the foreign species could interbreed "with native species and decrease biodiversity by crowding out native species" (Lake Superior *page #*). *(You may need to add a little further explanation to tie this together. Also, the word "species" is used six times in this paragraph. Try to use a different word here and there.)*

4 Cause and Effect Essay

These circumstances would make the competition for food and living spaces in the environment much worse *(This can be reworded to be a bit more formal: "would greatly increase the competition for resources and habitat within the environment.")* To put it simply, more of the foreign species means less food and living space for everything else. The native species would be pushed out of their natural environment and would either have to change *(Try "adapt.")* or leave to find *(Try "leave in search of.")* new living spaces *(Use "habitats" or "territories.")* and food sources. However, "some native animals cannot leave. Without proper habitat and food supplies, they die" (Eco-Pros).

As you can see, the introduction of a foreign species into an established environment could have devastating effects. Without predators to keep the foreign *("Foreign" has been used many times. Try another descriptor, such as "invasive.")* species in check, especially if the species has the ability to interbreed with native species, the non-native species would quickly become the leading population in the habitat. The resulting increase in population would create an increased *(A version of "increase" is used twice in one sentence. Change one of them.)* competition for resources and could lead to the evacuation or death of many native species.

Works Cited

Eco-Pros. *Invasive Non-native Species.* Environmental Education on the Web. 20 May 2006.

Web. 12 September 2010. <http://www.eco-pros.com/ invasive_non-native_species.htm>

The Lake Superior Work Group. *Lake Superior Aquatic Invasive Species Complete Prevention Plan.* 2009. Web. 12 September 2010. <http:// www.epa.gov/glnpo/lakesuperior/lakesuperior_ais_draft.pdf>

Version 3: The Final Draft

The third version of the essay is the final, revised copy so you can see how it has transformed from an outline, to a rough draft, to a polished essay ready to turn in.

4 Cause and Effect Essay

Foreign Invasion

There is a delicate balance to nature. Everything has its place on the food chain and in the habitat in which it lives. So when something comes along that disrupts that balance, the effects can be devastating. For instance, the effects of introducing a non-native species into an environment would be catastrophic for that ecosystem. The foreign species might not have predators in the new habitat, and they could outbreed the existing species, which would result in increased competition for resources and habitat.

Though a certain species may have several predators in its natural habitat, it may not have any at all in a foreign environment. Without predators to keep the foreign species in check, it could decimate the native population. The Lake Superior Work Group, a group of environmental scientists who wrote an Invasive Species Prevention Plan, presented the example of the sea lamprey in Lake Superior. The plan stated that because of "its successful predatory behavior—only one out of every seven fish attacked survive—the sea lamprey continues to have adverse effects on large fish species in the Great Lakes" (6).

Another contributing issue would be the breeding habits of the foreign population. When a group has "no established natural controls, such as predators to keep [it] in check, there can be a population explosion of the invasive non-native species causing an ecological catastrophe" (Eco-Pros). In addition, the foreign group could interbreed "with native species and decrease biodiversity by crowding out native species" (Lake Superior 6). In other words, the foreign species would overrun the native population.

These circumstances would greatly increase the competition for resources and habitat within the environment. To put it simply, more of the foreign species means less food and living space for everything else. The native species would be pushed out of their natural environment and would either have to adapt or leave in search of new territories and food sources. However, "some native animals cannot leave. Without proper habitat and food supplies, they die" (Eco-Pros).

As you can see, the introduction of a foreign species into an established environment could have devastating effects. Without predators to keep the invasive species in check, especially if the species has the ability to interbreed with native species, the non-native species would

4 Cause and Effect Essay

quickly become the leading population in the habitat. The resulting rise in population would create an increased competition for resources and could lead to the evacuation or death of many native species.

Works Cited

Eco-Pros. *Invasive Non-native Species.* Environmental Education on the Web. 20 May 2006. Web. 12 September 2010. <http://www.eco-pros.com/invasive_non-native_species.htm>

The Lake Superior Work Group. *Lake Superior Aquatic Invasive Species Complete Prevention Plan.* 2009. Web. 12 September 2010. <http://www.epa.gov/glnpo/lakesuperior/lakesuperior_ais_draft.pdf>

Exercise 4-1

Answer the following questions about the cause and effect essay. (*Answers on page 310.*)

1. What does a cause and effect essay do?

   _____

   _____

   _____

2. What are three ways of organizing your information within the essay?

   _____

   _____

   _____

3. What is a chain reaction?

   _____

   _____

   _____

4 Cause and Effect Essay

5

Critical Essay

Lesson 5-1: What Is It?

Critical essays are essays that analyze another's work, whether it is a book, an article, a movie, or even a piece of art. Generally, when you hear the word *critical*, it brings to mind something negative, but this isn't really the case. With this type of essay, you are not necessarily negatively criticizing someone's work, but exploring and analyzing it. As with most essays, critical essays require a bit of brainstorming ahead of time and some research as well, because your statements must be supported by outside sources. Aside from the regular essay structure (introduction, body, conclusion), critical essays have two main components: 1) a summary of the work and topic in question, and 2) the analysis of the topic in question.

There are classes in which the teacher wants you to use only the material you are analyzing and your own thoughts. If that is the case, then your job is a little easier, as you won't need to research other sources. But most of the time, you will need to support your ideas with outside sources.

Lesson 5-2: Getting Started
Step 1: Brainstorm Possible Topics and Make a List

You're writing a critical essay on *Harry Potter and the Deathly Hallows* by J.K. Rowling. For this type of essay, you generally focus on one main theme or element of the book. To choose your topic, you will need to do some serious brainstorming. If you are given a topic, you can still brainstorm to find a good focus or to get ideas of what you'd like to include in your paper. But, if you need to choose your own topic, you need to get a list going of some possibilities.

What are some main elements of the book?

- Settings.
  - Hogwarts.
  - Aunt Petunia's house.
  - The train station.
  - Diagon Alley.
- Characters.
  - Harry.
  - Ron.
  - Hermione.
  - Snape.
  - Dumbeldore.
  - Malfoy.
- Themes.
  - Everyone is special.
  - Magic is all around us if you look hard enough.
  - Keep your friends close and your enemies closer.
  - Love conquers all.
  - Stay away from creepy snake-looking guys that try to kill you.

Once you have a good list of possible elements, you need to brainstorm a little more. It's question time!

- Settings: For each setting you listed, ask questions such as:
  - ▶ Why did the author create this school of magic?
  - ▶ How does this setting affect the characters?
  - ▶ Why are certain scenes set at this location?
  - ▶ What impact does this setting have on the main character?
- Characters: For characters, ask questions such as:
  - ▶ Why does a certain character react the way he did to a certain situation?
  - ▶ Why does a character make a certain decision?
  - ▶ Why docs one character hate another character?
- Themes: Which theme do you think is the overall theme of the story?
- Brainstorm any other questions you can think of, such as:
  - ▶ Why did the author start or end thc book the way she did?
  - ▶ Why did she choose the title she did?
  - ▶ Would another title have been better?

Step 2: Narrow Your Focus and Choose Your Topic

Once you've done all this brainstorming, pick the topic that interests you the most and that you think you'll be able to find the most evidence to support. You need to have evidence for your topic from both the work in question and, often, from outside sources. In other words, there needs to be enough evidence in the book to support your claim, and you usually need to be able to find sources other than the book in question to back up your statements.

For our example, let's choose a theme for our topic; how about "love conquers all"? Our argument will be that this is the main theme of the book. Now, we just need to find evidence within the book and some outside sources to support our claim. Don't worry; there is no right or wrong answer. You can interpret the book any way you choose, as long as you can find the evidence that supports your claims.

Step 3: Research and Make Notes

Time to hit the library and internet. For our topic, we could look for:

- ▶ Scholarly articles that have analyzed the *Harry Potter and the Deathly Hallows*.

- ▶ Movie or book reviews.

- ▶ Interviews with J.K. Rowling.

- ▶ Books on literary themes that discuss the theme of love conquers all.

- ▶ Any other source that may include statements that support our claim that love conquers all is the main theme.

Record your information! Note cards work well, but however you do it, be sure to make a note of the information, paraphrases, and quotations you think you will use in your paper. Don't forget to record the information you'll need for your citation as well.

Lesson 5-3: Elements of the Essay
The Introduction

Your introduction should include the name of the book and author, as well as a short summary of the book and an introduction of the theme. Your thesis should be firmly stated. Don't say "I think" or "I believe." Assertively state "The main theme of this book is...." Remember: There are no right or wrong answers. You have researched and found sources to support this claim, so say it with confidence.

Depending on how in-depth or complex your essay is supposed to be, you could also give some background on the work or author in question, or on the theme, such as why this theme has been tradition-ally important in literature.

The Body

Once your introduction is done, it's time to tackle that theme.

Start with your internal or primary source, which is, in our exam-ple, *Harry Potter and the Deathly Hallows*. What information found in the book supports your claim that love conquers all is the main theme

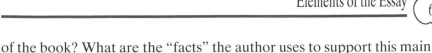

of the book? What are the "facts" the author uses to support this main theme? You can explore elements such as:

▶ Is there any symbolism or imagery that supports this theme?

▶ What scenes in the book outline this theme? Perhaps, the scene where Harry overcomes Voldemort because he can love?

▶ How do the characters' actions support this theme?

   ▶ Do Harry and his friends stick together no matter what?

   ▶ What do they do for each other?

   ▶ What choices have to be made that show that love conquers all?

   ▶ How do the characters interact?

   ▶ What are the differences between the villainous characters and the heroes?

What other evidence in the book proves your topic? Maybe the fact that Harry survived in the first place because of his mother's love? That Harry keeps surviving because of the love and sacrifices of the other characters? The fact that Harry finally conquers Voldemort because of his love and selfless sacrifice?

Next, you must evaluate the author's work, often using outside sources. This step basically takes a look at the "facts" the author presented in the work to support the main theme and analyzes whether or not these facts did their job. You'll support your analysis with your outside sources. You could discuss things such as:

   ▶ How well do the points outlined in the previous step support the author's main theme?

   ▶ If love conquers all is the main theme, did Rowling accomplish her goal in presenting this theme?

   ▶ Did the scenes and actions in the book present enough proof that the main theme is true?

   ▶ Did these scenes sufficiently support the main point of the book?

   ▶ How did they do this, or how could they have done a better job?

If you think she did a good job, state that. If you think she could have expanded her ideas or included more, state that, and maybe add some ideas about how the theme could have been developed further.

The Conclusion

The conclusion is the easy part, and it means you are almost done! Restate the author and title of the book in your conclusion, and, as always, restate your thesis and summarize your arguments and evidence.

Lesson 5-4: Putting It Together

When all is said and done, you should have a detailed outline that looks something like this from which to write your essay:

I. Introduction
    A. Introduce title of book and author
    B. Brief summary
    C. Thesis: Though there are many themes in this book, "love conquers all" is the central one.
    D. Background information or brief outline of the upcoming arguments

II. Primary source evidence
    A. Symbolism examples in story that support your position
        1. Citation from book
    B. Imagery examples in story that support your position
        1. Citation from book
    C. Scenes in the book that outline your point
        1. Harry overcoming Voldemort because he can love and Voldemort can't
        2. Scenes where Harry's friends come to the rescue
    D. Characters' actions in the book that support your arguments
        1. Harry's mother giving her life for him
        2. Friends coming to the rescue
        3. Dumbledore's mentorship

III. Evaluation
    A. Did the evidence you just discussed do its job?
        1. Support your answer with outside source

B. Was there anything the author could have done better or differently?
   1. Support your answer with outside source
C. Are there opposing views to your conclusions?
   1. Refute them with your internal evidence and outside sources
IV. Conclusion
   A. Restate author and book title
   B. Restate your position
   C. Summarize your arguments and evidence
   D. Close with a strong statement or suggestions for further analysis

Sample Essays

Look at the following essay that analyzes how elements in the movie *Nosferatu,* especially the main vampire character, Count Orlock, symbolize the social climate of post-war Germany. The essay briefly discusses German society during this time and focuses the essay on the conflicts the society dealt with by citing examples from the movie that illustrate these conflicts. The essay concludes that, though the horrific figure of Count Orlock and the film itself serve as warnings against anything foreign, the film also offers hope that the threat can be overcome.

Following is the detailed outline for the essay. Go through it, and then look at the rough draft to see how the essay falls into place. The parts of the essay are labeled in the rough draft with their corresponding numbers from the outline.

The Detailed Outline

I. Introduction
    A. Vampires have been around a while.
    B. Bram Stoker's *Dracula* made them popular.
       1. *Nosferatu* is one of the earliest vampire films.
       2. Brief summary of plot
    C. The vampire symbolizes what a society fears most.
    D. Thesis: *Nosferatu* in particular illustrates the social climate of post-war Germany.

Critical Essay

5

II.   Summary
  A.   Background on German society
    1.   Germany in turmoil after losing
    2.   Holte quote, pages 30–31
    3.   Germans were afraid of outsiders.
    4.   Murnau put these aspects of German society in the film.
  B.   The vampire monster is perfect to symbolize a society's fears.
    1.   Williams quote, page 9
    2.   His characteristics (wealth, foreign, powerful) symbolize a society's fears of those characteristics.
    3.   Serves as a warning

III.   Conflicts (Analysis)
  A.   Rich versus poor
    1.   Orlock is wealthy.
    2.   Williams quote, page 9
  B.   Morality versus immorality
    1.   Character of Ellen
    2.   Book of Vampires
    3.   Inviting the vampire into her room is immoral.
    4.   A virtuous wife being immoral to save the world
  C.   Foreign versus native
    1.   Germany defeated by foreign tyrants
    2.   German society was in chaos.
    3.   The film shows the difference in their societies.
    4.   Williams quote, page 3, 4
    5.   Orlock symbolizes the new world, fear, and loathing of anything foreign.

IV. Conclusion
  A.   Restate thesis
  B.   Restate arguments
    1.   Williams quote page 12
  C.   Concluding sentence
    1.   *Nosferatu* served as a warning.
    2.   Also offered hope

Version 1: The Rough Draft

Nosferatu

INTRODUCTION

(I A) The vampire has been a creature of fascination and horror for a long time. Both readers and audiences seem to love and hate them. **(I B)** There were a few early vampire tales, but the novel that made vampires popular was Bram Stoker's *Dracula*. **(I B1)** One of the earliest vampire films, based on Stoker's novel, is F. W. Murnau's *Nosferatu*, **(I B2)** in which a foreign vampire moves in and wreaks havoc. Throughout the years, the vampire has undergone vast transformations. **(I C)** The vampire is a symbol for what a society fears most. **(I D)** I think *Nosferatu* especially is a film that illustrates the social climate of a post-war Germany.

BODY OF ESSAY

(II A1) After World War I, Germany was a society haunted and in turmoil after their bitter defeat. **(II A2)** In *Nosferatu*, "the disassociation and confusion resulting from the breakdown of German society after the First World War can be seen. All aspects of cultural and political authority [were] called into question" (Holte page 2). **(II A3)** The German population was understandably afraid of outsiders, confused at a world that had been turned upside down. **(II A4)** Murnau imbued *Nosferatu* with these aspects of German society (Rickels 84).

(II B) The vampire is a monster that is particularly well suited as a symbol of societal fears. **(II B1)** Anne Williams states that the "word monster is derived from a Latin word that means both 'to warn' and 'to reveal'...that is, monsters embody a particular culture's worst fears" (Williams 9). **(II B2)** A monster that is wealthy, foreign, aristocratic, and powerful would be symbolically demonstrating the fears a society has of these traits. **(II B3)** This monster would also serve as a warning of those exhibiting these traits. This is exactly the type of vampire monster that is portrayed in *Nosferatu*.

(III A) *Nosferatu* shows the conflict between rich versus poor, or upper class versus lower class. **(III A1)** Orlock is a wealthy nobleman who is introduced into the native society in order to buy property. **(III A2)** Vampires often represent "an ancient, dark, violent...and... decadent aristocracy" (Williams 9). So, a rich foreigner buying property would be seen as supremely undesirable and threatening.

5 Critical Essay

(III B) Another conflict present in this film is morality versus immorality. **(III B1)** You can really see this with the character of Ellen. At the beginning of the film, Ellen is presented as a virtuous wife. **(III B2)** As stated in the "Book of Vampires" shown in the film, a virtuous woman such as Ellen is the only one who can defeat Orlock. **(III B3)** While she is performing a noble task in sacrificing herself for the greater good, she must act immorally by inviting the vampire into her bedchamber. The act of sucking blood is often viewed as an erotic, though horrific, act. **(III B4)** The film shows a virtuous wife purposefully committing an immoral act in order to save the world.

This idea introduces perhaps the most important conflict in this film. **(III C)** This is the conflict of old versus new, or foreign versus native. This represents several aspects of post-war German society. **(III C1)** Germany was defeated by forces they no doubt viewed as foreign tyrants. **(III C2)** As a result, German society was in chaos. **(III C3)** The film represents the difference between the old regime and the new, defeated society. **(III C4)** Williams states that the "paradoxical fear and desire evoked by the vampire...[expresses] a repulsion from the new and a desire for the old" (3–4).

Orlock, the monstrous, foreign nobleman, leaves his country and moves to Bremen, bringing with him ghastly changes German society must have felt a longing for the "old days," before a bitter defeat, before the intrusion of foreigners on their native soil. **(III C5)** The terrible creature Orlock symbolizes this fear of the "new" world in which the Germans found themselves. He also symbolizes fear and loathing of the foreign influences that were now a part of their society.

CONCLUSION

(IV A) The symbolism and techniques developed in this film combine to illustrate the social climate of post-war Germany. **(IV B)** The depiction of Orlock as a rat-like monstrosity illustrates the fear of the foreign or unknown. **(IV B1)** The fact that this portrayal is very different from those of other vampires suggests that "monstrosity is...a matter of cultural perspective" (Williams 12).

The horrific character of Orlock invades the peaceful, innocent town of Bremen, bringing with him pestilence and death. **(IV C1)** *Nosferatu* served as a warning against the dangers of foreign influences, **(IV C2)** but it also offered hope to a nation that had already experienced the realization of their foreign fears. There is hope that the foreign threat will, in the end, be overcome.

Works Cited

Holte, James C. *Dracula in the Dark : The Dracula Film Adaptations.* Westport, CT: Greenwood Publishing Group, Inc., 1997. National University Library: Ebrary. Web. 15 May 2007 <http://site.ebrary. com/lib/nuls/Doc?id=10004883&ppg=49>.

Rickels, Laurence A. *Nazi Psychoanalysis, Volume 1.*Minneapolis, MN: University of Minnesota Press, 2002. National University Library: Ebrary. Web. 15 May 2007 <http://site.ebrary.com/lib/nuls/ Doc?id=10151222&ppg=105>.

Williams, Anne, ed. *Three Vampire Tales.* Boston: Houghton, 2003. Print.

Version 2: The Edited Draft

The second version of the essay is the edited copy of the rough draft. This version has comments and revision suggestions marked in red. When proofreading your essays, you want to look for technical mistakes, such as spelling and punctuation errors, incorrect grammar, missing words, and awkward sentence structures. But you also want to look for areas where more extensive revision would be helpful. Maybe there is a statement that needs some additional information added, or a transition from one statement to another that could use a little beefing up. All of these things are part of the proofreading and editing process.

Nosferatu

The vampire has been a creature of fascination and horror for a long time. Both readers and audiences seem to love and hate them. *(This could be strengthened a bit if the word "seem" is removed. Make it strong; make a statement. This paper may be based on your opinion, but if you have strong statements to back up what you are saying and outside sources to support you, there is no reason for being wishy-washy. If you are going to make a statement, make it. Don't look like you are guessing by saying "seem.")* There were a few early vampire tales, *(Such as? Give examples.)* but the novel that made vampires popular was Bram Stoker's *Dracula*. One of the earliest vampire films, based on Stoker's novel, is F. W. Murnau's *Nosferatu*, in which a foreign vampire moves in and wreaks havoc. Throughout the years, the vampire has undergone vast transformations. The vampire is a symbol for what a society fears most *(Is this one of the characteristics that have changed?)*. I think *Nosferatu* especially is a film that illustrates the social climate of a post-war Germany. *(This is your thesis statement. It needs to be powerful. No "I think"! Make this sentence strong.)*

After World War I, Germany was a society haunted and in turmoil after their bitter defeat. *(The word "after" is used twice in this sentence. Reword.)* In *Nosferatu*, "the disassociation and confusion resulting from the breakdown of German society after the First World War can be seen. All aspects of cultural and political authority [were] called into question" (Holte *page #?*). The German population was understandably afraid of outsiders, confused at a world that had been turned upside down. Murnau imbued *Nosferatu* with these aspects of German society (Rickels 84). *(Who is Murnau? Did he write the movie? Direct it? Briefly tell us who he is.)*

The vampire is a monster that is particularly well suited as a symbol of societal fears. *(Why?)* Anne Williams states *(Who is she and where is she stating this?)* that the "word monster is derived from a Latin word that means both 'to warn' and 'to reveal'...that is, monsters embody a particular culture's worst fears" (Williams 9) *(You don't need her name here, because you introduced her and the source before the quote.)* A monster that is wealthy, foreign, aristocratic, and powerful would be symbolically demonstrating the fears a society has of these traits. This monster would also serve as a warning of those exhibiting these traits.

(A better transition is needed to introduce these conflicts.) *Nosferatu* shows the conflict between rich versus poor, or upper class versus

lower class. Orlock is a wealthy nobleman who is introduced into the native society in order to buy property. Vampires often represent "an ancient, dark, violent…and…decadent aristocracy" (Williams 9). So, a rich foreigner buying property would be seen as supremely undesirable and threatening. *(You could elaborate on this a little. Why, specifically, would a rich foreigner buying property be threatening to the losing side? What kind of property?)*

Another conflict present in this film is morality versus immorality. You can really see this with the character of Ellen *(This should be more formal. Avoid the use of personal pronouns such as "I," and "you," in formal papers)*. At the beginning of the film, Ellen is presented as a virtuous wife. *(How is this presented? Give some examples from the film to back up this statement.)* As stated in the "Book of Vampires" shown in the film, a virtuous woman such as Ellen is the only one who can defeat Orlock. While she is performing a noble task in sacrificing herself for the greater good, she must act immorally by inviting the vampire into her bedchamber. The act of sucking blood is often viewed as an erotic, though horrific, act. The film shows a virtuous wife purposefully committing an immoral act in order to save the world.

This idea introduces perhaps the most important conflict in this film. This is the conflict of old versus new or foreign versus native *(Which is it? Or if you are clarifying, make that more apparent by saying "or more specifically, foreign versus native.")*. This represents several aspects of post-war German society. Germany was defeated by forces they no doubt viewed as foreign tyrants. As a result, German society was in chaos. The film represents the difference between the old regime and the new, defeated society. Williams states that the "paradoxical fear and desire evoked by the vampire…[expresses] a repulsion from the new and a desire for the old" (3–4). *(Paraphrase the quote and elaborate a little more to stress and explain your point.)*

Orlock, the monstrous, foreign nobleman, leaves his country and moves to Bremen, bringing with him ghastly changes *(Such as?)* German society must have felt a longing for the "old days," before a bitter defeat, before the intrusion of foreigners on their native soil. The terrible creature Orlock symbolizes this fear of the "new" world in which the Germans found themselves. He also symbolizes fear and loathing of the foreign influences that were now a part of their society.

The symbolism and techniques developed in this film combine to illustrate the social climate of post-war Germany. The depiction of Orlock as a rat-like monstrosity illustrates the fear of the foreign or unknown. The fact that this portrayal is very different from those of other vampires suggests that *(You can get rid of the word "that." It isn't necessary.)* "monstrosity is…a matter of cultural perspective" (Williams 12). *(Add a transition into the concluding paragraph.)*

The horrific character of Orlock invades the peaceful, innocent town of Bremen, bringing with him pestilence and death. *Nosferatu* served as a warning against the dangers of foreign influences, but it also offered hope to a nation that had already experienced the realization of their foreign fears. *(How? You could recap the character of Ellen and her sacrifice here.)* There is hope that the foreign threat will, in the end, be overcome.

Works Cited

Holte, James C. *Dracula in the Dark : The Dracula Film Adaptations.* Westport, CT: Greenwood Publishing Group, Inc., 1997. National University Library: Ebrary. Web. 15 May 2007 <http://site.ebrary.com/lib/nuls/Doc?id=10004883&ppg=49>.

Rickels, Laurence A. *Nazi Psychoanalysis, Volume 1.* Minneapolis, MN: University of Minnesota Press, 2002. National University Library: Ebrary. Web. 15 May 2007 <http://site.ebrary.com/lib/nuls/Doc?id=10151222&ppg=105>.

Williams, Anne, ed. *Three Vampire Tales.* Boston: Houghton, 2003. Print.

Version 3: The Final Draft

The third version of the essay is the final, revised copy so you can see how it has transformed from an outline, to a rough draft, to a polished essay ready to turn in.

Nosferatu

The vampire has long been a creature of fascination and horror, both attracting and repelling readers and audiences alike. The novel that brought the vampire into global focus was Bram Stoker's *Dracula*. One of the earliest vampire films, based on Stoker's novel, is F.W. Murnau's *Nosferatu*. Throughout the years, the vampire has undergone vast transformations. One characteristic, however, has never changed: the vampire is a symbol for what a society fears most. *Nosferatu*, in particular, is a powerful film that illustrates the social climate of a post-war Germany.

In the aftermath of World War I, Germany was a society haunted and in turmoil after their bitter defeat. In *Nosferatu*, "the disassociation and confusion resulting from the breakdown of German society after the First World War can be seen. All aspects of cultural and political authority [were] called into question" (Holte 30–31). The German population was understandably afraid of outsiders, confused at a world that had been turned upside down. Murnau, himself a combat pilot turned propaganda film maker, imbued *Nosferatu* with these aspects of German society (Rickels 84).

The vampire is particularly well suited as a symbol of societal fears. A vampire is a monster, one who kills by getting close to his victims. He invades their homes and territory, leaving either death or new vampires in his wake. In Anne Williams's introduction to *Three Vampire Tales*, she states that the "word monster is derived from a Latin word that means both 'to warn' and 'to reveal'...that is, monsters embody a particular culture's worst fears" (9). A monster that is wealthy, foreign, aristocratic, and powerful would be symbolically demonstrating the fears a society has of these traits. This monster would also serve as a warning of those exhibiting these traits.

As it was the "losing" side that produced Count Orlock, the main vampire character in the film, it is natural that this character would represent the elements of the new world in which the Germans found themselves. *Nosferatu* depicts a number of conflict opposites. In each case, Orlock represents the new, frightening, and undesirable element.

A defeated country that has just come out of a long war is also a country with vastly reduced resources. Reflecting this, *Nosferatu* depicts the conflict of rich versus poor, or upper class versus lower class. Orlock is a wealthy nobleman who is introduced into the native society in order to buy property. Vampires often represent "an ancient, dark, violent...and...decadent aristocracy" (Williams 9). To a culture depleted by prolonged fighting and a bitter defeat, a rich foreigner buying native property would be seen as supremely undesirable and threatening.

Another conflict present in this film is morality versus immorality. This is particularly evident in association with the character of Ellen. At the beginning of the film, Ellen is presented as a virtuous wife. She is almost childlike in her innocence, as shown by the scene where she plays with the kitten. She sits faithfully at home, grieving for her traveling husband. As stated in the "Book of Vampires" shown in the film, a virtuous woman such as Ellen is the only one who can defeat Orlock. While she is performing a noble task in sacrificing herself for the greater good, she must act immorally by inviting the vampire into her bedchamber. The act of sucking blood is often viewed as an erotic, though horrific, act. The film shows a virtuous wife purposefully committing an immoral act in order to save the world.

This idea introduces perhaps the most important conflict in this film. This is the conflict of old versus new, or more specifically, foreign versus native. This represents several aspects of post-war German society. Germany was defeated by forces they no doubt viewed as foreign tyrants. As a result, German society was in chaos. The film represents the difference between the old regime and the new, defeated society. Williams states that, in essence, the vampire illustrates the longing of a new society has for the old regime, as well as its fears of the unknown.

Orlock, the monstrous, foreign nobleman, leaves his country and moves to Bremen, bringing with him ghastly changes. People begin to die, and life as they know it changes. German society must have felt a longing for the "old days," before a bitter defeat, before the intrusion of foreigners on their native soil. The terrible creature Orlock symbolizes this fear of the "new" world in which the Germans found themselves. He also symbolizes fear and loathing of the foreign influences that were now a part of their society.

This film "is a classic example of a post–World War I German expressionist film, emphasizing the ever-present horror beneath the surface of the ordinary and the irrational in the manner in which the tale is told" (29). The symbolism and techniques developed in this film combine to illustrate the social climate of post-war Germany. The depiction of Orlock as a rat-like monstrosity illustrates the fear of the foreign or unknown. The fact that this portrayal is very different from those of other vampires suggests that "monstrosity is...a matter of cultural perspective" (Williams 12). The culture that produced Orlock is one that was obviously reeling from a chaotic society produced by a recognized foreign threat.

It is important to note that though *Nosferatu* depicts the fears and horrors experienced by the German population after their defeat, it also expresses hope for the future. The horrific character of Orlock does invade the peaceful, innocent town of Bremen, bringing with him pestilence and death, but he is conquered at the end by the sacrifice of the young and noble Ellen. The elements of fear and hope blend to portray both the "desire to be...warned and comforted by the ritual re-enactment of the vampire's defeat" (11). *Nosferatu* served as a warning against the dangers of foreign influences, but it also offered hope to a nation that had already experienced the realization of its foreign fears. There is hope that the foreign threat will, in the end, be overcome.

Works Cited

Holte, James C. *Dracula in the Dark : The Dracula Film Adaptations.* Westport, CT: Greenwood Publishing Group, Inc., 1997. National University Library: Ebrary. Web. 15 May 2007 <http://site.ebrary.com/lib/nuls/Doc?id=10004883&ppg=49>.

Rickels, Laurence A. *Nazi Psychoanalysis, Volume 1.*Minneapolis, MN: University of Minnesota Press, 2002. National University Library: Ebrary. Web. 15 May 2007 <http://site.ebrary.com/lib/nuls/Doc?id=10151222&ppg=105>.

Williams, Anne, ed. *Three Vampire Tales*. Boston: Houghton, 2003. Print.

5 Critical Essay

Exercise 5-1

Answer the following questions about the critical essay. (*Answers on page 310.*)

1. What does a critical essay do?

_____

_____

_____

_____

_____

_____

2. What type of sources should you use to support your opinions of a work?

_____

_____

_____

_____

_____

_____

3. What kind of information should be included in the introduction?

_____

_____

_____

_____

_____

6

Compare and Contrast Essay

Lesson 6-1: What Is It?

The compare and contrast essay evaluates two topics by discussing their similarities and differences. This type of essay is used in just about every subject. A political science class could compare the economics of different countries; an art class could compare painters; a biology class could compare the findings of different experiments; a philosophy class could compare different methods of debate.

You could, for instance, compare and contrast Stephanie Meyer's novel *Twilight* to the movie version by discussing their differences or similarities. Or, for a longer, more complex essay, you can tackle both. For most assignments, you'll do both, and the length and complexity of your essay will be determined by your topic, how many topics you are including in the discussion, and how many aspects of that topic you include.

Lesson 6-2: Getting Started

Step 1: Choose a Topic

The first thing you need is a topic. Be sure to choose one that will give you plenty to compare or contrast. For our example, we'll compare and contrast the book version and movie version of *Twilight*.

Step 2: Make a List

Creating a list of the items you will discuss will help you keep your information organized. It will also give you an idea of what you will explore in your essay and the types of things you will need to research. In the compare column, note the similarities between both versions of *Twilight*. In the contrast column, note the differences. Your list may end up looking like this:

Compare	Contrast
Most of the same characters.	Movie characters didn't always appear as described in book, and there were some characters that appeared in one version but not the other.
Similar settings in both versions.	The Cullens' house was different in the movie than described in the book; the movie added a few new settings; minor differences in other settings.
The movie stayed close to the book's storyline.	The movie added a few scenes (such as the field trip scene), and there were instances in which things from the book happened but in a different way or setting.

Step 3: Research and Make Notes

Now that you have an idea of what you need to look for, you can begin your research. Some types of things you may want to look for could include:

▶ A list of specific scenes from the book and movie.

▶ Character lists and descriptions.

- ▶ Descriptions of the settings from the book and film.
- ▶ Reviews or critiques of both the book and film.
- ▶ Statistics on the popularity of both versions.
- ▶ Quotes from the author of the book and the producers, directors, or actors in the film.
- ▶ Polls from fans on their feelings about the conversion from book to movie format.
- ▶ Mentions of awards either version won or was nominated for.

As you research, make notes! Record all your information on note cards, in a spreadsheet, or in any other way that works best for you.

Lesson 6-3: Elements of the Essay

In addition to an introduction and conclusion, the body of a compare and contrast essay must explore the similarities and differences between two subjects in a clear fashion. This is generally handled in one of two ways.

Method 1

Lump all your similarities together and then all your differences. Your essay would follow this method.

I. Introduction

II. Section 1: Compare all the similarities of your two subjects.

III. Section 2: Contrast all the differences of your two subjects.

IV. Section 3: Analyze both subjects together. (This section isn't necessary, but it could be part of a larger wrap-up if you wish to present anything extra.)

V. Conclusion

For this example, the first section would discuss all the similarities between the book and the movie version of *Twilight*. Perhaps you could show that both have the same characters. This could be followed by an exploration of the similarities of the settings and of the similar storyline in both versions.

In the next section, you would contrast their differences. You could begin by discussing the differences in the characters, such as the presence of some in one version and not the other, or differences in their descriptions and appearances. Then discuss if there are any differences in the settings. For your last point, you could illustrate the differences in the storylines. Conclude your essay by summarizing everything you just proved.

Method 2

Present your information divided by subject instead of by similarities and differences. This method would look like this:

I. Introduction

II. Section 1: Present all the information about subject 1 (the book).

III. Section 2: Present all the information about subject 2 (the movie).

IV. Section 3: Analyze these together. For this section, discuss how the two are different, with perhaps a brief mention of their similarities.

V. Conclusion

Lesson 6-4: Putting It Together

The list you created gives you a rough outline of what will be discussed in your essay. You just need to add an introduction and conclusion. So, what will you need to include in your essay? Remember, there are two ways you can go about this.

Method 1

A detailed outline for this approach might look like this:

I. Introduction
  A. Opening remarks
    1. General comment or two about books that are made into movies
  B. Thesis statement: The movie version of Stephanie Meyer's novel *Twilight* stays true to the book.

II. Compare Similarities
  A. Characters
    1. Discuss main characters in book and movie
      a. Examples
    2. Discuss secondary characters in book and movie
      a. Examples
    3. Other supporting sources and evidence about their similarity
  B. Settings
    1. Discuss the settings in the book
      a. Examples
    2. Discuss how the settings in the movie are similar
      a. Examples
    3. Other supporting sources and evidence about their similarity
  C. Story and plotlines
    1. Discuss the book's story
      a. Examples
    2. Discuss how the movie's story is similar
      a. Examples
    3. Other supporting sources and evidence about their similarity

III. Contrast Differences
  A. Characters
    1. Discuss characters in the movie that are portrayed differently than in the book
      a. Examples

6 Compare and Contrast Essay

2. Discuss any new characters that appear in the movie that don't appear in the book or vice versa
   a. Examples
3. Other supporting sources and evidence about their differences

B. Settings
1. Discuss any settings in the movie that are different from the book
   a. Examples
2. Discuss any new settings that appear in the movie that don't appear in the book or that appear in the book that don't make it into the movie
   a. Examples
3. Other supporting sources and evidence about the difference in settings

C. Story and plotlines
1. Discuss any scenes in the movie that don't appear in the book
   a. Examples
2. Discuss any scenes in the book that were cut from the movie
   a. Examples
3. Other supporting sources and evidence about the difference in storyline

IV. Conclusion
A. Restate thesis
B. Summarize conclusions
1. As with any conversion from one format to another, there are a few differences in the book and film, such as:
   a. List a difference
   b. List another difference
2. For the most part, the similarities (possibly list a few) between the book and the movie far outweigh the differences.
C. Concluding sentence or two
1. (Maybe) Fans across the nation approve of the film version.
2. (Or) It's fun to see a book come to life on the big screen.

Method 2

A detailed outline for this approach might look like this:

I.   Introduction
   A.   Opening remarks
      1.   General comment or two about books that are made into movies
   B.   Thesis statement: The movie version of Stephanie Meyer's novel *Twilight* stays true to the book.

II. The book
   A.   Characters
      1.   Who are the characters in the books? Their importance? Traits?
         a.   Examples
         b.   Outside sources
   B.   Settings
      1.   What are the settings? Their importance?
         a.   Examples
         b.   Outside sources
   C.   Storylines and plotlines
      1.   What is the main storyline?
         a.   Examples
         b.   Outside sources
      2.   Side stories or plotlines?
         a.   Examples
         b.   Outside sources

III. The movie (Focus on the parts that are different so you aren't repeating the same information as above.)
   A.   Characters
      1.   In addition to the book characters, what other characters appear in the movie? What is their importance? Traits?
         a.   Examples
         b.   Outside sources
   B.   Settings
      1.   Are there any settings in the movie that don't appear in the book? What are they? Their importance?
         a.   Examples
         b.   Outside sources

6
Compare and Contrast Essay

C. Storylines and plotlines
  1. Is the main storyline different in any way from the book? Does it have a different focus?
     a. Examples
     b. Outside sources
  2. Are there side stories or plotlines that don't appear in the book?
     a. Examples
     b. Outside sources

IV. Conclusion: Analyze together
  A. Brief recap of similarities
  B. Restate thesis: As you can see, the movie stays true to the book.
     1. Though the movie didn't include Character A who appeared in the book, the ommision served to enhance such and such plotline.
     2. The settings and scenes in the movie were very similar to the book apart from Scene A, which was added to the film in order to explain a certain aspect that the audience wouldn't understand unless they'd read the book.
     3. Present any other evidence or outside source
  C. Good concluding sentence

Sample Essays

Look at the following essay comparing and contrasting two of Russia's most famous empresses, Catherine the Great, and Alexandra, the last Tsarina. The essay discusses various aspects of the women's lives, detailing the similarities and differences.

Following is the detailed outline for the essay. Go through it, and then look at the rough draft to see how the essay falls into place. The parts of the essay are labeled in the rough draft with their corresponding numbers from the outline.

The Detailed Outline

I. Introduction
   A. Ill-fated Alexandra, Catherine the Great
   B. Similarities
      1. Backgrounds
      2. Relationships with families and Russian people
   C. Differences
      1. In how they handles their personal lives
      2. Politically
   D. Thesis: They are both deserving of a place in history.

II. Background
   A. Similarities
      1. Born in small German states
      2. Domineering and ambitious mother/mother figures
         a. Catherine's mother, Princess Joanna, wanted a grand match she could control.
         b. Alexandra's grandmother, Queen Victoria, wanted the same thing.
      3. Arranged marriages into Russian imperial family
      4. Had to convert to Orthodoxy and change their names
         a. Alexandra's birth name was Alix.
         b. Catherine's birth name was Sophia Augusta Frederika.
   B. Differences
      1. Marriages
         a. Catherine didn't argue her parents' choice.
         b. Alexandra refused several suitors and married for love.
      2. Conversion
         a. Alexandra initially refused to marry the man she loved over the issue (Erickson paraphrase page 46).
         b. Catherine didn't balk and became very devout.

III. Relationships
   A. Similarities
      1. In-law troubles
         a. Alexandra
            1) Had to deal with a passionate, intriguing, arguing group of in-laws

2) She tried to stay out the way and ended up looking stuck up.

        3) Her mother-in-law controlled everything.

        4) Things were made worse because it took her 10 years to have an heir.

        5) The Russian court always saw her as an outsider.

    b. Catherine

        1) Also struggled with her in-laws, mostly the Empress Elizabeth who controlled every aspect of her life

        2) It also took Catherine 10 years to have an heir

        3) She also dealt with being seen as an outsider, though it wasn't as severe as Alex's treatment

B.   Differences

  1. In-laws

    a. Alexandra was despised at first and then loved.

        1) Minnie never wanted or approved of her.

        2) Once she got pregnant, her lot improved.

    b. Catherine was chosen by Elizabeth, and the court welcomed and helped her (Alexander quote page 30).

        1) Once she got pregnant, she was tossed aside and ignored.

  2. Children

    a. Alexandra

        1) A loving attentive mother who supervised every aspect of her children's rearing

        2) Breastfed her kids

        3) Took steps to make sure they were physically and morally well-developed

    b. Catherine

        1) Children were all illegitimate and taken from her right after birth.

        2) Children raised by Elizabeth

  3. The Russian people

    a. Catherine

        1) Was able to win the people over

        2) Was known as "the Great" even before her death

   b. Alexandra

    1) Was always despised and mistrusted

    2) Seen as pro-German

    3) Erickson quote page 222

    4) Was known as the German Bitch

    5) Was accused of being a German spy

IV. Deaths

  A. Catherine

    1. Died of apoplexy at 67

    2. Honored and buried as befitted an empress

  B. Alexandra

    1. Arrested and brutally murdered

    2. Buried in a pit in the woods for 70 years

    3. Reburied in 1998

V. Conclusion

  A. Both were amazing women.

  B. Both were strong and ambitious.

  C. Alexandra might have become as great as Catherine.

    1. Circumstances were against her and her mind broke under the strain.

  D. Catherine took the opportunities she was given and became one of the most celebrated leaders of her country.

  E. Ironic that Catherine who did much to help her people is now vilified while Alexandra, who accidentally did much to hurt her country, is now revered

  F. Both women, for good or bad, helped shape Russia into what it is today and are deserving of a place in history.

6 Compare and Contrast Essay

Compare and Contrast Essay

6

Version 1: The Rough Draft

Catherine and Alexandra

INTRODUCTION

(I A) Alexandra, the ill-fated last empress of Russia, and Catherine, who has been labeled "the Great" by posterity, are two of Russia's most famous royals. **(I B)** In many ways, these women were very similar, **(I B1)** both in their backgrounds **(I B2)** and with there struggles with their families and the Russian people. **(I C)** However there are many aspects in which they are completely different from one another, **(I C1)** most notably in how they dealt with their personal lives **(I C2)** and with regards to their political power and prowess. **(I D)** Regardless of their strengths or weaknesses, both women earned their place in history.

BODY OF ESSAY

(II A1) Alexandra, was born in Hesse-Darmstadt, a tiny German principality.[1] She was the daughter of Alice, the daughter of Queen Victoria of England. Like Alexandra, Catherine was born to a German family in the small principality of Anhalt-Zerbst.[2] **(II A2)** Both women were raised by ambitious and controlling women. **(II A2a)** Catherine's mother, Princess Joanna, was determined that her daughter would make a grand match, preferably one in which Joanna would be able to rule from behind the scenes. **(II A2b)** Although Alexandra's mother died when she was young, she was the granddaughter of Queen Victoria, who had the same aspirations for Alexandra as Joanna did for Catherine.

(II A3) Both women had husbands chosen for them, as was the custom for royalty and gentry in those days. **(II A4)** As a condition of their marriages into the Russian imperial family, both women were also required to convert to Orthodoxy and change their names. **(II A4a)** Alexandra's birth name was Alix, **(II A4b)** while Catherine was born Sophia Augusta Frederika.

(II B) Though Catherine and Alexandra had similar backgrounds and upbringings, the way in which they approached their duties differed

---

1. Carolly Erickson, *Alexandra: The Last Tsarina*, (New York: St. Martin's Press, 2001), 1.

2. John T. Alexander, *Catherine the Great*, (New York: Oxford University Press, 1989), 1.

greatly. **(II B1a)** First of all, Catherine did not argue her parent's choice of a spouse for her. She dutifully went to marry Peter, the future Tsar of Russia. **(II B1b)** Alexandra, on the other hand, managed to avoid being married off several times, often refusing because she did not love the man in question and rejected the idea of spending her life in a loveless union.[3] She even initially refused to marry Nicholas of Russia, her cousin whom she truly loved. The obstacle in this case was not a matter of heart, but of religion. **(II B2a)** In order to marry Nicolas, she would have to convert to Orthodoxy. Alix, a stout Lutheran, did not feel that she could renounce her religion, even if it meant a lifetime of loneliness. After speaking to several people, including her sister Ella who had also married into the Romanov family, Alexandra decided that she could make the sacrifice in order to marry Nicholas. It was explained to her that she didn't really have to renounce her religion. She could continue to worship as she pleased, as long as she went through the necessary Orthodox ceremonies that were required of the empress of Russia.[4]

(II B2b) Catherine, when it came to conversion, did not balk as Alexandra did. It wasn't that she was any less devoted to her Lutheran faith. It may be that she put more effort into learning about Orthodoxy. When it came time to choose, Catherine freely chose her new faith, and was ever after a devoted Orthodox.[5]

(III A1a) Alexandra's troubles continued with her soon-to-be in-laws. **(III A1a1)** The Romanov family was a passionate family, full of intrigues, arguments, and conflicting emotions. **(III A1a2)** Trying to avoid the ostracism, Alexandra attempted to stay out of the family's way. Instead, she was seen as stuck up. To make matters worse, a sort of uneasy rivalry developed between Alexandra and her mother-in-law, the Dowager Empress.

At the being of the marriage, Minnie seemed to hold the upper hand. **(III A1a3)** Minnie chose the rooms that Nicholas and Alexandra lived in, picked their servants, and was the dominant force in almost every other aspect of their lives. They asked her permission before going anywhere, and Nicholas always consulted her before making

---

3. Erickson, *Alexandra.*, 46.
4. Ibid., 48.
5. Alexander, *Catherine*, 21.
6. Erickson, *Alexandra*, 44.

any major decisions.[6] **(III A1a4)** Her position was not helped by the fact that she did not seem able to produce an heir, her sold purpose and primary duty. She did become pregnant relatively quickly, but gave birth to four girls before she finally, nearly a decade after her marriage, achieved that which she had been brought to Russia for and gave the country an heir. **(III A1a5)** But her new court and countrymen never truly accepted her.

(III A1b1) Catherine also struggled against in-laws, most notably the Empress Elizabeth, who controlled every aspect of her life. **(III A1b2)** As with Alexandra, matters were not helped by the fact that it also took Catherine nearly ten years to produce an heir for the throne. **(III A1b3)** Catherine also dealt with being seen as an outsider, though her problems in this area weren't as dire as Alexandra's.

(III B1) While both women had problems with their in-laws, relations for Alexandra were strained from the beginning **(III B1a1)** because Minnie (as her mother-in-law, the Dowager Empress, was known in the family) had made no secret of the fact that she had, for several years, been opposed to Alexandra as a wife for her oldest son. She relented only when it became obvious that Nicholas would never marry anyone else. **(III B1a2)** Though, when it was discovered that Alexandra was pregnant, the court celebrated. She was no longer criticized. Instead, she was pampered and protected.[7]

Catherine's problems started later in her marriage. **(III B1b)** The Empress Elizabeth, the guardian of Peter, Catherine's husband, chose Catherine, and issued the wedding invitation to her. The new court that Catherine entered not only welcomed her, but "facilitated [her] progress in adopting the culture and customs of her new homeland," unlike poor Alexandra who was thrown to the wolves and left to flounder.[8] **(III B1b1)** Catherine was pampered and protected right up until she gave birth. Then, her usefulness was over and her status as treasured daughter-in-law disappeared.

(III B2) The empresses relationships with their children also vastly differed. **(III B2a1)** Alexandra was a loving and attentive mother who supervised every aspect of her children's rearing. **(III B2a2)** She even

---

7. Ibid., 57.
8. Alexander, *Catherine*, 29–30.

breastfed her children herself. **(III B2a3)** She was not only very anxious for her children's health, but she was also concerned about the development of their moral character. She made every effort to make sure the children grew up conscious of the needs of others and free from any notions of privilege or haughtiness because of their station in life.

(III B2b) Catherine's experiences with her children were vastly different. **(III B2b1)** Her children were almost certainly fathered by several of her many lovers, not by her husband as was the case with Alexandra. While Alexandra took a personal role in the care and upbringing of her children, Catherine was given no choice on the matter. **(III B2b2)** As soon as she delivered her children, the Empress Elizabeth took them, named them, and raised them. Catherine had little to no contact with them and had no influence over their upbringing.[9]

(III B3) Both Alexandra and Catherine walked a fine line with the Russian people. As foreign princesses marrying into the Russian imperial family, they were viewed by the Russian people as outsiders, at least for a while. **(III B3a1)** Catherine was able to win the people, or at least those that could keep her in power, over. Whatever else she was, she was a great ruler. **(III B3a2)** She was known as "the Great" even before her death, throughout Europe and other areas abroad, as well as by the people of Russia.

(III B3b1) But Alexandra was always seen as a mistrusted outsider. **(III B3b2)** One thing that continued to hurt her was the accusation that she was pro-German because of her birth and background. This was an accusation that had been hurled at Alexandra since the early days of her marriage. **(III B3b3)** She had even become known as the German Bitch. This especially hurt her because she had always disliked her cousin Willy (the German Kaiser) and the German court. **(III B3b4)** She had also, by this time, lived in Russia for nearly half of her life and, in that time, "had become an ardent Russian patriot."[10] **(III B3b5)** But the people continued their accusations, even going so far as to call her a German spy.[11] **(IV)** Of all the differences between these two empresses of Russia, the greatest is that between their deaths. **(IV A1)** Catherine died at the age of 67 of an apoplexy. **(IV A2)** Her family,

---

9. Ibid., 62.

10. Erickson, *Alexandra*, 222.

11. Ibid., 223.

friends, and subjects openly mourned her, either genuinely or not. She was given a burial fit for an empress. **(IV B1)** Alexandra was taken into a little room, along with her family, and was brutally shot and stabbed to death. **(IV B2)** Her body was then dismembered, destroyed by acid and fire, and hidden in an unmarked, secret grave for 70 years. Only close friends and family mourned her death, those that were not killed themselves. **(IV B3)** And it wasn't until 1998 that she was finally laid to rest with the respect and style that she deserved.

CONCLUSION

(V A) Both Alexandra and Catherine were amazing women. **(V B)** They were both strong and ambitious. **(V C)** Under different circumstances, Alexandra might have even become a ruler as great as Catherine. She certainly had the qualities required. **(V C1)** But time and circumstances worked against her, and her once strong mind began to crack under the strain. **(V D)** Catherine, on the other hand, took the opportunities that were given to her and used them to make herself one of the most celebrated leaders of her country.

(V E) It is ironic that Catherine, who did much to help her people, would now be so vilified, while Alexandra, who did much, albeit inadvertently, to hurt her people, should now be revered. **(V F)** Both women, for good or bad, helped shape Russia into what it is today and are deserving of a place in history.

Works Cited

Alexander, John T. *Catherine the Great: Life and Legend*. New York: Oxford University Press, 1989.

Erickson, Carolly. *Alexandra: The Last Tsarina*. New York: St Martin's Press, 2001.

Version 2: The Edited Draft

The second version of the essay is the edited copy of the rough draft. This version has comments and revision suggestions marked in red italics. When proofreading your essays, you want to look for technical mistakes, such as spelling and punctuation errors, incorrect grammar, missing words, and awkward sentence structures. But you also want to look for areas where more extensive revision would be helpful. Maybe there is a statement that needs some additional information added, or a transition from one statement to another that could use a little beefing up. All of these things are part of the proofreading and editing process.

6 Compare and Contrast Essay

Catherine and Alexandra

Alexandra, the ill-fated last empress of Russia, and Catherine, who has been labeled "the Great" by posterity, are two of Russia's most famous royals. *(This isn't bad, but you could open it with a more general statement to lead into your subject.)* In many ways, these women were very similar, both in their backgrounds, and with there *(Change to "their.")* struggles with their families and the Russian people. However there are many aspects in which they are completely different from one another, most notably in how they dealt with their personal lives and with regards to their political power and prowess. Regardless of their strengths or weaknesses, both women earned their place in history.

Alexandra, was born in Hesse-Darmstadt, a tiny German principality.[1] She was the daughter of Alice, the daughter *(You might want to clarify this a bit. Because you are discussing Alexandra, stick with her relationship to the people you are mentioning.)* of Queen Victoria of England. Like Alexandra, Catherine was born to a German family in the small principality of Anhalt-Zerbst.[2] Both women were raised by ambitious and controlling women. Catherine's mother, Princess Joanna, was determined that her daughter would make a grand match, preferably one in which Joanna would be able to rule from behind the scenes. Although Alexandra's mother died when she was young, she was the granddaughter of Queen Victoria *(This has already been mentioned above)*, who had the same aspirations for Alexandra as Joanna did for Catherine.

Both women had husbands chosen for them, as was the custom for royalty and gentry in those days. As a condition of their marriages into the Russian imperial family, both women were also required to convert to Orthodoxy and change their names. Alexandra's birth name was Alix, while Catherine was born Sophia Augusta Frederika.

Though Catherine and Alexandra had similar backgrounds and upbringings, the way in which they approached their duties differed greatly. First of all, Catherine did not argue her parent's *(Change to "parents.")* choice of a spouse for her. She dutifully went to marry Peter, the future Tsar of Russia. Alexandra, on the other hand, managed to

1. Carolly Erickson, *Alexandra: The Last Tsarina*, (New York: St. Martin's Press, 2001), 1.
2. John T. Alexander, *Catherine the Great*, (New York: Oxford University Press, 1989), 1.

avoid being married off several times, often refusing because she did not love the man in question and rejected the idea of spending her life in a loveless union.[3] She even initially refused to marry Nicholas of Russia, her cousin whom she truly loved. *(Start a new paragraph here.)* The obstacle in this case was not a matter of heart, but of religion. In order to marry Nicolas *(This was spelled with an "h" above. Double-check the spelling and be consistent.)*, she would have to convert to Orthodoxy. Alix *(Though we know this is Alexandra's birth name, it's a good idea to stay consistent. Stick with Alexandra.)*, a stout Lutheran, did not feel <u>that</u> *(not needed)* she could renounce her religion, even if it meant a lifetime of loneliness. After speaking to several people, including her sister Ella who had also married into the Romanov family, Alexandra decided that she could make the sacrifice in order to marry Nicholas. It was explained to her that she didn't really have to renounce her religion. She could continue to worship as she pleased *(Both this bit and the previous sentence are stating the same information. Condense into one sentence.)*, as long as she went through the necessary Orthodox ceremonies that were required of the empress of Russia.[4]

Catherine, when it came to conversion, did not balk as Alexandra did. It wasn't *(This is technically fine, but in a formal essay, don't use contractions.)* that she was any less devoted to her Lutheran faith. It may be that she put more effort into learning about Orthodoxy. When it came time to choose, Catherine freely chose her new faith, and was ever after a devoted Orthodox.[5] *(This sentence sounds a little repetitive with the choose/chose. A simple rewording would make it stronger.)*

Alexandra's troubles continued with her soon-to-be in-laws. The Romanov family was a passionate family *(Can you use another word here to avoid the repeat of "family"?)*, full of intrigues, arguments, and conflicting emotions . Trying to avoid the ostracism *(What ostracism? This doesn't make much sense without more information.)*, Alexandra attempted to stay out of the family's way. Instead, she was seen as stuck up *(Reword to make it sound more formal.)*. To make matters worse, a sort of uneasy rivalry developed between Alexandra and her mother-in-law, the Dowager Empress.

---

3. Erickson, *Alexandra.*, 46.

4. Ibid., 48.

5. Alexander, *Catherine*, 21.

At the being *(beginning)* of the marriage, Minnie *(Is Minnie the Dowager Empress?)* seemed to hold the upper hand. Minnie chose the rooms that Nicholas and Alexandra lived in, picked their servants, and was the dominant force in almost every other aspect of their lives. They asked her permission before going anywhere, and Nicholas always consulted her before making any major decisions.[6] Her *(Who is "her"?)* position was not helped by the fact that she did not seem able to produce an heir, her sold *(sole)* purpose and primary duty. She did become pregnant relatively quickly, but gave birth to four girls before she finally, nearly a decade after her marriage, achieved that which she had been brought to Russia for *(Reword to "achieved that for which she had been brought to Russia.")* and gave the country an heir. But her new court and countrymen never truly accepted her.

Catherine also struggled against in-laws, most notably the Empress Elizabeth *(Is this her mother-in-law? What is their relationship?)*, who controlled every aspect of her life. As with Alexandra, matters were not helped by the fact that it also took Catherine nearly ten years to produce an heir for the throne. **(III A1b3)** Catherine also dealt with being seen as an outsider, though her problems in this area weren't as dire as Alexandra's. *(You have the word "also" several times here. Cut out a couple.)*

While both women had problems with their in-laws, relations for Alexandra were strained from the beginning because Minnie (as her mother-in-law, the Dowager Empress, was known in the family) *(Move this information up to where you first mention her.)* had made no secret of the fact that she had, for several years, been opposed to Alexandra as a wife for her oldest son. She relented only when it became obvious that Nicholas would never marry anyone else. Though, when it was discovered that Alexandra was pregnant, the court celebrated. She was no longer criticized. Instead, she was pampered and protected.[7]

Catherine's problems started later in her marriage. The Empress Elizabeth, the guardian of Peter, Catherine's husband, (Again, move this up to where you first mention her so your readers know who they are. Then you won't need to mention the relationships here, which will simplify this complicated sentence.) chose Catherine, and issued

---

6. Erickson, *Alexandra*, 44.

7. Ibid., 57.

the wedding invitation to her. The new court that Catherine entered not only welcomed her, but "facilitated [her] progress in adopting the culture and customs of her new homeland," unlike poor Alexandra who was thrown to the wolves and left to flounder.[8] Catherine was pampered and protected right up until she gave birth. Then, her usefulness was over and her status as treasured daughter-in-law disappeared.

The empresses *(Change to "empresses'.")* relationships with their children also vastly differed. Alexandra was a loving and attentive mother who supervised every aspect of her children's rearing. She even breastfed her children herself *(Why is this important?)*. She was not only very anxious for her children's health *(This is okay as is, but you could add the word "physical" to help differentiate between the two.)*, but she was also concerned about the development of their moral character. She made every effort to make sure the children grew up conscious of the needs of others and free from any notions of privilege or haughtiness because of their station in life.

Catherine's experiences with her children were vastly different. Her children were almost certainly fathered by several of her many lovers, not by her husband as was the case with Alexandra. While Alexandra took a personal roll *(role)* in the care and upbringing of her children, Catherine was given no choice on *(in)* the matter. As soon as she delivered her children, the Empress Elizabeth took them, named them, and raised them. Catherine had little to no contact with them and had no influence over their upbringing.[9]

Both Alexandra and Catherine walked a fine line with the Russian people. As foreign princesses marrying into the Russian imperial family, they were viewed by the Russian people as outsiders, at least for a while. *(Cut this last bit and reword to include this information without having to tack it on at the end.)* Catherine was able to win the people, or at least those that could keep her in power, over *(This is a little confusing and awkward. Reword.)* Whatever else she was, she was a great ruler. She was known as "the Great" even before her death, throughout Europe and other areas abroad, as well as by the people of Russia.

But Alexandra was always seen as a mistrusted outsider. One thing that continued to hurt her *(politically or personally?)* was the accusation

8. Alexander, *Catherine*, 29-30.

9. Ibid., 62.

that she was pro-German because of her birth and background. This was an accusation that had been hurled at Alexandra since the early days of her marriage. She had even become known as the German Bitch. This especially hurt her because she had always disliked her cousin Willy (the German Kaiser) and the German court. *(Rearrange this information a bit. The fact that she was seen as a pro-German outsider hurt her because she had never liked her cousin and had, by that time, spent most of her life in Russia—not the nasty nickname. So lump all the "outsider" information together and list all the names she was called (German Bitch, German spy) together.)* She had also, by this time, lived in Russia for nearly half of her life and, in that time, "had become an ardent Russian patriot."[10] But the people continued their accusations, even going so far as to call her a German spy.[11]

Of all the differences between these two empresses of Russia, the greatest is that between their deaths. Catherine died at the age of 67 of an apoplexy *(What is this?)*. Her family, friends, and subjects openly mourned her, either genuinely or not *(not needed)*. She was given a burial fit for an empress. Alexandra was taken into a little room, along with her family, and was brutally shot and stabbed to death *(Reword to get rid of at least one of these commas. Commas aren't bad, but, in this case, the over use of them make the sentence unnecessarily choppy.)*. Her body was then dismembered, destroyed by acid and fire, and hidden in an unmarked, secret grave for 70 years. *(Watch the sentence structures of your paragraphs. The last several sentences have the same structure— long with several commas chopping them up. Vary the sentence structure to keep the reader interested.)* Only close friends and family mourned her death, those that were not killed themselves *(Reword to simplify.)*. And *(Beginning a sentence with "And" isn't fatal, but it isn't necessary here.)* it wasn't until 1998 that she was finally laid to rest with the respect and style that she deserved *(Citations for all this info?)*.

Both Alexandra and Catherine were amazing women. They were both strong and ambitious. Under different circumstances, Alexandra might have even *(not needed)* become a ruler as great as Catherine. She certainly had the qualities required. But time and circumstances worked against her, and her once strong mind began to crack under

---

10. Erickson, *Alexandra*, 222.

11. Ibid., 223.

the strain. Catherine, on the other hand, took the opportunities that were given to her and used them to make herself one of the most celebrated leaders of her country.

It is ironic that Catherine, who did much to help her people, would now be so vilified, while Alexandra, who did much, albeit inadvertently, to hurt her people, should now be revered *(Again, reword to simplify this sentence.)*. Both women, for good or bad, helped shape Russia into what it is today and are deserving of a place in history.

Works Cited

Alexander, John T. *Catherine the Great: Life and Legend*. New York: Oxford University Press, 1989.

Erickson, Carolly. *Alexandra: The Last Tsarina*. New York: St Martin's Press, 2001.

6 Compare and Contrast Essay

Version 3: The Final Draft

The third version of the essay is the final, revised copy so you can see how it has transformed from an outline, to a rough draft, to a polished essay ready to turn in.

Compare and Contrast Essay 6

Catherine and Alexandra

When thinking of the empresses of Russia, two names automatically come to mind. Alexandra, the ill-fated last empress of Russia, and Catherine, who has been labeled "the Great" by posterity, are two of Russia's most famous royals. In many ways, these women were very similar, both in their backgrounds, and with their struggles with their families and the Russian people. However there are many aspects in which they are completely different from one another, most notably in how they dealt with their personal lives and with regards to their political power and prowess. Regardless of their strengths or weaknesses, both women earned their place in history.

Alexandra was born in Hesse-Darmstadt, a tiny German principality.[1] She was the daughter of Princess Alice of Great Britain, and the granddaughter of Queen Victoria. Like Alexandra, Catherine was born to a German family in the small principality of Anhalt-Zerbst.[2] Both women were raised by ambitious and controlling women. Catherine's mother, Princess Joanna, was determined that her daughter would make a grand match, preferably one in which Joanna would be able to rule from behind the scenes. Although Alexandra's mother died when she was young, her grandmother had the same aspirations for Alexandra as Joanna did for Catherine.

Both women had husbands chosen for them, as was the custom for royalty and gentry in those days. As a condition of their marriages into the Russian imperial family, both women were also required to convert to Orthodoxy and change their names. Alexandra's birth name was Alix, while Catherine was born Sophia Augusta Frederika.

Though Catherine and Alexandra had similar backgrounds and upbringings, the way in which they approached their duties differed greatly. First of all, Catherine did not argue her parents' choice of a spouse for her. She dutifully went to marry Peter, the future Tsar of Russia. Alexandra, on the other hand, managed to avoid being married off several times, often refusing because she did not love the man in

---

1. Carolly Erickson, *Alexandra: The Last Tsarina*, (New York: St. Martin's Press, 2001), 1.

2. John T. Alexander, *Catherine the Great: Life and Legend*, (New York: Oxford University Press, 1989), 1.

question and rejected the idea of spending her life in a loveless union.[3] She even initially refused to marry Nicholas of Russia, her cousin, whom she truly loved.

The obstacle in this case was not a matter of heart, but of religion. In order to marry Nicholas, she would have to convert to Orthodoxy. Alexandra, a stout Lutheran, did not feel she could renounce her religion, even if it meant a lifetime of loneliness. After speaking to several people, including her sister Ella who had also married into the Romanov family, Alexandra decided that she could make the sacrifice in order to marry Nicholas. It was explained to her that she could continue to worship as she pleased, as long as she went through the necessary Orthodox ceremonies that were required of the empress of Russia.[4]

Catherine, when it came to conversion, did not balk as Alexandra did. It was not that she was any less devoted to her Lutheran faith. It may be that she put more effort into learning about Orthodoxy. When it came time to choose, Catherine freely embraced her new faith and was ever after a devoted Orthodox.[5]

Alexandra's troubles continued with her soon-to-be in-laws. The Romanov family was a passionate clan, full of intrigues, arguments, and conflicting emotions. Trying to avoid the ostracism faced by other members of the family who didn't fit in, Alexandra attempted to stay out of the family's way. Instead, her behavior was seen as hauteur. To make matters worse, a sort of uneasy rivalry developed between Alexandra and her mother-in-law, Minnie, the Dowager Empress.

At the beginning of the marriage, Minnie seemed to hold the upper hand. Minnie chose the rooms that Nicholas and Alexandra lived in, picked their servants, and was the dominant force in almost every other aspect of their lives. They asked her permission before going anywhere, and Nicholas always consulted her before making any major decisions.[6] Alexandra's position was not helped by the fact that she did not seem able to produce an heir, her sole purpose and primary duty.

6 Compare and Contrast Essay

---

3. Erickson, *Alexandra*, 46.

4. Ibid., 48.

5. Alexander, *Catherine*, 21.

6. Erickson, *Alexandra*, 44.

She did become pregnant relatively quickly, but gave birth to four girls before she finally, nearly a decade after her marriage, achieved that for which she had been brought to Russia and gave the country an heir. But her new court and countrymen never truly accepted her.

Catherine also struggled against in-laws, most notably with her husband's guardian, the Empress Elizabeth, who controlled every aspect of her life. As with Alexandra, matters were not helped by the fact that it took Catherine nearly ten years to produce an heir for the throne. Catherine also dealt with being seen as an outsider, though her problems in this area weren't as dire as Alexandra's.

While both women had problems with their in-laws, relations for Alexandra were strained from the beginning because Minnie had made no secret of the fact that she had, for several years, been opposed to Alexandra as a wife for her oldest son. She relented only when it became obvious that Nicholas would never marry anyone else. When it was discovered that Alexandra was pregnant, the court celebrated. She was no longer criticized. Instead, she was pampered and protected.[7]

Catherine's problems started later in her marriage. The Empress Elizabeth chose Catherine and issued the wedding invitation to her. The new court that Catherine entered not only welcomed her, but "facilitated [her] progress in adopting the culture and customs of her new homeland," unlike poor Alexandra, who was thrown to the wolves and left to flounder.[8] Catherine was pampered and protected right up until she gave birth. Then, her usefulness was over and her status as treasured daughter-in-law disappeared.

The empresses' relationships with their children also vastly differed. Alexandra was a loving and attentive mother who supervised every aspect of her children's rearing. She even breastfed her children herself, something that was not usually done in noble or royal families. She was not only very anxious for her children's physical health, but she was also concerned about the development of their moral character. She made every effort to make sure the children grew up conscious of the needs of others and free from any notions of privilege or haughtiness because of their station in life.

---

7. Ibid., 57.
8. Alexander, *Catherine*, 29–30.

Catherine's experiences with her children were vastly different. Her children were almost certainly fathered by several of her many lovers, not by her husband, as was the case with Alexandra. While Alexandra took a personal role in the care and upbringing of her children, Catherine was given no choice in the matter. As soon as she delivered her children, the Empress Elizabeth took them, named them, and raised them. Catherine had little to no contact with them and had no influence over their upbringing.[9]

Both Alexandra and Catherine walked a fine line with the Russian people. As foreign princesses marrying into the Russian imperial family, they were initially viewed by the Russian people as outsiders. Catherine was able to win the right people over. Whatever else she was, she was a great ruler. She was known as "the Great" even before her death, throughout Europe and other areas abroad, as well as by the people of Russia.

But Alexandra was always seen as a mistrusted outsider. One thing that continued to hurt her, both politically and personally, was the accusation that she was pro-German because of her birth and background. This was an accusation that had been hurled at Alexandra since the early days of her marriage. This especially hurt her because she had always disliked her cousin Willy (the German Kaiser) and the German court. She had also, by this time, lived in Russia for nearly half of her life and, in that time, "had become an ardent Russian patriot."[10] But the people continued their accusations, even going so far as to call her the German Bitch and claim that she was a German spy.[11]

Of all the differences between these two empresses of Russia, the greatest is that between their deaths. Catherine died at the age of 67 of an apoplexy (most likely a stroke). Her family, friends, and subjects openly mourned her. She was given a burial fit for an empress.[12] Alexandra and her family were taken into a little room, where they were brutally shot and stabbed to death. Her body was then dismembered, destroyed by acid and fire, and hidden in an unmarked, secret grave

---

9. Ibid., 62.

10. Erickson, *Alexandra*, 222.

11. Ibid., 223.

12. Alexander, *Catherine*, 298–306.

for 70 years. Only her surviving close friends and family mourned her death. It wasn't until 1998 that she was finally laid to rest with the respect and style that she deserved.[13]

Both Alexandra and Catherine were amazing women. They were both strong and ambitious. Under different circumstances, Alexandra might have become a ruler as great as Catherine. She certainly had the qualities required. But time and circumstances worked against her, and her once-strong mind began to crack under the strain. Catherine, on the other hand, took the opportunities that were given to her and used them to make herself one of the most celebrated leaders of her country.

It is ironic that Catherine, who did much to help her people, would now be so vilified, while Alexandra, who inadvertently did much to hurt her people, should now be revered. Both women, for good or bad, helped shape Russia into what it is today and are deserving of a place in history.

---

13. Erickson, *Alexandra*, 301–315.

Works Cited

Alexander, John T. *Catherine the Great: Life and Legend*. New York: Oxford University Press, 1989.

Erickson, Carolly. *Alexandra: The Last Tsarina*. New York: St Martin's Press, 2001.

Exercise 6-1

Answer the following questions about the compare and contrast essay. (*Answers on page 310.*)

1. What are the two methods of writing this type of essay?

    _____

    _____

    _____

    _____

2. What are the similarities discussed in the essay?

    _____

    _____

    _____

    _____

3. What are the differences?

    _____

    _____

    _____

    _____

6 Compare and Contrast Essay

7

Definition Essay

Lesson 7-1: What Is It?

The definition essay defines a particular topic. When writing this type of essay, it is best to describe your topic using all possible avenues. For example, if you are writing an essay on cats, don't just look up the definition of the actual word. You can literally define the word *cat*, but add to it by discussing the history of cats, how many types there are, where they live, countries they are worshipped in; describe how cats look, feel, smell, and act. Do cats have natural predators? What do cats like to eat? Explore all aspects of your topic in order to fully define it.

With most subjects, it is helpful to narrow your focus. For instance, if you want to write about cats, you could choose a specific breed. Instead of writing a general essay on the cat species as a whole, you could focus on the Siamese cat, exploring its unique qualities.

Definition essays are also used to define terms or ideas such as "love," "faith," or "patriotism." You can use personal experiences, examples, and stories to help define these concepts along with other evidence, such as dictionary definitions or

7 Definition Essay

scholarly articles. As with other essays, you'll need to narrow your focus. For example, if your topic was faith, what type of faith are you defining? Religious faith, faith in yourself, faith in another? Then, as with an object, use all your personal knowledge and appropriate outside sources to help further define your topic.

The thesis for this essay is usually the literal definition. However, don't just use the dictionary definition. Come up with a definition in your own words. Make it as precise and clear as you can. Define your topic by the way it's used, by how it's made, by its characteristics. If you are writing about Siamese cats, your definition/thesis could be "Siamese cats are a breed whose sleek, dark features and pale body fur make them distinctive in the feline world." If your topic is the club hammer, your definition could be "Club hammers are tools with a double-faced head that are useful for tasks such as light demolition work and pounding masonry nails." For something like familial love, the definition could be "Familial love is the emotion a person feels toward people to whom he is related." You want to keep it as basic and precise as you can, while still giving a clear definition.

Lesson 7-2: Getting Started
Step 1: Choose a Topic

First choose a topic. You are going to need to find a lot of information for your essay in order to fully define your subject, so pick a topic that has some depth and breadth to it. This type of essay can actually be a lot of fun, especially if you are able to choose your own topic.

If you are assigned a topic, you can still find an aspect of that topic that interests you to focus on. Are you supposed to write on a Renaissance artist? Look a few up and find one you think is cool. Does your art professor want you to write about baroque architecture? Find a specific building that is interesting and focus on it. For every topic, no matter how boring or uninteresting you think it is, there is probably at least one aspect of it that you'll find interesting enough. You just need to brainstorm a bit.

Step 2: Narrow Your Topic by Making a List

Once you've decided on a general topic, you'll need to narrow your focus. You could write an entire book on something like love or religion or even something tangible like food or books. To narrow your topic, make a list to help you focus on a single category or component. If you want to write on books, what kind specifically:

▶ Romance novels?

▶ Biographies?

▶ Murder mysteries?

▶ Historical novels?

Narrow that focus to something that is manageable within the guidelines of your assignment. If you are supposed to write a three-page essay, you'll probably only be able to discuss one or two aspects of the topic you are defining. If you have 15 pages to fill, you can explore several aspects.

Step 3: Research and Make Notes

The research will be extensive for this type of essay. Even if you know all there is to know about your subject, you'll still need some outside sources to support your information. If you choose doughnuts as your topic, you need to find everything you can to define these wonderful, mouth-watering treats. Imagine describing them to someone who has never had one before. He wants to know everything about them, from how they were invented to how many different kinds there are now.

Remember: It is always better to have too much information than too little, so try not to cut corners here. And don't forget to record your notes! Copy the quotes, paraphrase the info, and make sure you get your citation information. You will not believe how much time this will save you when it comes time to do your outline and write your paper.

Lesson 7-3: Elements of the Essay
Introduction

One way to open your introduction is with a general remark, anecdote, or quotation. If you are writing an essay on doughnuts, you could start with a sentence like "Doughnuts are found in most supermarkets, cafes, and convenience stores." And then lead into your topic. For a definition essay, you will most likely be defining a certain aspect of doughnut history or preparation. Don't forget your thesis; let your reader know what you will be defining.

Body

The body of the essay is where you will be fully defining your topic. Depending on how in-depth your essay is, you could have one paragraph for each aspect of your definition or a page or more for each aspect. For example, if you are defining doughnuts, you could have a paragraph describing different types, a paragraph discussing how they are made, and a paragraph on the doughnut's place in popular culture.

Define your topic as fully as possible. Back up your arguments and remarks with outside sources when appropriate, and be sure to cite the sources you use.

Conclusion

In your conclusion, you need to restate your thesis and summarize all the information you've included in your essay. Remind the reader about the main points in your paper and close it with a nice concluding remark. Whatever it is that you want your reader to take away from your essay, bring it up here. If your paper is on doughnuts, and you've argued that they are America's most popular sweet snack, you won't want to close the essay with a discussion on the decline of doughnut production. Restate your arguments and drive your point home.

Lesson 7-4: Putting It Together

All of your notes should be incorporated into your outline, nicely organized and ready to go. A detailed outline of an essay on doughnuts should look something like this:

I. Introduction
   A. Opening remarks, anecdote, quotation
      1. Quotation from a poem about doughnuts
   B. Thesis: Doughnuts are a sweet, cake-like dessert often shaped in a ring and fried.

II. Body
   A. History of doughnuts
      1. Where did they originate?
      2. Who invented them?
      3. How did they get to the United States?
      4. Has the recipe changed over the years?
   B. Characteristics of doughnuts
      1. Different flavors
      2. Different shapes
      3. Different types of dough
      4. Classic doughnuts
      5. New varieties
   C. Doughnuts and culture
      1. Jokes
      2. Special occasions
      3. Image in popular culture

III. Conclusion
   A. Restate thesis
   B. Summarize information

Sample Essays

Look at the following essay that defines the religion or theological theory of pantheism. The essay focuses on examples of pantheistic societies and their beliefs to define the term, along with basic dictionary and encyclopedic definitions. To make this essay more in-depth, perhaps for a college-level paper, more aspects could be explored. For example, instead of focusing only on pantheistic societies and their beliefs, you could also discuss pantheistic elements in works of literature, poetry, and art.

For our example, we'll stay with a basic essay model. Following is the detailed outline for the essay. Go through it, and then look at the rough draft to see how the essay falls into place. The parts of the essay are labeled in the rough draft with their corresponding numbers from the outline.

The Detailed Outline

I.   Introduction
    A.   Opening statements
        1.   Many believe man and nature came from the same source and are connected.
        2.   Many religions have developed from this idea.
            a.   Pantheism
    B.   Thesis: A good way to understand pantheism is by looking at the beliefs of pantheistic societies.

II. Basic Definitions
    A.   *Webster's Dictionary* definition
    B.   *Collier's Encyclopedia* definition

III. Beliefs of pantheism
    A.   Nature is holy
    B.   Nash quote page 90: "identified deities"
    C.   Nash quote page 90: "conditioned human behavior"
    D.   Nash quote page 20: "environmental ethics"
    E.   Nash quote page 20: circle of life
    F.   Nash quote page 20: Baruch Spinoza quote

IV. Pantheistic societies
    A. Greece and Rome
        1.   Believed in many nature gods
        2.   Poseidon/Neptune
        3.   Also many minor nature deities, such as nymphs and sprites
    B.   Native Americans
        1.   Nash quote page 117: humans and other forms of life formed a society
        2.   They didn't waste anything.
            a.   Nash quote page 118
        3.   Everything had a conscious life.
            a.   Nash quote page 117: bear and plant people

4. They felt everything was connected.
   a. Capps quote page 119
5. Nash quote page 118: selling land is equal to selling family

V. Conclusion
   A. Restate thesis
   B. Restate evidence
      1. All things are connected.
      2. All should be treated with respect.
      3. Nash quote page 118: Chief Seattle quote

Version 1: The Rough Draft

Pantheism

INTRODUCTION

(I A1) Many societies and cultures, both ancient and modern, in the Old and New Worlds, believe that man and nature originated form the same source. Some call that source "God"—others believe it to be a different supernatural force. But most believe that the common background of man and nature connects them in a spiritual and ethical way. **(I A2)** Many religions have developed from this concept. **(I A2a)** One theological philosophy that has developed is pantheism. **(I B)** A good way to understand pantheism is by looking at the beliefs of pantheistic societies

BODY OF ESSAY

(II) So basically, what's pantheism? **(II A)** *Webster's Dictionary* defines it as "1. the doctrine that God is the transcendent reality of which the material universe and man are only manifestations: it involves a denial of God's personality and expresses a tendency to identify God and nature. 2. any religious belief or philosophical doctrine which identifies the universe with God" (1043).

(II B) *Collier's Encyclopedia* states that pantheism is "a point of view which considers that the world, despite its apparent diversity is 'really' a unity, and a unity of such a spiritual kind as to deserve the name 'God'" (Ramsey 393). So pantheism is the belief in nature and that all the things like rocks, trees, animals, man, and even the Earth deserve respect as they are manifestations of God and so they should be treated they same way a person should treat God.

(III A) For pantheists, nature is holy. **(III B)** Because nature is perceived to be something that is sacred, many pantheistic societies "...identified deities with natural objects and processes" (Nash 90). **(III C)** Considering the fact that these societies worshipped nature, it is logically "...reasoned that this belief conditioned human behavior toward nature in the direction of reverence and respect" (Ibid).

(III D) Pantheism is a belief in "...both ecological consciousness and environmental ethics" (Nash 20). Life is a never-ending circle; **(III E)** "when a person [dies], the matter that was his body became something else: soil and food for a plant, for instance, which might nourish a deer and, in turn, a wolf or another person" (Ibid). All things were seen as being holy. **(III F)** Baruch Spinoza said "put forward the pantheistic notion that every being or object—wolves, maple trees, humans, rocks, stars—was a temporary manifestation of a common God-created substance...A tree or a rock had as much value and right to exist as a person" (Ibid).

(IV A) One example of a society that believed in pantheism was Greece. **(IV A)** Rome was also a pantheistic society. **(IV A1)** Both cultures believed in an array of gods, most of whom were deities of Nature. **(IV A2)** Poseidon, known as Neptune to the Romans, is probably the best known of these gods. He was the god of the sea (Nash 90). **(IV A3)** The Greeks and Romans also had manor and goddesses called nymphs and sprites that watched over rivers, trees, and even flowers.

(IV B) Another group of people that could be called pantheists are the Native Americans, as **(IV B1)** "central to most Indian religions and ethical systems was the idea that humans and other forms of life constituted a single society" (Nash 117). **(IV B2)** The Native American Indians didn't waste or unnecessarily desecrate anything that was a part of nature: **(IV B2a)** "Respect and courtesy were mandatory in all interactions with nature. Even when Indians took another life to sustain their own, it was done ritually with reverence and gratitude" (Nash 118). **(IV B3)** The Native Americans saw everything as having a conscious life. **(IV B3a)** "Indians regarded bears, for example, as the bear *people*. Plants were also people" (Nash 117). **(IV B4)** Native Americans believed that everything was connected in some mystical way. **(IV B4a)** To them, "everything in the world about them was filled with Spirits and powers that controlled or otherwise affected the lives of the tribesman. The sun, the mountains, the beaver, the snake, the eagle—each had its mysterious force, or medicine" (Capps 119). **(IV B5)** Because they believed that the very land on which they lived was a living entity, "buying and selling a piece of the earth was as foreign to most Indian cultures as marketing a brother or mother" (Nash 118).

CONCLUSION

(V A) As you can see, it's possible to gain an understanding of what pantheism is by studying those who believe in it. **(V B1)** One of the concepts of pantheism is that all things upon the Earth—from the smallest rock to the widest ocean to a human being—are

7 Definition Essay

all manifestations of the same God or creator and therefore are all connected and related. **(V B2)** If this is the case, then all should be treated with the same respect and courtesy that would be shown to a family member. **(V B3)** As Chief Seattle once said, "All things are connected, like the blood which unites one family" (Nash 118).

Works Cited

Capps, Benjamin. *The Old West: The Indians*. New York: Time Life Books, 1976. Print.

Nash, Roderick Frazier. *The Rights of Nature*. Madison, WI: The University of Wisconsin Press, 1989. Print.

Ramsey, Ian T. "Pantheism." *Collier's Encyclopedia*. Volume 18, 1970. Print.

Webster's Encyclopedia Unabridged Dictionary of the English Language. Avenal, New Jersey: Gramercy Books, 1989. Print.

Version 2: The Edited Draft

The second version of the essay is the edited copy of the rough draft. This version has comments and revision suggestions marked in red. When proofreading your essays, you want to look for technical mistakes, such as spelling and punctuation errors, incorrect grammar, missing words, and awkward sentence structures. But you also want to look for areas where more extensive revision would be helpful. Maybe there is a statement that needs some additional information added, or a transition from one statement to another that could use a little beefing up. All of these things are part of the proofreading and editing process.

Pantheism

Many societies and cultures, both ancient and modern, in the Old and New Worlds, believe that man and nature originated form *(Change to "from.")* the same source. Some call that source "God"— *(Use a semicolon instead of a dash here.)* others believe it to be a different supernatural force. But most believe that the common background of man and nature connects them in a spiritual and ethical way. Many religions have developed from this concept. One theological philosophy that has developed is pantheism. A good way to understand pantheism is by looking at the beliefs of pantheistic societies.

So basically, what's pantheism? *(Reword to make more formal.)* *Webster's Dictionary* defines it as "1. the doctrine that God is the transcendent reality of which the material universe and man are only manifestations: it involves a denial of God's personality and expresses a tendency to identify God and nature. 2. any religious belief or philosophical doctrine which identifies the universe with God" (1043). *(Paraphrase to get rid of the numbers.)*

Collier's Encyclopedia states that pantheism is "a point of view which considers that the world, despite its apparent diversity is 'really' a unity, and a unity of such a spiritual kind as to deserve the name 'God'" (Ramsey 393). So pantheism is the belief in nature and that all the things like rocks, trees, animals, man, and even the Earth deserve respect as they are manifestations of God and so they should be treated they same way a person should treat God. *(This is too long and a little awkward and confusing. Revise.)*

For pantheists, nature is holy. Because nature is perceived to be something that is sacred, many pantheistic societies "...identified deities with natural objects and processes" (Nash 90). Considering the fact that these societies worshipped nature, it is logically "...reasoned that this belief conditioned human behavior toward nature in the direction of reverence and respect" (Ibid). *(Ibid is no longer used in MLA. Just cite the page number again.)*

Pantheism is a belief in "...both ecological consciousness and environmental ethics" (Nash 20). Life is a never-ending circle; "when a person [dies], the matter that was his body became something else: soil and food for a plant, for instance, which might nourish a deer and, in turn, a wolf or another person" (Ibid). *(Change all instances of "Ibid" in this essay.)* All things were seen as being holy. Baruch Spinoza *(Who is this?)* said, "Put forward the pantheistic notion that every being or object—wolves, maple trees, humans, rocks, stars—was a temporary manifestation of a common God-created substance...A tree or a rock had as much value and right to exist as a person" (Ibid).

One example of a society that believed in pantheism was Greece. Rome was also a pantheistic society *(Combine these sentences.)*. Both cultures believed in an array of gods, most of whom were deities of Nature. Poseidon, known as Neptune to the Romans, is probably the best known of these gods *(Zeus is probably better known, and he also controlled a force of nature.)*. He was the god of the sea (Nash 90). The Greeks and Romans also had manor *(Change to "minor.")* gods and goddesses called nymphs and sprites that watched over rivers, trees, and even flowers.

Another group of people that could be called pantheists are the Native Americans *(The tenses of the words "could" and "are" are not consistent. For most essays, stay in the present tense.)*, as "central to most Indian religions and ethical systems was the idea that humans and other forms of life constituted a single society" (Nash 117). The Native American Indians didn't *(Spell out instead of using the contraction.)* waste or unnecessarily desecrate anything that was a part of nature: "Respect and courtesy were mandatory in all interactions with nature. Even when Indians took another life to sustain their own, it was done ritually with reverence and gratitude" (Nash 118). The Native Americans saw everything as having a conscious life. "Indians regarded bears, for example, as the bear *people*. Plants were also people" (Nash 117). *(You could paraphrase this into your own words.)*

Native Americans believed that everything was connected in some mystical way. To them, "everything in the world about them was filled with Spirits and powers that controlled or otherwise affected the lives of the tribesman. The sun, the mountains, the beaver, the snake, the eagle—each had its mysterious force, or medicine" (Capps 119). Because they believed that the very land on which they lived was a living entity, "buying and selling a piece of the earth was as foreign to most Indian cultures as marketing a brother or mother" (Nash 118).

As you can see, it's *(Either spell out or eliminate altogether.)* one of the concepts of pantheism that all things upon the Earth—from the smallest rock to the widest ocean to a human being—are all manifestations of the same God or creator and therefore are all connected and related.

If this is the case, then all should be treated with the same respect and courtesy that would be shown to a family member. As Chief Seattle once said, "All things are connected, like the blood which unites one family" (Nash 118).

Works Cited

Capps, Benjamin. *The Old West: The Indians*. New York: Time Life Books, 1976. Print.

Nash, Roderick Frazier. *The Rights of Nature*. Madison, WI: The University of Wisconsin Press, 1989. Print.

Ramsey, Ian T. "Pantheism." *Collier's Encyclopedia*. Volume 18, 1970. Print.

Webster's Encyclopedia Unabridged Dictionary of the English Language. Avenal, New Jersey: Gramercy Books, 1989. Print.

Version 3: The Final Draft

The third version of the essay is the final, revised copy so you can see how it has transformed from an outline, to a rough draft, to a polished essay ready to turn in.

7 Definition Essay

Pantheism

Many societies and cultures, both ancient and modern, in the Old and New Worlds, believe that man and nature originated from the same source. Some call that source "God"; others believe it to be a different supernatural force. But most believe that the common background of man and nature connects them in a spiritual and ethical way. Many religions have developed from this concept. One theological philosophy that has developed is pantheism. A good way to understand pantheism is by looking at the beliefs of pantheistic societies.

First of all, what exactly is pantheism? *Webster's Dictionary* defines it as a belief in which "God is the transcendent reality of which the material universe and man are only manifestations: it involves a denial of God's personality and expresses a tendency to identify God and nature." It also defines it as "any religious belief or philosophical doctrine which identifies the universe with God" (1043).

Collier's Encyclopedia states that pantheism is "a point of view which considers that the world, despite its apparent diversity is 'really' a unity, and a unity of such a spiritual kind as to deserve the name 'God'" (Ramsey 393). Basically, pantheism is the belief that everything upon the Earth—rocks, trees, animals, man, even the Earth itself—is a manifestation of God and therefore deserves the same respect and treatment as one would show to God.

For pantheists, nature is holy. Because nature is perceived to be something that is sacred, many pantheistic societies "...identified deities with natural objects and processes" (Nash 90). Considering the fact that these societies worshipped nature, it is logically "...reasoned that this belief conditioned human behavior toward nature in the direction of reverence and respect" (90).

Pantheism is a belief in "...both ecological consciousness and environmental ethics" (Nash 20). Life is a never-ending circle; "when a person [dies], the matter that was his body became something else: soil and food for a plant, for instance, which might nourish a deer and, in turn, a wolf or another person" (20). All things were seen as being holy. Baruch Spinoza, a Dutch philosopher, said "put forward the pantheistic notion that every being or object—wolves, maple trees, humans, rocks, stars—was a temporary manifestation of a common God-created substance.... A tree or a rock had as much value and right to exist as a person" (20).

Greece and Rome are two examples of pantheistic societies. Both cultures believed in an array of gods, most of whom were deities of nature. Poseidon, known as Neptune to the Romans, is one of the best known of these gods. He is the god of the sea (Nash 90). The Greeks and Romans also had minor gods and goddesses called nymphs and sprites that watched over rivers, trees, and even flowers.

Another group of people that can be called pantheists are the Native Americans, as "central to most Indian religions and ethical systems was the idea that humans and other forms of life constituted a single society" (Nash 117). The Native American Indians did not waste or unnecessarily desecrate anything that was a part of nature: "Respect and courtesy were mandatory in all interactions with nature. Even when Indians took another life to sustain their own, it was done ritually with reverence and gratitude" (Nash 118). The Native Americans saw everything as having a conscious life. They regarded bears and even plants as equal to people. (Nash 117).

Native Americans believed that everything was connected in some mystical way. To them, "everything in the world about them was filled with Spirits and powers that controlled or otherwise affected the lives of the tribesman. The sun, the mountains, the beaver, the snake, the eagle—each had its mysterious force, or medicine" (Capps 119). Because they believed that the very land on which they lived was a living entity, "buying and selling a piece of the earth was as foreign to most Indian cultures as marketing a brother or mother" (Nash 118).

As you can see, it is one of the concepts of pantheism that all things upon the Earth—from the smallest rock to the widest ocean to a human being—are all manifestations of the same God or creator and therefore are all connected and related. If this is the case, then all should be treated with the same respect and courtesy that would be shown to a family member. As Chief Seattle once said, "All things are connected, like the blood which unites one family" (Nash 118).

Works Cited

Capps, Benjamin. *The Old West: The Indians*. New York: Time Life Books, 1976. Print.

Nash, Roderick Frazier. *The Rights of Nature*. Madison, WI: The University of Wisconsin Press, 1989. Print.

7 Definition Essay

Ramsey, Ian T. "Pantheism." *Collier's Encyclopedia*. Volume 18, 1970. Print.

Webster's Encyclopedia Unabridged Dictionary of the English Language. Avenal, NJ: Gramercy Books, 1989. Print.

Exercise 7-1

Answer the following questions about the definition essay. (*Answers on page 310.*)

1. What does a definition essay do?

_____

_____

_____

_____

2. What should you do after choosing a topic but before you research?

_____

_____

_____

_____

3. What are the main elements of this essay?

_____

_____

_____

_____

8

Descriptive Essay

Lesson 8-1: What Is It?

The descriptive essay describes a person, place, object, experience, or event. Through the use of vivid details utilizing all the senses, you will describe every aspect of your topic.

Descriptive essays could be put in the narrative non-fiction category. In other words, they are very similar to fiction, only the content of the essay is true, not made up. So, just as if you were writing a fictional short story, you want to add in all sorts of details to help the reader experience what you are describing, just as you experienced it. Point out the exciting, interesting, unusual aspects of what you are describing.

If you are describing an episode from your childhood when you found a jar in the woods, you can start by saying you found a jar. Develop that general statement by telling us where it was and what was in it. What was it about this jar or its location or contents that made the experience memorable for you? Was it full of fake gold you thought was real? Was it half buried beneath a tree? What made the whole experience stand out for you?

Make Them Believe It

One way to bring your writing to life is to add description using the five senses. If you are writing your essay about going to a fair, describe for the reader what she'd see, hear, smell, touch, and feel. Is it cold outside? Can you smell popcorn and cotton candy, or maybe the grease and metallic smell of the rides? Are there animals around? What sounds do you hear? The laughter and screams of those on the rides? The vendors selling their wares? What does the funnel cake taste like? Describing all of these details as vividly as you can will help draw your reader into your essay and let him truly experience whatever you are describing. You don't have to use all five senses, of course, but adding a few in here and there can really help make the experience real for your reader.

Even something mundane can become interesting when you use descriptive details. For example, if you were to write about eating a cheese sandwich, you could describe the smell of the bread, the taste of cheese on your tongue as you bite into it, the feel of the bread between your fingers, the sight of the cheese piled onto the bread, and the consistency of the cheese as you chew. Each detail you describe should be designed to draw the reader further into your essay, so that he experiences what you are writing about as thoroughly as you did.

Another thing to keep in mind is that you want to show your reader what is going on; don't just tell her. For instance, something like "It was cold the night of the fair," is fine. It lets the reader know what the temperature was that night. But it doesn't draw him into the essay and make him a part of the experience you are trying to describe. Instead, describe it fully. Don't just say it was cold; say "A chilling breeze blew across the fairgrounds, raising the gooseflesh on my skin as it nipped at my bare arms." Or was it hot? Don't say "It was hot." Say "Beads of sweat rolled down the back of my neck as the sun beat down on my unprotected head." Make your reader feel the cold or heat. Show her it was cold or hot; don't just tell it.

Lesson 8-2: Getting Started

Step 1: Choose a Topic

Two important things to think of when choosing a topic for a descriptive essay are 1) what are you going to describe? and 2) why do you want to describe it? The "what" will obviously give you your main topic. The "why" will help you narrow your focus a bit and give a meaning and, in fact, a thesis to your essay.

Say you want to describe a recent ride on a motorcycle. What is it about that experience that you want your reader to really understand? Did it make you feel free and alive? Or did you almost have a terrifying crash? If you want to describe the first scenario, you'll want to emphasize the exciting aspects of the ride: the wind blowing through your hair, the feel of the bike thundering beneath you, the scenery flying by. If you want to describe the near-crash scenario, you could describe the same things, but with a different emphasis and tone. For example, you could describe the wind blowing through your hair, the thundering bike, and the scenery speeding by, but where these things were exciting and freeing in one description, you'd want to describe them as frightening and dangerous in the other description. It all depends on how you want to spin it, so this is something you need to figure out before you start.

Step 2: List Your Details

This type of essay won't usually require a lot of research as you will mostly be describing events, objects, people, places, and other subjects that you have personally experienced, but you can make up a list of details that you would like to use in your essay. This list will help keep you on topic and on track once you start writing.

Let's use our motorcycle experience as the topic for an example. We'll make it the fun and exciting scenario. We want to write this essay to show our reader how thrilling and freeing riding a motorcycle can be. What type of details will we want to emphasize? Don't forget to use the five senses!

8

Descriptive Essay

▶ Seeing the bike and climbing on.

▶ Hearing the motor roar to life.

▶ The smell of the tires as you peel out of the parking lot.

▶ The sight of the trees rushing past you as the bike picks up speed.

▶ The taste of the bug that you swallow because your mouth was hanging open as you laughed.

▶ The feel of the wind as you fly down the road.

Lesson 8-3: Elements of the Essay

Your essay, even though it is a descriptive piece illustrating a personal experience, still needs to be clear and organized. Start in a logical place and progress through the experience as you would in real life. For a nice, basic essay, you can use one paragraph for each main point you'd like to describe. (We'll pick three main points we want to emphasize about the motorcycle riding experience.) For a longer, more thorough essay, you could either pick more points to focus on, or just expand your discussion of the few you've chosen.

The Introduction

Introduce your topic with a little general background information and progress into your thesis. For example, your introduction might look like this:

> I always wanted to ride a motorcycle. My father had one when I was growing up, but I was never allowed to touch it. My mother thought it was too dangerous. It wasn't until I was a little older that I was finally able to ride. It was everything I had imagined it would be. Riding that motorcycle was the most interesting, daring, and thrilling experience of my life.

The last line serves as your thesis, the three main points on which your essay will focus.

The Body

Go through your three main points, describing them with as much vivid detail as you can. Look back at your list of details and add them into your descriptions for each main point (interesting, daring, thrilling). Talk about what was so interesting about the bike. What did it look like? What did it sound like? Was it the biggest, shiniest bike on the block or a rusty bucket of bolts that barely puttered when you turned it on?

Move on to your next main point. Why was riding the bike so daring? Where you still a teenager, living at home? Was it still against the rules? Or was it just the knowledge that you were traveling down the road at 60 miles per hour with nothing between you and the road but a bit of leather? Show the reader what made this first ride of yours so daring.

Then focus on what was so thrilling about your ride. The speed? The sheer power of the machine beneath you? Did you meet up with a big biker gang? Did you race someone? Or was it the thrill of flying down the road with the wind in your face that made it so thrilling? Give the reader detail, make him feel what you felt.

The Conclusion

As with other forms of essays, restate your thesis and summarize your main points in the conclusion. Maybe something like this:

> I never rode a motorcycle again, but I'll never forget what an Interesting, daring, and thrilling experience it was. The sight of that red, flame-painted Harley, knowing I was breaking all the rules while I was flying through the wind on that bike will stay with me for the rest of my life.

Lesson 8-4: Putting It Together

Once you have all the elements and details ready to go, put them into outline form. This will help you keep everything organized and ensure that you include all the details you want to include. It will also make writing the essay much easier, as you'll have all your information ready. You'll just need to link it all together.

A detailed outline for this essay might look something like this:

I.   Introduction
   A.   Opening lines
      1.   Wanting to ride when I was a kid
      2.   Not allowed, too dangerous
      3.   Never stopped the desire
   B.   Thesis: Riding that motorcycle was the most interesting, daring, and thrilling experience of my life.

II. Body
   A.   Interesting
      1.   First sight of the bike
         a.   What it looked like
         b.   What make and model it was
         c.   Engine specs (or other interesting info)
   B.   Daring
      1.   The sound of the motor
      2.   Smell of the rubber, squeal of the tires
      3.   Everyone looking at me
      4.   Felt dangerous
   C.   Thrilling
      1.   The sight of the trees rushing past
      2.   The feel of the wind, feeling like flying
      3.   Meeting up with the biker gang

III. Conclusion
   A.   Restate thesis
   B.   Summarize main points
      1.   The sight of that red flame painted Harley
      2.   Knowing I was breaking all the rules
      3.   Flying through the wind on that bike
   C.   Closing line or two

8   Descriptive Essay

Sample Essays

Look at the following essay that describes an experience a woman had in a flower shop. She accompanied her mother to pick out flowers for her grandmother's funeral and ended up learning something about her mother she never knew before.

Following is the detailed outline for the essay. Go through it, and then look at the rough draft to see how the essay falls into place. The parts of the essay are labeled in the rough draft with their corresponding numbers from the outline.

The Detailed Outline

I.   Introduction
    A.   Mom was always a hero to me.
        1.   Raised five kids
    B.   Didn't see her as a "person"
    C.   Grandma died.
    D.   Went to the flower shop
    E.   Finally saw the person behind my mom

II. The flower shop
    A.   Description
        1.   Christmas trees
        2.   The smell of flowers
        3.   The décor
    B.   Mom always loved Christmas.
        1.   Loved the singing and presents
        2.   Loved to decorate
        3.   Loved having her family around
            a.   Ryan lived in California.
            b.   I was married.
            c.   This year we were together for the funeral.
    C.   Meeting Cheryl
        1.   Mom was polite and positive.
        2.   Cheryl gets out the book.
        3.   We tell Cheryl what we are looking for.
    D.   Mom was always the strong one.
        1.   Still had to do the funeral
        2.   Coordinate family
        3.   Take care of Grandpa
        4.   Mom never slowed down
    E.   I realize how much Mom has been doing.
        1.   Caring for Grandma

  2. Caring for Grandpa

  3. Doctors' appointments

  4. Caring for her own kids

 F. I talk to Mom.

  1. Mom feels anxious.

  2. We realize it's because she's used to having so much to do.

III. Conclusion: Lessons learned

 A. Didn't realize until then how much she'd been through

 B. I don't think I could be so strong.

 C. My mom is amazing.

Version 1: The Rough Draft

The Flower Shop

> INTRODUCTION

(I A) My mother was always a hero to me. **(I A1)** She raised five kids while my dad worked and went to school. We all turned out pretty decent, so she must have done an okay job, **(I B)** but I don't know if I ever really saw her as a "person." She was just my mom. But one day, that all changed. **(I C)** My grandmother died the year I was married, and my family flew up to stay with me for the funeral. **(I D)** I accompanied my mom to the flower shop to pick out flowers for my grandmother's casket. **(I E)** And, for the first time, I saw my mom as someone new. She wasn't just my mom. She was a wife, a daughter, a sister. And she was stronger than I ever knew possible.

> BODY OF ESSAY

(II) The bell over the shop door tinkled it's greeting as we entered. **(II A)** The shop was filled with Christmas trees, all decorated with a different theme. **(II A1)** There was one with teddy bears tucked in between the branches, and one decorated entirely with plastic marshmallows and graham crackers. **(II A2)** The heavy aroma of roses and carnations coated the air, and I inhaled deeply, filling my lungs with the fragrant scent. **(II A3)** The walls were covered with shelves of candles and small floral arrangements. Twinkling white lights enveloped every available surface.

The woman behind the counter was arranging what looked like a wedding bouquet, while a gentleman was helping a young man pick out a floral arrangement for his sweetheart. I glanced at my mom nervously, wondering how she felt seeing all these happy people. **(II B)** Christmas had always been her favorite time of year. **(II B1)** She loved the singing and the present giving. **(II B2)** She anxiously waited to decorate her home and Christmas tree, and to daily luxuriate in the strong scent of pine (sometimes strengthened with candles) that emitted from the beautifully adorned tree in the living room.

(II B3) Most importantly, she loved to have her family gathered around her. That hadn't happened for several years now. **(II B3a)** My oldest brother, Ryan, lived in California, and had a young wife and two small children, which made traveling all the way to Tennessee difficult for them. **(II B3b)** I had recently married and moved to Utah, making this my first Christmas away from home. **(II B3c)** Though this year, we

8

Descriptive Essay

were all gathered at my home. It should have been a happy time, with our whole family together again. But we were missing someone.

My mom looked around the shop with a faint smile. She usually loved flower shops. They were always happy, fairyland places that were filled with love and hope in the form of the flowers that dripped and curved from every crack and crevice. We didn't pause for to long. The ever-present anxiety my mom had been living under seemed to boost her adrenaline and propelled her toward the counter and the next duty on the list. "Things to do, people to take care of, can't stop now. Got to hurry." I could almost here the thoughts churning in her mind.

(II C) The woman behind the counter saw us and put the wedding bouquet down as she came toward us, a cheery smile on her face. "Hi. I'm Cheryl. What can I help you with today?"

(II C1) My mom smiled back, automatically polite and positive as she had been through out the ordeal of the last few months. "Well, I need to order some flowers," she said.

Cheryl wiped her hands on her apron, the green juice from the flowers leaving tracks across the white canvas. "We can help you with that. What are you looking for? Are these for a wedding, or dance, or Christmas present?"

"Well, they are actually for a funeral. I need a spray for the casket."

(II C2) Cheryl's smile faded and she looked sympathetically at my mother. "Oh. I'm so sorry." Her smile gradually crept back, but this time instead of gaiety, it held empathy and warmth. "We can help you with those to. Let me get some books for you to look at. Do you have something in mind?"

(II C3) "Well, the casket is emerald green, so I was thinking of something with a lot of greenery, and maybe some pink or white roses, and baby's breath.

"That sounds lovely. We have several arrangements that are similar to that. Let me find the pictures for you here." Cheryl began flipping through books until she found the picture she was looking for. "Here we are." The book opened to a beautiful spray of flowers, white rose, pink lilies and baby's breath arranged in Christmas ferns, lying on top of a green, lacquered coffin.

"Oh," my mom sighed. "Those are gorgeous. She would love those."

"Are these for someone in your family?" Cheryl politely asked.

"Yes. My mother," my mom said matter-of-factly as she continued to look through the book. **(II D)** She was always the strong one. She had to be especially strong now. **(II D1)** There were the funeral arrangements to take care of, **(II D2)** family to be coordinated, and of course, **(II D3)** we still had my 80-year-old grandfather to look after. He wasn't dealing with his wife's death very well. **(II D4)** My mom simply didn't have time to slow down, let alone mourn. I don't know how she did it.

"Oh, I'm so sorry. That's terrible," Cheryl said. "It must be hard, especially so close to the holidays. Was it sudden?"

"No. She had cancer. She was diagnosed just seven months ago. But we were glad that she was able to go before it got too painful for her. We didn't want her to suffer."

"Oh, of course. That is a blessing. You look so tired. Have you been caring for her?"

Laurie looked at the kind, compassionate face of the florist, and I could see her choking back tears. **(II E)** The last few months had been so hard on her. **(II E1)** She cared for her mother through her illness, **(II E2)** kept her house clean and my grandfather taken care of, **(II E3)** not to mention dealing with all the doctor's appointments and medication runs and **(II E4)** all the demands of my siblings and myself.

I answered for her. "Yes, my mom has been taking care of everyone.

"Wow, it sounds like you were run off your feet!" Cheryl said in surprise.

"Yeah, it was pretty hectic," my mom said with a smile.

Cheryl grinned sympathetically at my mom. "Let's find a beautiful bouquet for your mother," she said.

After the flowers were chosen and paid for, my mom and I wandered around the shop a bit longer. I looked up to see my mother staring into space, a slight frown furrowed between her brows.

(II F) "What's wrong?" I asked.

She blinked and looked at me. "I don't know," she said with a little laugh. **(II F1)** "I keep getting these pangs of anxiety like I'm supposed to be somewhere, or that I'm forgetting something important."

I smiled at her. **(II F2)** "That's because taking care of everyone else is all you've been doing for the last several months. Your used to having something to do all the time."

8

Descriptive Essay

My mom laughed. I hadn't heard that sound in quite a while. "You know, you're right. I guess I didn't realize how much I actually been through. I haven't had the time too stop and think." She looked at the gift table in front of her. "This if the first time in a long time that I don't have anything to do, and everyone is being taken care of. What am I going to do with myself?"

I grinned at her. "Whatever you want."

She smiled back. "Let's go get some lunch."

> ### Conclusion

(III) A wait seemed to be lifted from her shoulders, and we walked out the door with an extra bounce in our steps. It was a sad time, but I learned a lot about my mom that day. **(III A)** I hadn't realize until that moment just how much my mother had been through either. I knew the basics. I knew she'd been caring for everyone and everything. But I don't think I truly realized until we were standing in that flower shop just how strong my mom had had to be.

(III B) I don't know that I could have been as strong as she had proven to be. I hope I never have to try. **(III C)** But I do know that my mother is and amazing woman, and that moment in the flower shop will live in my memory for a lifetime.

Version 2: The Edited Draft

The second version of the essay is the edited copy of the rough draft. This version has comments and revision suggestions marked in red. When proofreading your essays, you want to look for technical mistakes, such as spelling and punctuation errors, incorrect grammar, missing words, and awkward sentence structures. But you also want to look for areas where more extensive revision would be helpful. Maybe there is a statement that needs some additional information added, or a transition from one statement to another that could use a little beefing up. All of these things are part of the proofreading and editing process.

The Flower Shop

My mother was always a hero to me. She raised five kids while my dad worked and went to school. We all turned out pretty decent, so she must have done an okay job, but I don't know if I ever really saw her as a "person." She was just my mom. One day, that all changed. *(Start new paragraph.)* My grandmother died the year I was married, and my family flew up to stay with me for the funeral *(What year was this? And why did they come stay with the narrator?)*. I accompanied my mom to the flower shop to pick out flowers for my grandmother's casket. And, for the first time, I saw my mom as someone new. She wasn't just my mom. She was a wife, a daughter, a sister. And she was stronger than I ever knew possible. *(In this paragraph, there are two sentences that start with "but" and two that start with "and." This is okay, but only if you use it sparingly. I'd change one of each.)*

The bell over the shop door tinkled it's *(Remove apostrophe.)* greeting as we entered. The shop was filled with Christmas trees, all decorated with a different theme. There was one with teddy bears tucked in between the branches, and one decorated entirely with plastic marshmallows and graham crackers. The heavy aroma of roses and carnations coated the air, and I inhaled deeply, filling my lungs with the fragrant scent *(You can't really inhale the scent. Change it to "air.")*. The walls were covered with shelves of candles and small floral arrangements. Twinkling white lights enveloped every available surface.

The woman behind the counter was arranging what looked like a wedding bouquet, while a gentleman was helping *(Just say "helped.")* a young man pick out a floral arrangement for his sweetheart. I glanced at my mom nervously, wondering how she felt seeing all these happy people. Christmas had always been her favorite time of year. She loved the singing and the present giving. She anxiously waited *(All year? The weeks leading up to Christmas? When?)* to decorate her home and Christmas tree, and to daily luxuriate in the strong scent of pine (sometimes strengthened with candles) that emitted from the beautifully adorned tree in the living room.

Most importantly, she loved to have her family gathered around her. That hadn't happened for several years now. My oldest brother, Ryan, lived in California, and had a young wife and two small children, which made traveling all the way to Tennessee difficult for them. I had recently married and moved to Utah, making this my first Christmas away from home. Though this year, we were all gathered at my home. It should have been a happy time, with our whole family together again. But we were missing someone. *(We've already been told why the family has gathered together, so this bit of mystery isn't necessary and doesn't fit. Take a look at the last couple lines, starting with "making this my first Christmas away from home" and revise, keeping in mind what the reader has already been told.)*

My mom looked around the shop with a faint smile. She usually loved flower shops. They were always happy, fairyland places that were filled with love and hope in the form of the flowers that dripped and curved from every crack and crevice. We didn't pause for to *(too)* long. The ever-present anxiety my mom had been living under seemed to boost her adrenaline and propelled her toward the counter and the next duty on the list. "Things to do, people to take care of, can't stop now. Got to hurry." I could almost here *(Change to "hear.")* the thoughts churning in her mind. *(Put this last line before the line of dialogue. As it's written, the reader assumes someone is speaking out loud and then telling them it was inner dialogue is a bit confusing.)*

The woman behind the counter saw us and put the wedding bouquet down as she came toward us *(How did she come toward them if she was behind the counter?)*, a cheery smile on her face. "Hi. I'm Cheryl. What can I help you with today?"

My mom smiled back, automatically polite and positive as she had been through out the ordeal of the last few months *(Was she only polite and positive through the ordeal, or was she polite and positive before that as well?)*. "Well, I need to order some flowers," she said.

Cheryl wiped her hands on her apron, the green juice from the flowers leaving tracks across the white canvas. "We can help you with that. What are you looking for? Are these for a wedding, or dance, or Christmas present?"

"Well, they are actually for a funeral. I need a spray for the casket."

Cheryl's smile faded and she looked sympathetically at my mother. "Oh. I'm so sorry." Her smile gradually crept back *(Saying that it "crept" implies it was gradual, so you don't need both words.)*, but this time instead of gaiety, it held empathy and warmth. "We can help you with those to *(too)*. Let me get some books for you to look at. Do you have something in mind?"

"Well, the casket is emerald green, so I was thinking of something with a lot of greenery, and maybe some pink or white roses, and baby's breath. *(Insert a closing quotation mark.)*

"That sounds lovely. We have several arrangements that are similar to that. Let me find the pictures for you here." Cheryl began flipping through books until she found the picture she was looking for. "Here we are." The book opened to a beautiful spray of flowers, white rose*(s)*, pink lilies and baby's breath arranged in Christmas ferns, lying on top of a green, lacquered coffin.

"Oh," my mom sighed. "Those are gorgeous. She would love those."

"Are these for someone in your family?" Cheryl politely asked.

"Yes. My mother," my mom said matter-of-factly as she continued to look through the book. *(Start a new paragraph, because these thoughts are connected to the narrator, not the mother.)* She was always the strong one. She had to be especially strong now. There were the funeral arrangements to take care of, family to be coordinated, and of course, we still had my 80-year-old grandfather to look after. He wasn't dealing with his wife's death very well. My mom simply didn't have time to slow down, let alone mourn. I don't know how she did it.

"Oh, I'm so sorry. That's terrible," Cheryl said. "It must be hard, especially so close to the holidays. Was it sudden?"

"No. She had cancer. She was diagnosed just seven months ago (Saying "just" implies that is was sudden, yet she says it wasn't sudden. Remove the "just" so it's not contradictory, or change the first line to something like "Not really."). But we were glad that she was able to go before it got too painful for her. We didn't want her to suffer."

"Oh, of course. That is a blessing. You look so tired. Have you been caring for her?"

Laurie *(Who is this? The mother? The narrator?)* looked at the kind, compassionate face of the florist, and I could see her choking back tears *(Who was choking back tears? The florist? The mother?)*. The last few months had been so hard on her. She cared for her mother through her illness, kept her house clean and my grandfather taken care of, not to mention dealing with all the doctor's appointments and medication runs and all the demands of my siblings and myself *(The narrator had gotten married and moved away, so was she still making demands on her mother?)*.

I answered for her. "Yes, my mom has been taking care of everyone.

"Wow, it sounds like you were run off your feet!" Cheryl said in surprise.

"Yeah, it was pretty hectic," my mom said with a smile.

Cheryl grinned sympathetically *(This would be stronger if you showed this instead of telling us. Did she do something that showed her sympathy? A hand pat or hug, for example?)* at my mom. "Let's find a beautiful bouquet for your mother," she said.

After the flowers were chosen and paid for, my mom and I wandered around the shop a bit longer. I looked up *(Add a detail here. What did she look up from?)* to see my mother staring into space, a slight frown furrowed between her brows.

"What's wrong?" I asked.

She blinked and looked at me. "I don't know," she said with a little laugh. "I keep getting these pangs of anxiety like I'm supposed to be somewhere, or that I'm forgetting something important."

I smiled at her. "That's because taking care of everyone else is all you've been doing for the last several months. Your *(Should be "you're.")* used to having something to do all the time."

My mom laughed. I hadn't heard that sound in quite a while *(What did the laugh sound like? Nervous? Amused? Giggly? Beautiful? Scary?)*. "You know, you're right. I guess I didn't realize how much I *(had?)* actually been through. I haven't had the time too *(Change to "to.")* stop and think." She looked at the gift table in front of her. "This if *(Change to "is.")* the first time in a long time that I don't have anything to do, and everyone is being taken care of. *(This works okay, but it might sound better if the last half of this sentence was moved so it began the sentence: "This is the first time everyone is taken care of and I don't have anything to do.")* What am I going to do with myself?"

I grinned at her. "Whatever you want."

She smiled back. "Let's go get some lunch."

A wait *(Change to "weight.")* seemed to be lifted *(Change to "seemed to lift.")* from her shoulders, and we walked out the door with an extra bounce in our steps. It was a sad time, but I learned a lot about my mom that day. I hadn't realized until that moment just how much my mother had been through either. I knew the basics. I knew she'd been caring for everyone and everything. But I don't think I truly realized until we were standing in that flower shop just how strong my mom had had to be.

I don't know that I could have been as strong as she had proven to be. I hope I never have to try. But I do know that my mother is and *(Change to "an.")* amazing woman, and that moment in the flower shop will live in my memory for a lifetime.

Version 3: The Final Draft

The third version of the essay is the final, revised copy so you can see how it has transformed from an outline, to a rough draft, to a polished essay ready to turn in.

8 Descriptive Essay

The Flower Shop

My mother was always a hero to me. She raised five kids while my dad worked and went to school. We all turned out pretty decent, so she must have done an okay job, but I don't know if I ever really saw her as a "person." She was just my mom. One day, that all changed. In 2001, the year I was married, my grandmother died. She was going to be buried near my home, so my family flew up to stay with me for the funeral. I accompanied my mom to the flower shop to pick out flowers for my grandmother's casket. For the first time, I saw my mom as someone new. She wasn't just my mom. She was a wife, a daughter, a sister. And she was stronger than I ever knew possible.

The bell over the shop door tinkled its greeting as we entered. The shop was filled with Christmas trees, all decorated with a different theme. There was one with teddy bears tucked in between the branches, and one decorated entirely with plastic marshmallows and graham crackers. The heavy aroma of roses and carnations coated the air, and I inhaled deeply, filling my lungs with the fragrant air. The walls were covered with shelves of candles and small floral arrangements. Twinkling white lights enveloped every available surface.

The woman behind the counter was arranging what looked like a wedding bouquet, while a gentleman helped a young man pick out a floral arrangement for his sweetheart. I glanced at my mom nervously, wondering how she felt seeing all these happy people. Christmas had always been her favorite time of year. She loved the singing and the present giving. She anxiously waited during the weeks leading up to Christmas to decorate her home and Christmas tree, and to daily luxuriate in the strong scent of pine (sometimes strengthened with candles) that emitted from the beautifully adorned tree in the living room.

Most importantly, she loved to have her family gathered around her. That hadn't happened for several years now. My oldest brother, Ryan, lived in California, and had a young wife and two small children, which made traveling all the way to Tennessee difficult for them. With my marriage, this would have been my first Christmas away from home as well. Though I knew my mother was happy to have her family together for the holidays, the reason filled us all with sadness.

My mom looked around the shop with a faint smile. She usually loved flower shops. They were always happy, fairyland places that were filled with love and hope in the form of the flowers that dripped and curved from every crack and crevice. We didn't pause for too long. The ever-present anxiety my mom had been living under seemed to boost her adrenaline and propelled her toward the counter and the next duty on the list. I could almost hear the thoughts churning in her mind: "Things to do, people to take care of, can't stop now. Got to hurry."

The woman behind the counter saw us and put the wedding bouquet down as she leaned toward us, a cheery smile on her face. "Hi. I'm Cheryl. What can I help you with today?"

My mom smiled back, automatically polite and positive as she had always been. "Well, I need to order some flowers," she said.

Cheryl wiped her hands on her apron, the green juice from the flowers leaving tracks across the white canvas. "We can help you with that. What are you looking for? Are these for a wedding, or dance, or Christmas present?"

"Well, they are actually for a funeral. I need a spray for the casket."

Cheryl's smile faded and she looked sympathetically at my mother. "Oh. I'm so sorry." Her smile crept back, but this time instead of gaiety, it held empathy and warmth. "We can help you with those too. Let me get some books for you to look at. Do you have something in mind?"

"Well, the casket is emerald green, so I was thinking of something with a lot of greenery, and maybe some pink or white roses, and baby's breath."

"That sounds lovely. We have several arrangements that are similar to that. Let me find the pictures for you here." Cheryl began flipping through books until she found the picture she was looking for. "Here we are." The book opened to a beautiful spray of flowers, white roses, pink lilies, and baby's breath arranged in Christmas ferns, lying on top of a green, lacquered coffin.

"Oh," my mom sighed. "Those are gorgeous. She would love those."

"Are these for someone in your family?" Cheryl politely asked.

"Yes. My mother," my mom said matter-of-factly as she continued to look through the book.

She was always the strong one. She had to be especially strong now. There were the funeral arrangements to take care of, family to be coordinated, and of course, we still had my 80-year-old grandfather to

8 Descriptive Essay

look after. He wasn't dealing with his wife's death very well. My mom simply didn't have time to slow down, let alone mourn. I don't know how she did it.

"Oh, I'm so sorry. That's terrible," Cheryl said. "It must be hard, especially so close to the holidays. Was it sudden?"

"No. She had cancer. She was diagnosed seven months ago. But we were glad that she was able to go before it got too painful for her. We didn't want her to suffer."

"Oh, of course. That is a blessing. You look so tired. Have you been caring for her?"

I could see my mom choking back tears as she looked at the kind, compassionate face of the florist. The last few months had been so hard on her. She cared for her mother through her illness, kept her house clean and my grandfather taken care of, not to mention dealing with all the doctors' appointments, medication runs, and the demands of my siblings.

I answered for her. "Yes, my mom has been taking care of everyone."

"Wow, it sounds like you were run off your feet!" Cheryl said in surprise.

"Yeah, it was pretty hectic," my mom said with a smile.

Cheryl grinned and patted my mom's hand. "Let's find a beautiful bouquet for your mother," she said.

After the flowers were chosen and paid for, my mom and I wandered around the shop a bit longer. I looked up from the display of candles to see my mother staring into space, a slight frown furrowed between her brows.

"What's wrong?" I asked.

She blinked and looked at me. "I don't know," she said with a little laugh. "I keep getting these pangs of anxiety like I'm supposed to be somewhere, or that I'm forgetting something important."

I smiled at her. "That's because taking care of everyone else is all you've been doing for the last several months. You're used to having something to do all the time."

My mom laughed. I hadn't heard that sound in quite a while. It was beautiful. "You know, you're right. I guess I didn't realized how much I had actually been through. I haven't had the time to stop and think." She looked at the gift table in front of her. "This is the first time everyone is taken care of and I don't have anything to do. What am I going to do with myself?"

I grinned at her. "Whatever you want."

She smiled back. "Let's go get some lunch."

A weight seemed to lift from her shoulders, and we walked out the door with an extra bounce in our steps. It was a sad time, but I learned a lot about my mom that day. I hadn't realized until that moment just how much my mother had been through either. I knew the basics. I knew she'd been caring for everyone and everything. But I don't think I truly realized until we were standing in that flower shop just how strong my mom had had to be.

I don't know that I could have been as strong as she had proven to be. I hope I never have to try. But I do know that my mother is an amazing woman, and that moment in the flower shop will live in my memory for a lifetime.

Exercise 8-1

Answer the following questions about the descriptive essay. (*Answers on page 311.*)

1. What does a descriptive essay do?

_____

_____

_____

_____

_____

_____

2. What are two important questions to ask yourself choosing a topic?

_____

_____

_____

_____

_____

_____

3. How can you help bring your essay to life?

_____

_____

_____

_____

_____

_____

8 Descriptive Essay

9

Division and Classification Essay

Lesson 9-1: What Is It?

Division and classification essays consist of two parts. The first part, division, looks at a general topic and divides it into smaller categories that are more specific. The second part, classification, takes the categories from the first part and further separates them into even more specialized groups. The purpose of this type of essay is to more fully understand a topic by seeing how all the components of that topic fit together and influence the larger topic.

For example, you may write about the various groups that are used to classify dogs. In the division part of the essay, you may choose two groups—say, the herding group and the sporting group—and describe the characterizations of each. Then, you can separate each group into the breeds that it consists of and describe each of them.

Lesson 9-2: Getting Started
Step 1: Choose a Topic and Make a List

Be sure to choose a topic that can be broken down into smaller parts. This might be the one

9 Division and Classification Essay

essay where choosing a broader topic is a good idea. As with most essays, making a list is helpful. What do you know about your chosen topic? List everything that comes to mind, then list everything you might need to research. If you are writing an essay on your favorite band, maybe you know all the names of their songs, but not when they first got together. The more items you brainstorm, the better. Making a list will also help you narrow your focus. If you know all the songs of your favorite band, but not much about the band's pre-music life, you might want to focus your essay on their music instead of on their lives leading up to forming a group. A list will also help when it comes to dividing and classifying. If you notice that most of their songs are either love ballads, party anthems, or instrumentals, you have three classifications right there, just waiting to be further divided.

Let's say you are going to write an essay on author Eleanor Burford. Burford wrote under eight different pseudonyms, or pen names, but we'll just use three as an example. For the first section of your essay, the division section, you could discuss these pen names, breaking down the larger topic of Eleanor Burford into the smaller categories of her pen names of Victoria Holt, Jean Plaidy, and Philippa Carr.

Now, for the classification section of your essay, you would discuss these categories in order to further classify them:

Category 1: Under the pen name Jean Plaidy, Burford wrote historical fiction, novels about real historical figures such as King George III and the Tudors.

Category 2: Under the pen name Philippa Carr, Burford wrote a sort of family saga, in which each book was about the daughter of the main character of the preceding book.

Category 3: Under the pen name of Victoria Holt, Burford wrote Gothic romances.

Step 2: Divide, Classify, and Research

Once you've chosen your topic, and made your list, you'll need to research for your sources and additional information. If this is a topic you know something about (for instance, your favorite band), then you can begin your division and classification before starting on your research. However, you might still need to do some research before you can fully break down your topic.

Either way, you are going to need outside sources to support any claims, arguments, or statements you make in your essay. You need to know how the smaller categories of your topic affect the larger picture. For our example, we'll use Eleanor Burford and her pen names for our topic. If Burford writes under several different names, what does each name do for her? Does she make more money with one name and the series that goes with it?

We've already divided and classified our topic, so we can move on to the research. For this particular topic, a few things we might want to research are:

- ▶ Burford's biography.
- ▶ Titles of books.
- ▶ Publication dates.
- ▶ Which pen name came first.
- ▶ Popularity of each series under each name.

As you research, record the information, quotes, and paraphrases you think you'd like to use on note cards. Don't forget to get the citation information you'll need as well!

Lesson 9-3: Elements of the Essay

This type of essay has four main elements. The introduction will introduce your topic, present your thesis, and give your reader a taste of what will be discussed in the body of the essay, which includes the division and classification sections. The division section will divide the topic into the main sections and give some information on each of them. The classification section will further divide the sections of your topic and discuss the significance of each. The conclusion will tie everything up with a neat summary.

9

Division and
Classification Essay

Lesson 9-4: Putting It Together

You should have all your information ready and waiting to go. Once you put it all in outline form, the essay writing will take care of itself. Be sure to introduce your topic in your introduction. A detailed outline for our example essay would look like this:

I. Introduction
    A. Eleanor Burford
        1. Popular and mysterious
        2. Born in London suburb in 1906 or 1910
        3. Died on *The Sea Princess* between Athens and Egypt
    B. Thesis: Writing under several different pen names helped Burford to reach larger audiences and, as a result, become more successful.
    C. Introduce divisions: Philippa Carr, Jean Plaidy, Victoria Holt

II. Body (Division and Classification)
    A. Philippa Carr
        1. Began writing historical fiction under this name in 1972
        2. Definition of historical fiction
        3. This series was a family saga.
        4. Titles in this series
            a. *The Miracle at St. Bruno's, The Lion Triumphant, The Witch from the Sea*
        5. Sold more than 3 million books under this name
    B. Jean Plaidy
        1. Published her first book under this name in 1945
        2. Historical novels, many of which followed the royal families
            a. The Tudors, the Plantagenets
        3. Titles under this name
            a. *The Revolt of the Eagles, The Prince of Darkness, Red Rose of Anjou*
        4. Best-known and most popular pen name
        5. Sold more than 14 million copies
    C. Victoria Holt
        1. Wrote Gothic romances
        2. Wrote under this name from 1960 to 1993

3. Definition of Gothic romance
4. Wrote 32 books under this name
5. Titles
   a. *The Demon Lover, The Judas Kiss, The Time of the Hunter's Moon*
6. More than 56 million books sold under this name

III. Conclusion
   A. Restate thesis: As you can see, writing under several different names helped Burford to become successful in several different genres.
   B. Summary
      1. Using more than one name gives an author the ability to branch out into different genres
      2. Can reach more audiences
      3. Can gain more readers
      4. They become more successful, challenged and satisfied

Sample Essays

The following essay is the result of the brainstorming, researching and outlining we just completed on author Eleanor Burford. The sources in this essay are cited using the Chicago/Turabian style that is most often used in humanities and history classes. Go through the outline, and then look at the rough draft to see how the essay falls into place. The parts of the essay are labeled in the rough draft with their corresponding numbers from the outline.

9 Division and Classification Essay

Version 1: The Rough Draft

Eleanor Burford

> INTRODUCTION

(I A1) Eleanor Burford was a very popular and mysterious writer. (I A2) Some thing she was born in a suburb of London in either 1906 or 1910, but no one knows for sure. (I A3) She died in 1993 on the ship *The Sea Princess* between Athens and Egypt.[1] (I B) Writing under several different pen names helped Burford become more successful. Burford wrote under eight different pen names in addition to her own name.[2] (I C) Three of the most popular of these pen names were Philippa Carr, Jean Plaidy, and Victoria Holt.

> BODY OF ESSAY

(II A1) Burford began writing under the name Philippa Carr in 1972.[3] She wrote a series of historical fiction novels. (II A2) Historical fiction is a genre that is set in the past. Often, these stories include historical figures, places, or events. (II A3) This series was a family saga meaning, it followed a family of women, each book detailing the story of the daughter of the woman in the book before. (II A4a) Some of the titles in this series include *The Miracle at St. Bruno's*, *The Lion Triumphant*, and *The Witch from the Sea*. (II A5) Burford sold more than 3 million books under this name.

(II B1) In 1945, Burford published her first book under the name Jean Plaidy. (II B2) This book soon turned into a series of historical novels which included several sub-series following the royal families of Europe. (II B2a) Some of the families these books fictionalized are the Tudors, and the Plantagenet's. (II B3a) Titles in this series include *The Revolt of the Eaglets*, *The Prince of Darkness*, and *Red Rose of Anjou*. (II B4)

---

1. Bruce Lambert, "Eleanor Hibbert, Novelist Known As Victoria Holt and Jean Plaidy," *The New York Times*, January 21, 1993, http://www.nytimes.com/1993/01/21/books/eleanor-hibbert-novelist-known-as-victoria-holt-and-jean-plaidy.html.
2. D C Wands and P G Wands, "Jean Plaidy," http://www.fantasticfiction.co.uk/p/jean-plaidy/.
3. "Eleanor Burford Book Dates," *Eleanor Alice Burford Hibbert*, http://jeanplaidy.tripod.com/id49.htm.

Jean Plaidy is perhaps the best known and most popular of Burford's pen names. **(II B5)** The novels of Jean Plaidy sold more than 14 million copies.[4]

(II C1) Under the name Victoria Holt, Burford wrote Gothic romances. **(II C2)** She wrote these novels from 1960 until her death in 1993.[5] **(II C3)** A Gothic romance is "a romance that deals with desolate and mysterious and grotesque events" according to the online dictionary Dictionary.com. They are often dark and mysterious. **(II C4)** Burford wrote 32 books under this name, **(II C5a)** some of which include *The Demon Lover, The Judas Kiss*, and *The Time of the Hunter's Moon*.[6] **(IIC 6)** More than 75 million copies of Victoria Holt's books have been sold.[7]

CONCLUSION

(III A) As you can see, righting under several different names helped Burford to become successful in several different genres. **(III B1)** Using more then one name gives an author the ability to branch out into different genres, **(III B2–3)** thereby reaching more diverse audiences, and gaining a greater readership. **(III B4)** This in turn helps them become more successful and offers them greater opportunities for challenges and satisfaction in their field of work.

---

4. "Jean Plaidy," Random House, Inc. Online, http://www.randomhouse.com/author/results.pperl?authorid=24084.
5. "Eleanor Burford Book Dates," *Eleanor Alice Burford Hibbert*, http://jeanplaidy.tripod.com/id49.htm.
6. Ibid.
7. Richard Dalby, "All About Jean Plaidy," *Book and Magazine Collector* no. 109, April 1993, http://jeanplaidy.tripod.com/id17.htm.

9 Division and Classification Essay

Works Cited

Dalby, Richard. "All About Jean Plaidy." *Book and Magazine Collector,* no. 109. April 1993. http://jeanplaidy.tripod.com/id17.htm.

"Eleanor Burford Book Dates." *Eleanor Alice Burford Hibbert.* http:// jeanplaidy.tripod.com/id49.htm.

"Jean Plaidy." Random House, Inc. Online. http://www.randomhouse. com/author/results.pperl?authorid=24084.

Lambert, Bruce. "Eleanor Hibbert, Novelist Known As Victoria Holt and Jean Plaidy." *The New York Times.* January 21, 1993. http://www. nytimes.com/1993/01/21/books/eleanor-hibbert-novelist-known- as-victoria-holt-and-jean-plaidy.html.

Wands, D.C. and P G Wands. "Jean Plaidy." http://www.fantasticfiction. co.uk/p/jean-plaidy/.

Version 2: The Edited Draft

The second version of the essay is the edited copy of the rough draft. This version has comments and revision suggestions marked in red. When proofreading your essays, you want to look for technical mistakes, such as spelling and punctuation errors, incorrect grammar, missing words, and awkward sentence structures. But you also want to look for areas where more extensive revision would be helpful. Maybe there is a statement that needs some additional information added, or a transition from one statement to another that could use a little beefing up. All of these things are part of the proofreading and editing process.

Eleanor Burford

Eleanor Burford was a very popular and mysterious writer. Some thing *(Change to "think.")* she was born in a suburb of London in either 1906 or 1910, but no one knows for sure *(This is too wordy. Revise.)*. She died in 1993 on the ship *The Sea Princess* between Athens and Egypt.[1] Writing under several different pen names helped Burford become more successful *(Briefly mention how.)*. Burford wrote under eight different pen names in addition to her own name.[2] Three of the most popular of these pen names were Philippa Carr, Jean Plaidy, and Victoria Holt.

Burford began writing under the name Philippa Carr in 1972.[3] *(In looking through the rest of the essay, this seems to be the last name she wrote under, and it is the least popular of the three discussed here, while the last name you have listed is the earliest name she used and the most popular. Maybe add a few words or a line about how you are arranging the flow of the essay—going in order chronologically or by popularity from least to most.)* She wrote a series of historical fiction novels *(She wrote them under this name, or just in general?)*. Historical fiction is a genre that is set in the past. Often, these stories include historical figures, places, or events. This series was a family saga, *(Is it family saga along with being historical?)* meaning it followed a family of women, each book detailing the story of the daughter of the woman in the book before *(How many books were there?)*. Some of the titles in this series include *The Miracle at St. Bruno's*, *The Lion Triumphant*, and *The Witch from the Sea*. Burford sold more than 3 million books under this name. *(This needs a citation.)*

In 1945, Burford published her first book *(Was it her first book ever or just under this name?)* under the name Jean Plaidy. This book soon turned into a series of historical novels that included *(Make this present tense as the series still contains these novels.)* several sub-series following the royal families of Europe. *(How many books did she write under this*

---

1. Bruce Lambert, "Eleanor Hibbert, Novelist Known As Victoria Holt and Jean Plaidy," *The New York Times*, January 21, 1993, http://www.nytimes.com/1993/01/21/books/eleanor-hibbert-novelist-known-as-victoria-holt-and-jean-plaidy.html.

2. D.C. Wands and P.G. Wands, "Jean Plaidy," http://www.fantasticfiction.co.uk/p/jean-plaidy/.

3. "Eleanor Burford Book Dates," *Eleanor Alice Burford Hibbert*, http://jeanplaidy.tripod.com/id49.htm.]

9 Division and Classification Essay

name?) Some of the families these books fictionalized are the Tudors, and the Plantagenet's *(Delete apostrophe.)*. Titles in this series include *The Revolt of the Eaglets*, *The Prince of Darkness*, and *Red Rose of Anjou*. Jean Plaidy is perhaps the best known and most popular of Burford's pen names. *(Books under this name sold significantly less than books under Victoria Holt and there were quite a few more of Jean Plaidy's books. So this statement seems incorrect.)* The novels of Jean Plaidy *(It's a little confusing with all the name changes. Maybe say "The novels sold under this name" or "under the name of Jean Plaidy.")* sold more than 14 million copies.[4]

Under the name Victoria Holt, Burford wrote Gothic romances. She wrote these novels from 1960 until her death in 1993.[5] A Gothic romance is "a romance that deals with desolate and mysterious and grotesque events" *(This quote needs a citation.)* according to the online dictionary Dictionary.com *(This is unnecessarily wordy. Revise a bit.)*. They are often dark and mysterious. *(Add a few more characteristics here to help give the reader a good idea of what these books are like.)* Burford wrote 32 books under this name, some of which include *The Demon Lover*, *The Judas Kiss*, and *The Time of the Hunter's Moon*.[6] More than 75 million copies of Victoria Holt's books have been sold.[7]

As you can see, righting *(Change to "writing.")* under several different names helped Burford to become successful in several different genres. Using more then *(Change to "than.")* one name gives an author the ability to branch out into different genres, thereby reaching more diverse audiences *(Change to the grammatically correct "a more diverse audience.")*, and gaining a greater readership. This in turn helps them become more successful and offers them greater opportunities for challenges and satisfaction in their field of work.

---

4. "Jean Plaidy," Random House, Inc. Online, http://www.randomhouse.com/author/results.pperl?authorid=24084

5. "Eleanor Burford Book Dates," *Eleanor Alice Burford Hibbert*, http://jeanplaidy.tripod.com/id49.htm.

6. Ibid.

7. Richard Dalby, "All About Jean Plaidy," *Book and Magazine Collector* no. 109, April 1993, http://jeanplaidy.tripod.com/id17.htm.]

Works Cited

Dalby, Richard. "All About Jean Plaidy." *Book and Magazine Collector*, no. 109. April 1993. http://jeanplaidy.tripod.com/id17.htm.

"Eleanor Burford Book Dates." *Eleanor Alice Burford Hibbert*. http://jeanplaidy.tripod.com/id49.htm.

"Jean Plaidy." Random House, Inc. Online. http://www.randomhouse.com/author/results.pperl?authorid=24084.

Lambert, Bruce. "Eleanor Hibbert, Novelist Known As Victoria Holt and Jean Plaidy." *The New York Times*. January 21, 1993. http://www.nytimes.com/1993/01/21/books/eleanor-hibbert-novelist-known-as-victoria-holt-and-jean-plaidy.html.

Wands, D.C. and P G Wands. "Jean Plaidy." http://www.fantasticfiction.co.uk/p/jean-plaidy/.

Version 3: The Final Draft

The third version of the essay is the final, revised copy so you can see how it has transformed from an outline, to a rough draft, to a polished essay ready to turn in.

9 Division and Classification Essay

Eleanor Burford

Eleanor Burford was a very popular and mysterious writer. She was born in a suburb of London in either 1906 or 1910. She died in 1993 on the ship *The Sea Princess* between Athens and Egypt.[1] Writing under several different pen names helped Burford to reach larger audiences and, as a result, become more successful. Burford wrote under eight different pen names in addition to her own name.[2] Three of the most popular of these pen names were Philippa Carr, Jean Plaidy, and Victoria Holt.

Burford began publishing under the name Jean Plaidy in 1945 with the book *Together They Ride*.[3] She soon it turned into a series of 108 historical novels that included several sub-series following the royal families of Europe.[4] Some of the families these books fictionalized are the Tudors and the Plantagenets. Titles in this series include *The Revolt of the Eaglets*, *The Prince of Darkness*, and *Red Rose of Anjou*. Burford sold more than 14 million copies under this name.[5]

Under her most popular name, Victoria Holt, Burford wrote Gothic romances. She wrote these novels from 1960 until her death in 1993.[6] A Gothic romance is defined by Dictionary.com as "a romance that deals with desolate and mysterious and grotesque events." They often have dark, sinister elements, with mysterious, spooky settings such as old, isolated castles. These stories generally include some type of mystery, often involving ghosts and murder. Burford wrote 32 books under this

1. Bruce Lambert, "Eleanor Hibbert, Novelist Known As Victoria Holt and Jean Plaidy," *The New York Times*, January 21, 1993, http://www.nytimes.com/1993/01/21/books/eleanor-hibbert-novelist-known-as-victoria-holt-and-jean-plaidy.html.
2. D C Wands and P G Wands, "Jean Plaidy," http://www.fantasticfiction.co.uk/p/jean-plaidy/.
3. "Eleanor Burford Book Dates," *Eleanor Alice Burford Hibbert*, http://jeanplaidy.tripod.com/id49.htm.
4. "Jean Plaidy Book Titles," *Eleanor Alice Burford Hibbert*, http://jeanplaidy.tripod.com/id18.htm.
5. "Jean Plaidy," Random House, Inc. Online, http://www.randomhouse.com/author/results.pperl?authorid=24084.
6. Ibid.
7. "Gothic Romance," Dictionary.com, http://dictionary.reference.com/browse/gothic+romance.

name, some of which include *The Demon Lover, The Judas Kiss*, and *The Time of the Hunter's Moon*.[8] More than 75 million copies of Victoria Holt's books have been sold.[9]

Burford began writing under the name Philippa Carr in 1972.[10] These books were historical fiction, as were most of her works. Historical fiction is a genre that is set in the past. Often, these stories include historical figures, places, or events. This particular series was a family saga. It followed a family of women, each book detailing the story of the daughter of the woman in the book before. Some of the titles in this series include *The Miracle at St. Bruno's, The Lion Triumphant*, and *The Witch from the Sea*. Burford sold more than 3 million books under this name.[11]

As you can see, writing under several different names helped Burford to become successful in several different genres. Using more than one name gives an author the ability to branch out into different genres, thereby reaching a more diverse audience and gaining a greater readership. This, in turn, helps an author become more successful and offers greater opportunities for challenges and satisfaction in the author's field of work.

8. Ibid.
9. Richard Dalby, "All About Jean Plaidy," *Book and Magazine Collector* no. 109, April 1993, http://jeanplaidy.tripod.com/id17.htm.]
10. "Eleanor Burford Book Dates," *Eleanor Alice Burford Hibbert*, http://jeanplaidy.tripod.com/id49.htm.
11. "Jean Plaidy," Random House, Inc. Online, http://www.randomhouse.com/author/results.pperl?authorid=24084.

9 Division and Classification Essay

Works Cited

Dalby, Richard. "All About Jean Plaidy." *Book and Magazine Collector,* no. 109. April 1993. http://jeanplaidy.tripod.com/id17.htm.

"Eleanor Burford Book Dates." *Eleanor Alice Burford Hibbert.* http://jeanplaidy.tripod.com/id49.htm.

"Gothic Romance." *Dictionary.com.* http://dictionary.reference.com/browse/gothic+romance

"Jean Plaidy Book Titles." *Eleanor Alice Burford Hibbert.* http://jeanplaidy.tripod.com/id18.htm

"Jean Plaidy." Random House, Inc. Online. http://www.randomhouse.com/author/results.pperl?authorid=24084.

Lambert, Bruce. "Eleanor Hibbert, Novelist Known As Victoria Holt and Jean Plaidy." *The New York Times.* January 21, 1993. http://www.nytimes.com/1993/01/21/books/eleanor-hibbert-novelist-known-as-victoria-holt-and-jean-plaidy.html.

Wands, D.C. and P G Wands. "Jean Plaidy." http://www.fantasticfiction.co.uk/p/jean-plaidy/.

Exercise 9-1

Answer the following questions about the division and classification essay. (*Answers on page 311.*)

1. What is the purpose of the division and classification essay?

    _____

    _____

    _____

2. What does the division part of the essay do?

    _____

    _____

3. What does the classification part of the essay do?

    _____

    _____

9 Division and Classification Essay

10

Evaluation Essay

Lesson 10-1: What Is It?

The evaluation essay is similar to the argumentative/persuasive essay in that you are often trying to persuade readers to your point of view. Movie or book reviews are types of evaluative essays. The focus in such essays is often geared toward the author's (that's you) point of view.

For example, if you were writing an evaluation essay about a movie that you didn't like, you could describe the plot, emphasizing all the negative things about the movie. You are still giving a truthful representation of the movie, but in focusing on the negative, your reader will more likely have a negative opinion of the movie.

You also need to include your thesis (which in this case would be your overall opinion) and the evidence to support it, but do so in a non-aggressive manner. You want to convince your readers that you are right, but not be so abrasive that it turns people against you. A logical and neutral tone is more convincing than if you are aggressive.

Evaluation Essay

10

Lesson 10-2: Getting Started
Step 1: Choose a Topic

Evaluation essays can be used for a variety of topics, from book reviews to employee performance reviews. Choose something you are interested in. If you are assigned a topic, choose an aspect of that topic that interests you. In either case, you are looking for a focus that you have an opinion about and that you'll be able to find evidence to support. As with several other types of essays, evaluation essays can be used to persuade your audience to your way of thinking. However, your arguments will be much more effective and convincing if you have outside sources to support your claims.

Step 2: Make a List

Just as with any other form of essay, the easiest way to get going is to make a list. For this type of essay, you'll want to look at two things: your main source (the book, movie, piece of art, or whatever it is you are evaluating) and outside sources that will back up your arguments (if these are required for your assignment).

Think about what you want to discuss. What is your topic and what is your point of view on that topic? Are you reviewing a book? Did you like it? Jot down the things you liked, such as characters, settings, specific scenes, dialogue, imagery, or storyline. Did you hate it? Write down the things you hated. Are you looking at it from a non-biased point of view in order to present general information on the topic? Are you trying to prove a point about a larger issue? What elements of the piece you are evaluating prove that point? Make a list of the important items you might want to cover.

Next, if your assignment requires you to use sources other than the one being evaluated, write down a few things you can research. For book, movie, or artistic reviews, you could look at what other critics are saying. Maybe you are evaluating a book that is always bringing up images of butterflies. Do you want to know why? Your readers might, too. Look it up; research the symbolism of that creature. Are you evaluating one of Lady Gaga's songs to prove she really loves the paparazzi? Research articles on her, find out how many times she's been photographed, or look up analyses of her outfits. Perhaps the movie you are evaluating is a remake of an older movie. You could look up articles and news releases comparing the two versions.

Step 3: Research and Make Notes

You'll need to research for two types of information: your main topic and your sources. If you are doing a book or movie review, you'll need to read or see the material you will be discussing. Once you come up with your thesis (your main opinion or judgment about the piece you are evaluating), you'll need to research statistics, quotes, articles, charts, eyewitness testimonies, and anything else that might provide evidence to back up your statements. You'll especially need to find examples from the subject you are evaluating.

Are you evaluating a plan for a new building project for your town? Find information on building specifications, funding, time tables, labor reviews, and statistics on how the building is supposed to help the community. Perhaps compare this plan to other towns' plans. Point out specific examples from the plan that illustrate your point.

Are you evaluating a new book in a series? How does it measure up to the other books in the series? Is it selling better or worse than the other books? Will it be made into a movie? What are other critics or audiences saying? Is the plot believable, are the characters relatable, and is the ending satisfying? Point out examples from the book that prove your point.

Though your opinion is key in this essay, it needs to be supported from within the subject and often from outside sources. Remember: It's always better to have too much information than to start writing your paper and discover you need more.

While you are researching, record your notes! You need this information for your outline, so make note cards, type up a spread sheet, or find another method that suits you, but make sure you are recording the information, quotations, and paraphrases you think you'll use in your essay.

Evaluation Essay

10

Lesson 10-3: Elements of the Essay

For an evaluative essay, the main elements you'll need to include are your thesis, the subject you'll be evaluating, your actual evaluation, and your conclusion.

Thesis

Your thesis should be included in your introduction. It should let your reader know what point you are proving or what your point of view is on your topic. Are you reviewing a young adult book you felt was too violent? Your thesis could be, "*Mockingjay*, by Suzanne Collins, depicts a violent and oppressive society inappropriate for young audiences." If you liked it, you could say, "Suzanne Collins's *Mockingjay* is a gripping tale of self-discovery and survival that will leave you on the edge of your seat and begging for more." If your paper is using this book to prove a point about a larger issue, such as what could happen because of the prevalence of violence in our own society, your thesis could be "Suzanne Collins's *Mockingjay* depicts what could happen to a society that becomes too desensitized to the suffering of others."

Your Evaluation Topic

If you are reviewing a book or film, include the book publication and author information, film release dates, and any other pertinent information a reader might need to know if she wanted to find the item. You can present some of this information in the introduction or the body of the essay, but be sure that it is in the beginning. Also give a brief, but thorough, summary of the item you are evaluating by telling your reader what the book or film is about.

Your Evaluation

This is where you'll get into the specifics of proving your point. Use examples from the subject and, if your assignment requires it, use outside sources to back up your points. For instance, if you are reviewing a book with the point of view that it is too violent, show several examples from the book that illustrate this. You could also present opposing arguments that you can refute with your evidence.

Conclusion

Wrap up your evaluation, restate your thesis, and summarize your evidence. You could add a line encouraging or discouraging the reader to explore the item you evaluated for themselves or maybe direct readers to other sources if they are interested in more information on your subject.

Lesson 10-4: Putting It Together

Once you have all your information ready to go, get it organized in an outline. Start with the general information about what you are evaluating. For an example, let's use the newest book in a series. We'll pretend the fifth *Percy Jackson* book just came out. Your basic outline for your introduction should look something like this:

I. Introduction
   A. General information about the book
      1. *Percy Jackson and the Last Olympian*
      2. Author: Rick Riordan
      3. Published in the United States by Hyperion in May 2009
   B. Thesis: *Percy Jackson and the Last Olympian* is yet another exciting and brilliant installment in the Percy Jackson series. (If you didn't like it, your thesis could be something like "This book is a disappointing ending to a great series." If this book is an example of a greater point, it could be "This book illustrates the classic literary plot of sacrificing the one to save the many.")

II. Body
   A. Full of action
      1. Example from the book
         a. Fight against the Typhon monster
      2. Another example from the book
         a. Final showdown with Kronos
      3. Outside evidence
         a. Statistics on reader responses
   B. Developed characters
      1. Example from the book
         a. Examples about Percy or his friends

    2. Another example from the book
      a. The villains
    3. Outside evidence
      a. Quote an interview with the author discussing this

C. Interesting plot twists
    1. Example from the book
      a. The revelation of the real "last Olympian"
    2. Another example from the book
      a. Luke's suicide
    3. Outside evidence
      a. Quote from the author about this subject

III. Conclusion
    A. Restate thesis
    B. Summarize arguments

Sample Essays

Look at the following essay that discusses the theme of cultural integration in the short story "Gussuk" by Mei Mei Evans. This essay was written for a literature class in which this story was an assigned reading. The instructor preferred students to take examples from the story itself rather than outside sources. However, outside sources could be added to this essay to make it a longer, more in-depth paper.

For our example, we'll stay with a more basic essay model. Following is the detailed outline for the essay. Go through it, and then look at the rough draft to see how the essay falls into place. The parts of the essay are labeled in the rough draft with their corresponding numbers from the outline.

The Detailed Outline

I. Introduction
    A. Opening statements
      1. Alaska is remote compared to the rest of the country.
      2. The native populations have been able to maintain their cultural identities.
    B. Thesis: This balancing act creates confusion as the natives try to maintain their cultural while integrating with mainland Americans.

II. Summary of short story "Gussuk"
   A. Story title
   B. Author information: Mei Mei Evans
      1. Associate professor of humanities and director of the MA program at Alaska Pacific University
      2. Asian American
      3. Has experience with the Eskimo culture
   C. Story summary
      1. Lucy is a Chinese American woman on her first nursing assignment in Alaska.
      2. She struggles with her identity and being accepted.

III. Evidence of cultural confusion—looks can be deceiving
   A. Lucy's clothing sets her apart—Evans quote page 237
   B. Robert mistakes her for a native—Evans quote page 237
   C. She has a conflict of identity.

IV. Evidence of cultural confusion—acting native or American
   A. Lucy tries to act native but they seem unsure of how to act.
   B. Example of Mercy's dinner
   C. Mercy makes ethnic slurs and rude comments about Lucy.
      1. Evans quote page 242–43
      2. Obvious the slurs are part of every day speech
      3. Lucy ignores the insult in order to fit in.

V. Evidence of cultural confusion—economic and social differences
   A. Villagers are unhappy and drink to get drunk.
   B. Live in poverty
   C. Many leave the village for work.
   D. Lucy's trailer is better than the other homes, setting her apart.

VI. Conclusion
   A. Restate thesis: It's difficult for different cultures to integrate.
   B. Restate evidence
      1. Racial slurs and patterns of behavior might be acceptable for one culture but not another.
      2. Appearances can be deceiving.
   C. Closing statement: Cultures can integrate but it may be difficult.

Version 1: The Rough Draft

Gussuk

INTRODUCTION

(I A1) Alaska, though part of the United States of America, differs from the majority of the states in that it is geographically remote from the rest of the country. **(I A2)** Alaska is very isolated, so the native people kept their cultural identities. **(I B)** However, this balancing act invariably causes confusion as the natives strive to maintain their native culture while integrating with the more "mainland" Americans.

BODY OF ESSAY

(II A) This cultural integration is addressed in Mei Mei Evans's short story "Gussuk." **(II B1)** Evans, an associate professor of humanities and the director of the Master of Arts program at Alaska Pacific University, **(II B2)** is herself an Asian American, **(II B3)** and has experience with this unique culture. **(II C1)** "Gussuk" is the story of Lucy, a young Chinese-American woman, who ventures into the wilds of Alaska on her first nursing job. **(II C2)** Wile falling in love with the remote beauty of the area, Lucy struggles with her identity and with being accepted among the natives that she so resembles.

The future conflicts of Lucy's identity is apparent in the first three paragraphs of the story. **(III A)** Her clothing immediately marks her as different and she "felt conspicuous...in her khaki skirt and tasseled loafers—clothes she had worn more to make a good impression than because she liked them. The women giggled and looked away when she tried to meet their eyes, which added to Lucy's feeling of self-consciousness" (Evans 237). **(III B)** Then, a young man, Robert, comes to help her down from the plane. They each "noticed their resemblance to each other," so much so that Robert mistakes her for a native and tries to address her in his native tongue, Yup'ik (237). **(III C)** Already there is a conflict of identity.

Her situation is unusual. Though Lucy may look like a native, she is clearly a *gussuk*. **(IV A)** Wanting to fit in, Lucy tries to act like a native. Yet the natives themselves seem unsure of how to act. They try to get Lucy to act native, yet seem intent on acting as American as possible. **(IV B)** For example, Mercy, invites Lucy to dinner. Mercy serves her children Hamburger Helper, a very American meal. But she instructs Lucy to eat a "native" meal of dried fish and seal oil.

(IV C) Mercy, while appearing to approve of Lucy, then launches into a conversation full of ethnic slurs and rude comments about Lucy's appearance and private life. **(IV C1)** Mercy tells Lucy, "You look Eskimo. Now you gotta act Eskimo" and then proceeds to call Lucy an *avuk*, or half-breed, and asks inappropriate questions about Lucy's life (242–43). **(IV C2)** Though Mercy may not have been so openly insulting to a more traditional looking *gussuk*, it's obvious that these slurs are a part of the natives' everyday speech. It was a normal, and accepted term for them, but not for Lucy. **(IV C3)** However, Lucy chooses to ignore the insult.

However, as much as Lucy might have thought that she was accepted as one of the villagers, she remained firmly apart. **(V)** Not only are Lucy and the villagers culturally different, but their economic backgrounds must also add to the complexity of this situation. **(V A)** The villagers are obviously not happy. They drink to get drunk, **(V B)** they live in poverty with human waste receptacles 10 feet from where they eat. **(V C)** Many leave the village in order to find work as soon as they are able. **(V D)** Lucy's trailer is better equipped than most of the homes in the village, which sets her apart from them even more. But Lucy does not seem to realize this for quite a while.

CONCLUSION

(VI A) This story is a very good illustration of just how difficult it is for different cultures to integrate with one another, even when those cultures live in the same country. **(VI B1)** Racial slurs and patterns of behavior that are acceptable and normal for one culture may be, at best, confusing, and more likely very insulting to other cultures. **(VI B2)** This story also illustrates that appearances can be deceiving. Going on looks alone, Lucy should have been able to integrate very well with the villagers. But they're cultural differences, the differences beneath the surface, were too great to overcome.

(VI C) This is not to say that cultures can never integrate well, or that in the future this will always be the case. But this story serves to show the difficulties involved in such an undertaking.

Works Cited

Evans, Mei Mei. "Gussuk." *Imagining America: Stories from the Promised Land—A Multicultural Anthology of American Fiction*. Eds. Wesley Brown and Amy Ling. New York: Persea Books, 2002. Print.

Version 2: The Edited Draft

The second version of the essay is the edited copy of the rough draft. This version has comments and revision suggestions marked in red. When proofreading your essays, you want to look for technical mistakes, such as spelling and punctuation errors, incorrect grammar, missing words, and awkward sentence structures. But you also want to look for areas where more extensive revision would be helpful. Maybe there is a statement that needs some additional information added, or a transition from one statement to another that could use a little beefing up. All of these things are part of the proofreading and editing process.

Gussuk

Alaska, though part of the United States of America, differs from the majority of the states in that it is geographically remote from the rest of the country. Alaska is very isolated, so the native people kept their cultural identities. *(This could be reworded to be a bit more formal. Also, there are parts of Alaska that aren't remote. Also, if they maintained their cultural identities, does that mean they aren't American at all?)* However, this balancing act invariably causes confusion as the natives strive to maintain their native culture while integrating with the more "mainland" Americans.

This cultural integration is addressed in Mei Mei Evans's short story "Gussuk." Evans, an associate professor of humanities and the director of the Master of Arts program at Alaska Pacific University, is herself an Asian American, and has experience with this unique culture. *(Is it the Asian American culture or the Eskimo American culture described in the story?)* "Gussuk" is the story of Lucy, a young Chinese-American woman, who ventures into the wilds of Alaska on her first nursing job. Wile *(Change to "while.")* falling in love with the remote beauty of the area, Lucy struggles with her identity and with being accepted among the natives that she so resembles.

The future conflicts of Lucy's identity is *(Change to "are," because "conflicts" is plural.)* apparent in the first three paragraphs of the story. Her clothing immediately marks her as different and she "felt conspicuous...in her khaki skirt and tasseled loafers—clothes she had worn more to make a good impression than because she liked them. The women giggled and looked away when she tried to meet their eyes, which added to Lucy's feeling of self-consciousness" (Evans 237) *(Set this quote up first. When does her clothing mark her as different? What is the context?)*. Then, a young man, Robert, comes to help her down from the plane. They each "noticed their resemblance to each other," so much so that Robert mistakes her for a native and tries to address her in his native tongue, Yup'ik (237). Already there is a conflict of identity *(Why? What is it? Add a brief line or two with a little more explanation.)*.

Her situation is unusual. Though Lucy may look like a native, she is clearly a *gussuk (What is this? Those who have not read the story may not know, so a brief definition would be good here.)*. Wanting to fit in, Lucy tries to act like a native. Yet the natives themselves seem unsure of how to act. They try to get Lucy to act native, yet seem intent on acting as American as possible. For example, Mercy, invites Lucy to dinner *(Who is Mercy?)*. Mercy serves her children Hamburger Helper, a very American meal. But she instructs Lucy to eat a "native" meal of dried fish and seal oil.

Mercy, while appearing to approve of Lucy, then launches into a conversation full of ethnic slurs and rude comments about Lucy's appearance and private life. Mercy tells Lucy, "You look Eskimo. Now you gotta act Eskimo" and then proceeds to call Lucy an *avuk*, or half-breed, and asks inappropriate questions about Lucy's life (242–43). Though Mercy may not have been so openly insulting to a more traditional looking *gussuk*, it's *(Spell out. Contractions are generally avoided in formal essays)* obvious that these slurs are a part of the natives' everyday speech. *(How is this obvious? Maybe include examples from the story to prove this point.)* It was a normal, *(Delete comma.)* and accepted term for them, but not for Lucy. However, Lucy chooses to ignore the insult *(Why?)*.

The way in which Lucy handles this situation sets the tone for her stay among the villagers. She wants to be accepted by the villagers, to be one of them, yet she is clearly very different—perhaps not in looks, but definitely in culture. *(This needs a little more explanation. Is ignoring the insults and differences how she handles all the situations she finds herself in?)*

However, as much as Lucy might have thought that she was accepted as one of the villagers, she remained firmly apart. Not only are Lucy and the villagers culturally different, but their economic backgrounds must also add to the complexity of this situation *(Must it? Or does it?)*. The villagers are obviously not happy. They drink to get drunk *(What other reason might there be, or not be?)*, they live in poverty with human waste receptacles 10 feet from where they eat. Many leave the village in order to find work as soon as they are able *(Do they leave as soon as they are able to do so, or leave as soon as they find work?)*. Lucy's trailer is better equipped than most of the homes in the village, which sets her apart from them even more. But Lucy does not seem to realize this for quite a while.

This story is a very good illustration of just how difficult it is for different cultures to integrate with one another, even when those cultures live in the same country. Racial slurs and patterns of behavior that are acceptable and normal for one culture may be, at best, confusing, and more likely very insulting to other cultures. This story also illustrates that appearances can be deceiving. Going on looks alone, Lucy should have been able to integrate very well with the villagers. But *(Use "but" sparingly. "However" is a better and more formal choice.)* they're *(Change to "their.")* cultural differences, the differences beneath the surface, were too great to overcome.

This is not to say that cultures can never integrate well, or that in the future this will always be the case. But this story serves to show the difficulties involved in such an undertaking.

Works Cited

Evans, Mei Mei. "Gussuk." *Imagining America: Stories from the Promised Land—A Multicultural Anthology of American Fiction*. Eds. Wesley Brown and Amy Ling. New York: Persea Books, 2002. Print.

Version 3: The Final Draft

The third version of the essay is the final, revised copy so you can see how it has transformed from an outline, to a rough draft, to a polished essay ready to turn in.

Gussuk

Alaska, though part of the United States of America, differs from the majority of the states in that it is geographically isolated from the rest of the country. Many parts of Alaska are very remote. As a result, the native populations have been able to maintain their cultural identities. While being essentially "American," by virtue of the fact that Alaska is a part of the United States, many native Eskimos have the unique experience of being American while, at the same time, maintaining much of their native culture. However, this balancing act invariably causes confusion as the natives strive to maintain their native culture while integrating with the more "mainland" Americans.

This cultural integration is addressed in Mei Mei Evans's short story "Gussuk." Evans, an associate professor of humanities and the director of the Master of Arts program at Alaska Pacific University, is herself an Asian American, and has experience with the Eskimo culture. "Gussuk" is the story of Lucy, a young Chinese-American woman, who ventures into the wilds of Alaska on her first nursing job. While falling in love with the remote beauty of the area, Lucy struggles with her identity and with being accepted among the natives that she so resembles.

The future conflicts of Lucy's identity are apparent in the first three paragraphs of the story. As Lucy steps out of the plane, she notices the group of villagers who have come to meet her. Her clothing immediately marks her as different and she "felt conspicuous...in her khaki skirt and tasseled loafers—clothes she had worn more to make a good impression than because she liked them. The women giggled and looked away when she tried to meet their eyes, which added to Lucy's feeling of self-consciousness" (Evans 237). Then, a young man, Robert, comes to help her down from the plane. They each "noticed their resemblance to each other," so much so that Robert mistakes her for a native and tries to address her in his native tongue, Yup'ik (237). Already there is a conflict of identity. Lucy looks like a native, yet clearly is different.

Her situation is unusual. While clearly a *gussuk*, a derogatory term for a white person or, more generally, an outsider, and something the villagers use to describe her no matter how much they appear to accept her, Lucy also looks like a native. Wanting to fit in, Lucy tries to act like a native. Yet the natives themselves seem unsure of how to act. They try to get Lucy to act native, yet seem intent on acting as American as possible. For example, one of the characters, Mercy, invites Lucy to dinner. Mercy serves her children Hamburger Helper, a very American meal. But she instructs Lucy to eat a "native" meal of dried fish and seal oil.

Mercy, while appearing to approve of Lucy, then launches into a conversation full of ethnic slurs and rude comments about Lucy's appearance and private life. Mercy tells Lucy, "You look Eskimo. Now you gotta act Eskimo" and then proceeds to call Lucy an *avuk*, or half-breed, and asks inappropriate questions about Lucy's life (242–43). Though Mercy may not have been so openly insulting to a more traditional-looking *gussuk*, it is obvious that these slurs are a part of the natives' everyday speech. Village children fling the term carelessly, laughingly, not in a subversive way that would suggest they knew it was wrong to use such ethnic slurs. It was a normal and accepted term for them, but not for Lucy. However, in order to fit in, Lucy chooses to ignore the insult.

The way in which Lucy handles this situation sets the tone for her stay among the villagers. She wants to be accepted by the villagers, to be one of them, yet she is clearly very different, perhaps not in looks, but definitely in culture. Lucy goes through most of the story trying to ignore the insults and obvious differences between her and the villagers in an effort to fit in, but in the end finds she cannot.

However, as much as Lucy might have thought that she was accepted as one of the villagers, she remained firmly apart. Not only are Lucy and the villagers culturally different, but their economic backgrounds also add to the complexity of this situation. The villagers are obviously not happy. They drink not for recreation, but to get drunk. They live in poverty with human waste receptacles 10 feet from where they eat. Many leave the village as soon as they are able in order to find work. Lucy's trailer is better equipped than most of the homes in the village, which sets her apart from them even more. But Lucy does not seem to realize this for quite a while.

This story is a very good illustration of just how difficult it is for different cultures to integrate with one another, even when those cultures live in the same country. Racial slurs and patterns of behavior that are acceptable and normal for one culture may be, at best, confusing, and more likely very insulting to other cultures. This story also illustrates that appearances can be deceiving. Going on looks alone, Lucy should have been able to integrate very well with the villagers. However, their cultural differences, the differences beneath the surface, were too great to overcome.

This is not to say that cultures can never integrate well, or that in the future this will always be the case. Yet, this story serves to show the difficulties involved in such an undertaking.

Works Cited

Evans, Mei Mei. "Gussuk." *Imagining America: Stories from the Promised Land—A Multicultural Anthology of American Fiction*. Eds. Wesley Brown and Amy Ling. New York: Persea Books, 2002. Print.

Exercise 10-1

Answer the following questions about the evaluation essay. (*Answers on page 311.*)

1. What does the evaluation essay do, and what are some examples of this type of essay?

2. In what type of manner should you present your opinion?

3. What are some types of supporting evidence can you research for this essay?

11

Literary Analysis Essay

Lesson 11-1: What Is It?

Literary analysis essays examine a piece of literature. There are several specific types of literary criticisms, but a basic literary analysis simply looks at a theme or element of a particular work and tries to discover the meaning behind it. You do this by:

▶ Identifying the theme or element in question.

▶ Giving an interpretation (your thesis) of that theme or element.

▶ Discussing the background of the piece in question.

▶ Analyzing the evidence you've found to support your interpretation.

Lesson 11-2: Getting Started
Step 1: Choose a Topic and Make a List

First, of course, you must choose a topic. As with most other essays, making a list is a good way

11 Literary Analysis Essay

to start. Just sit down for a few minutes and brainstorm. List all the possible themes that could be in the book. Is there one that sticks out in particular (the theme of adultery in *The Scarlet Letter*, for example)? Once you have a good list of possible themes, pick out the one that interests you the most. Or, if you want to make it easy on yourself, pick the topic for which it will be the easiest to find information and examples. If you've been assigned a topic, brainstorm ideas for your focus. If you are supposed to write an essay on animal symbolism in *Lord of the Flies*, try to find an aspect of that symbolism that interests you. Brainstorm all the instances of animal-related symbolism in the book and go from there.

Some things you can discuss when you are doing a literary analysis include (but are certainly not limited to):

- Imagery.
- Characters.
- Plot.
- Themes.
  - Feminism.
  - Society.
  - Ideals.
  - Culture.
  - Any other theme that may be present in the story.
- Social commentary in the book.
- Settings.
- Time periods.
- Symbolism.

Once you have a topic, spend a few more minutes and brainstorm some examples from the piece that illustrate your topic. List as many as you can find. It is always best to have too many than to have too few. Once you have a nice list of examples, you can pick and choose which you'd like to include in your essay.

There are specific types of literary analysis essays (or criticisms, as they are also called) that focus on particular themes. These may seem a bit complicated, but they are really just a way of focusing the discussion of your essay. For example, if you were discussing a literary piece, using feminist criticism to analyze the work, you'd look at how the story affects or portrays women.

Here is a list of several common types of literary criticisms and what they would focus on:

▶ African American criticism analyzes a piece of literature in terms of how it affects, illustrates, and portrays African-American culture, history, and issues.

▶ Cultural criticism looks at a piece of literature from a cultural point of view, examing the behavior and values presented in the piece.

▶ Deconstructive criticism focuses on the assumption that there are so many different and conflicting interpretations and meanings of a text possible that, in a way, the text has no meaning. This is not to say that a text is pointless or that it doesn't have value. Rather, it means that no one interpretation is more correct than another. You can use this theory to discover many possible meanings of a text.

▶ Feminist criticism analyzes a piece of literature in terms of how it deals with the position of women.

▶ Lesbian and gay criticism looks at how a literary piece deals with homosexual issues.

▶ Marxist criticism focuses on social classes and economic power. It looks at the division of the classes, capitalist or imperialist ideals, and how the literary work reflects the society and economic climate it portrays.

▶ New historical looks at a piece of literature as a product of the culture that produced it. In other words, it's seen as a sort of artifact that can tell the reader about the culture, time period, society, mannerisms, and people that existed when the piece was written.

▶ Psychoanalytic criticism examines a piece of literature the way a psychologist would look at you, studying oedipal themes, fears, motivations, family dynamics, denial, repression, projection, insecurities, and other psychological issues.

▶ Reader response criticism analyzes how the literary piece makes the reader respond to the specific elements of the text.

Step 2: Research and Make Notes

Depending on your assignment, you might need to do a bit of study and research in order to get good outside sources, such as other literary criticisms of your work, to support the arguments you will make in your analysis. How many sources you'll need will depend on your specific assignment and topic. Again, it doesn't hurt to have too much information. You can choose the best sources when it comes time to write the paper. If your assignment requires you to focus only on the text you are analyzing, be sure you find a solid list of examples to illustrate.

Don't forget to make notes! You'll need these for your outline. Record all the information, quotations, and paraphrases you think you might include in your essay. And don't forget the citation information!

Lesson 11-3: Elements of the Essay
The Introduction

Your introduction needs to include the title and author of the piece you are evaluating. Start with a general line or two, working your way to a very specific thesis statement. Your thesis statement should firmly state your position. Does your essay prove that the color red is the most important imagery element in *The Scarlet Letter*? Say so: *The color red is the most important element of imagery in* The Scarlet Letter.

The Body

The body of your essay will go through each of the arguments that will prove your thesis. Depending on your assignment, you will need examples from the piece you are analyzing as well as outside sources to back up your claims. Be sure to put any examples you use from the piece in context. In other words, don't start tossing in quotes from the literary piece you are discussing without rhyme or reason. Give your reader a little background so he knows what is going on, and be sure to incorporate the quotes within one of your sentences.

The Conclusion

Once you've gone through all of your arguments, and supported them with your examples and outside sources, it's time for your conclusion. The conclusion needs to restate your thesis and briefly summarize the arguments you presented.

Lesson 11-4: Putting It Together

A detailed outline for a literary analysis exploring the theme of heroic ideals in the medieval story *Sir Gawain and the Green Knight* might look like this:

I. Introduction
   A. Opening statements
   B. Thesis: The famous medieval romance *Sir Gawain and the Green Knight* illustrates the fact that these ideal heroes did not exist.
   C. Transition
II. Body
   A. What was the heroic ideal?
      1. Qualities and traits
         a. Outside source
      2. Courtly love
         a. Outside source
   B. The character of Sir Gawain
      1. Qualities and traits
         a. Quotes from the book
         b. Outside source
   C. Does Gawain embody the heroic ideal?
      1. Examples of Gawain's behavior

a. Examples from the book

    b. Outside sources

III. Conclusion

    A. Brief summary of arguments

    B. Restate thesis: *Sir Gawain and the Green Knight* illustrates the fact that these ideal heroes did not exist.

    C. Concluding sentence

Sample Essays

Look at the following essay that discusses the theme of cavalier ideals in the poem "To Althea, from Prison," by Richard Lovelace. The essay first defines cavalier ideals (a philosophical style that was popular in the early 17th century), by highlighting the three main ideals of women, wine, and royalism. The essay then uses examples from the poem to show how these ideals are illustrated in the piece. This essay does not use outside sources as the assignment required the author to use only examples from the piece being analyzed. For a longer and more in-depth essay, outside sources could be included.

This particular essay was written by a student who was studying history, so the historical information she included in the essay was information she already knew. However, in the case of someone who did not have a bank of historical facts in her brain, those areas would be great opportunities for outside sources.

Also note the citations in this essay. As the only source used was the poem being analyzed, the numbers in the parenthetical citations refer to the lines of the poem, not page numbers of a source.

The detailed outline for the essay begins on page 186. Go through it, and then look at the rough draft to see how the essay falls into place. The parts of the essay are labeled in the rough draft with their corresponding numbers from the outline. Also, the poem that the essay discusses is included, so you can see the lines to which the essay refers, and so you can see how a relatively short poem has many elements to discuss and explore.

To Althea, From Prison

I

> When Love with unconfined wings
> Hovers within my Gates;
> And my divine Althea brings
> To whisper at the Grates;
> When I lye tangled in her haire
> And fettered to her eye;
> The Gods that wanton in the Aire,
> Know no such Liberty.

II

> When flowing Cups run swiftly round
> With no allaying Thames,
> Our carelesse heads with Roses bound,
> Our hearts with Loyall Flames;
> When thirsty griefe in Wine we steepe,
> When Healths and draughts go free,
> Fishes that tipple in the Deepe,
> Know no such Libertie.

III

> When (like committed linnets) I
> With shriller throat shall sing
> The sweetness, Mercy, Majesty,
> And glories of my KING;
> When I shall voyce aloud, how Good
> He is, how Great should be;
> Enlarged Winds that curle the Flood,
> Know no such Liberty.

IV

> Stone Walls do not a Prison make,
> Nor Iron bars a Cage;
> Mindes innocent and quiet take
> That for an Hermitage;
> If I have freedome in my Love,
> And in my soule am free;
> Angels alone that sore above,
> Injoy such Liberty.

The Detailed Outline

I. Introduction
   A. Opening statements
      1. Cavalier style ruled the day.
      2. Their poetry is full of colorful images and sentiments.
      3. Cavalier ideals of women, wine, and royalism are exalted.
   B. Introduce poem information
      1. Author: Richard Lovelace
      2. Wrote the poem in prison
   C. Thesis: This poem is the ultimate Cavalier ideals poem.
   D. What the essay will discuss
      1. The idea that, though imprisoned, he can find freedom through his ideals of women, wine, and king

II. Poem information
   A. Written in prison in 1642
   B. Published in 1649
   C. Supports Cavalier ideals
   D. Those ideals make him free despite his imprisonment.

III. Stanza 1: Women
   A. Personifies love in lines 1 and 2
   B. He is imprisoned but his love can't be caged.
   C. Describes his love, Althea as divine in lines 3–6.
   D. Describes his imprisonment in these lines
      1. Tangled
      2. Fettered
      3. "Fettered to her eye" is both tender and refers to imprisonment.
   E. The last lines (7–8) sum up his love for Althea/women.
      1. "Wanton" has a sexual connotation.
   F. Conclusion: Love can make you free even in prison.

IV. Stanza 2: Wine
   A. First two lines (9–10) personify cups of wine.
      1. Also suggests the wine was undiluted as was the custom
   B. Lines 11–12
      1. Describes devotion to the crown
      2. "Careless heads" could describe being drunk and danger of being beheaded as a royalist.

      3.   Royalists tended to be very carefree and careless but were very loyal.

  C. Lines 13–14

      1.   Refer to drinking and imprisonment

      2.   Many grieving people drink.

         a. Cavaliers had reason to grieve because the monarchy was overthrown.

      3.   "Steep" is associated with making wine or soaking something.

  D. Lines 15–16

      1.   "Tipple" alludes to drinking.

      2.   Fish in the deep ocean are free from the danger of being caught.

      3.   Lovelace feels he is more free because of his ideals.

V. Stanza 3: King

  A. Compares himself to "commited linnets" whose condition parallels his own

  B. He sings of his king.

      1.   His song is more piercing to let the world know of his loyalty.

  C. Although he is caged as a bird, he is free through his ideals.

VI. Stanza 4: Summary of ideals

  A. A hermitage is the home of a hermit.

      1.   Can use the prison time to think

  B. They aren't really imprisoned anyway as their ideals set them free.

  C. The last lines make a statement about his values and how they affect him.

      1.   Love cannot be taken away.

      2.   His soul will always be free.

      3.   Only the angels enjoy more freedom.

VII. Conclusion

  A. Restate thesis: The poem is a wonderful example of Cavalier ideals.

  B. Restate evidence

      1.   The poem explores the ideals of women, wine, and king one by one.

      2.   The imagery helps create the concept of Cavalier ideals.

Version 1: The Rough Draft

The Freedom of Cavalier Ideals

INTRODUCTION

(I A1) During the early 17th century, Cavalier style ruled the day. (I A2) The Cavaliers' poetry is full of colorful images and sentiments. (I A3) The Cavalier ideals of women, wine, and royalism are exalted in every way possible. (I B1) Richard Lovelace, a poet during this period, (I B2) wrote a poem while he was in prison entitled, "To Althea, from Prison." (I C) This poem is the ultimate Cavalier values poem. (I D1) Through it he explores the idea that though his physical body is imprisoned, he can still find freedom through the love of the things he holds most dear, namely, women, wine, and King. These ideals keep his soul free and his spirits high even when he is locked behind stone walls.

BODY OF ESSAY

(II A) This poem was written in prison in 1642 and (II B) was published in 1649, the year Charles I was executed. (II C) "To Althea, from Prison" supports his Cavalier ideals with the imagery used in each line. (II D) Lovelace goes through each of the Cavalier's prime values and explains why these values make him as free as the "angels," even when he is imprisoned.

(III) The first stanza is devoted to the love of women, in this case Althea. (III A) Lovelace starts by personifying his love, describing it as a bird or breath of wind by writing, "When Love with unconfined wings/ Hovers within my Gates" (1–2). Love is not a tangible, animate thing; it cannot hover of fly. However, this is precisely why it can come to him. (III B) He is imprisoned, but his love is something that cannot be caged.

(III C) In the next few lines, he describes his love, Althea:

> And my divine Althea brings
> To whisper at the Grates;
> When I lye tangled in her haire
> And fettered to her eye, (3–6)

By describing her as "divine," he is exalting womanhood, as he often does in his poems. (III D) He also uses words that describe his imprisonment. (III D1) To be "tangled" in something generally implies being unable to get free. (III D2) The word "fettered" is another word for being chained. These are strange words to use when describing his love. (III D3) However, being "fettered to her eye" could mean that when he looks in her eyes it is impossible to pull himself away, which is a very tender sentiment. the word "fettered" is a good reference to his imprisonment. These images describe both his physical imprisonment and his emotional state that sets him free from the physical.

(III E) The last lines "The Gods that wanton in the Aire/Know no such Liberty," (7–8) sum up his love for Althea, or women. Some versions of this poem use the word "birds" instead of "gods". Either helps to express the idea that even those beings that can play freely in the air **(III E1)** (the word "wanton" has a definite sexual connotation) are not as free as he is, even though he is in prison. **(III F)** The Cavalier love of women makes them free despite their physical circumstances.

(IV) The second stanza is dedicated to the Cavaliers' love of wine. **(IV A)** The first two lines, "When flowing Cups run swiftly round/With no allaying Thames," (9–10) personifies the cups, suggesting they can run. It also creates the image of over-flowing cups of wine being past around the drunk Cavaliers. The Thames is the major river that flows through London. Wine was often watered down to prevent the drinkers from getting too drunk. The word "allaying" means to reduce or to ease. **(IV A1)** Saying that there is "no allaying Thames" suggests that the wine is undiluted.

(IV B1) The next lines, "Our carelesse heads with Roses bound/Our hearts with Loyall Flames," (11–12) describes the Cavalier's staunch loyalty to the crown. **(IV B2)** The words "carelesse heads" could mean several things. A drunken person is pretty careless and tends to not think at full capacity. Their faces are often red and flushed with the wine. Also, being a royalist during this period was a dangerous thing to be. Heads were separated from necks at an alarming rate. Being so openly royalist would have been a risky situation. **(IV B3)** However, because of their attitudes and outlook on life, Cavalier's were generally careless with their sentiments and demeanor. They tended to take a "head in the sand" approach to life. They did have very loyal hearts though, and many of them followed Charles II into exile.

(IV C1) The following lines, "When thirsty griefe in Wine we steepe/ When Healths and draughts go free", makes reference to both drinking and his imprisonment. **(IV C2)** A general tendency in many people when they experience great grief is to drown their sorrows in liquor. **(IV C2a)** The Cavaliers definitely had reason to grieve. Charles I was on his way to losing his throne and his head, and his son and heir was in exile.

Many of his followers were in prison and their lands were confiscated. **(IV C3)** The word "steep" is commonly associated with the process of making wine, and refers to the extreme soaking of something. If the Cavaliers are steeped in wine, they are pretty drunk.

(IV D) The ending lines of this stanza sum up the idea that the Cavalier love of wine makes them more free than the "Fishes that tipple in the Deepe" (15). **(IV D1)** The word "tipple" is a definite allusion to drinking. **(IV D1)** Fish in the deepest waters are generally free from being bothered or caught, **(IV D3)** but Lovelace feels that he is freer because of his Cavalier ideals.

(V) Stanza three is royalism at its best. **(V A)** He starts, in the first line, with a reference to his imprisoned state by comparing himself to "committed linnets", which are caged finches. He writes:

> When (like committed linnets) I
> With shriller throat shall sing,
> The sweetness, Mercy, Majesty,
> And glories of my KING;
> When I shall voyce aloud, how Good
> He is, how Great should be;(17–22)

The condition of the linnets parallels his own situation. **(V B)** He is also caged, however, instead of the song of the linnets, he sings about his kind. **(V B1)** His song is also "shriller", meaning louder, piercing, more acute. He wants the world to know of his loyalty and the greatness of his ling.

The last lines sum again sum up how his ideals set him free. **(V C)** Although he is caged like a bird, he is still more free and powerful than the "[e]nlarged winds, that curl the flood" (23) because of his love for his king.

(VI) The last stanza is a summary of the previous ideals and how they set him free:

> Stone Walls do not a Prison make,
> Nor Iron bars a Cage;
> Mindes innocent and quiet take
> That for an Hermitage. (25–28)

(VI A) A hermitage is the home of a hermit; a recluse. (VI A1) Lovelace is saying that for an innocent and peaceful man, a prison can be almost a blessing instead of a punishment. The time spent away from others can be used to think and to contemplate. (VI B) Besides, they are not really imprisoned as their ideals set them free in mind and spirit.

The last lines make a statement about his view on his values and how they affect him.

> If I have freedome in my Love,
> And in my soule am free,
> Angels alone that soar above,
> Injoy such Liberty. (29–32)

(VI C1) Love is something that cannot be taken away by physical imprisonment. Lovelace is saying that he will always have the freedom to love. If his soul is free, then he cannot really be caged. (VI C2) He has a free and guiltless soul and is assured in his convictions and so his soul will always be free, regardless of the circumstances his body is in. Because only his physical body is caged, but his emotional and spiritual self is free and happy in his feelings and convictions, (VI C3) than only the angels in the heavens enjoy the same liberty that he does, though he is imprisoned.

CONCLUSION

(VII A) This is a beautiful and uplifting poem about how Lovelace's values and ideals make him feel free even in the most dire of situations. (VII B1) It is a wonderful example of Cavalier poetry that explores the ideals of these poets, one by one, and how each affects the sentiments and attitudes of the Cavaliers. (VII B2) The imagery of this poem helps to create and maintain the concept of Cavalier ideals that Lovelace so firmly believed in.

11 Literary Analysis Essay

Version 2: The Edited Draft

The second version of the essay is the edited copy of the rough draft. This version has comments and revision suggestions marked in red. When proofreading your essays, you want to look for technical mistakes, such as spelling and punctuation errors, incorrect grammar, missing words, and awkward sentence structures. But you also want to look for areas where more extensive revision would be helpful. Maybe there is a statement that needs some additional information added, or a transition from one statement to another that could use a little beefing up. All of these things are part of the proofreading and editing process.

The Freedom of Cavalier Ideals

During the early 17th century, Cavalier style ruled the day. The Cavaliers' poetry is full of colorful images and sentiments. The Cavalier ideals of women, wine, and royalism are exalted in every way possible. Richard Lovelace, a poet during this period, wrote a poem while he was in prison entitled, "To Althea, from Prison." This poem is the ultimate Cavalier values poem. Through it *(Insert comma.)* he explores the idea that though his physical body is imprisoned, he can still find freedom through the love of the things he holds most dear, namely, women, wine, and King. These ideals keep his soul free and his spirits high even when he is locked behind stone walls.

This poem was written in prison in 1642 and was published in 1649, the year Charles I was executed. "To Althea, from Prison" supports his *(Lovelace's or Charles I's?)* Cavalier ideals with the imagery used in each line. Lovelace goes through each of the Cavalier's prime values and explains why these values make him as free as the "angels," even when he is imprisioned. *(Change to "imprisoned." Also, this paragraph could be condensed and added to the first paragraph. Other than the information about when the poem was published, you have already stated most of this information. Combine it with your introductory* paragraph.)

The first stanza is devoted to the love of women, in this case Althea. Lovelace starts by personifying his love, describing it as a bird or breath of wind by writing, "When Love with unconfined wings/Hovers within my Gates" (1–2). Love is not a tangible, animate thing; it cannot hover of *(Change to "or.")* fly. However, this is precisely why it can come to him. He is imprisoned, but his love is something that cannot be caged.

In the next few lines, he describes his love, Althea:

> And my divine Althea brings
> To whisper at the Grates;
> When I lye tangled in her haire
> And fettered to her eye; (3–6)

By describing her as "divine," he is exalting womanhood, as he often does in his poems. *(Start a new paragraph.)* He also uses words that describe his imprisonment. To be "tangled" in something generally implies being unable to get free. The word "fettered" is another word for being chained. These are strange words to use when describing his love *(Why?)*. However, being "fettered to her eye" could mean that when he looks in her eyes it is impossible to pull himself away, which is a very tender sentiment. the *(Capitalize "the.")* word "fettered" is a good reference to his imprisonment. These images describe both his physical imprisonment and his emotional state that sets him free from the physical.

The last lines *(of this stanza?)* "The Gods that wanton in the Aire/ Know no such Liberty," (7–8) sum up his love for Althea, or women. Some versions of this poem use the word "birds" instead of "gods". Either helps to express the idea that even those beings that can play freely in the air (the word "wanton" has a definite sexual connotation) *(This could be stronger if it is its own sentence, instead of an aside in parentheses.)* are not as free as he is, even though he is in prison. The Cavalier love of women makes them free despite their physical circumstances.

The second stanza is dedicated to the Cavaliers' love of wine. The first two lines, "When flowing Cups run swiftly round/With no allaying Thames," (9–10) personifies *(As this refers to the first two lines, it should be "personify.")* the cups, suggesting they can run. It also creates the image of over-flowing cups of wine being past *(Change to "passed.")* around the drunk Cavaliers. The Thames is the major river that flows through London. Wine was often watered down to prevent the drinkers from getting too drunk. The word "allaying" means to reduce or to ease. *(Rewrite these three sentences so they are a little more cohesive. As is, they seem to have no relation until you sum it up with this last sentence.)* Saying that there is "no allaying Thames" suggests that the wine is undiluted.

The next lines, "Our carelesse heads with Roses bound/Our hearts with Loyall Flames," (11–12) describes *(Again, this should be "describe" as it refers to "the next lines.")* the Cavalier's staunch loyalty to the crown. The words "careless heads" could mean several things. A drunken person is pretty careless *(A similar phrase, "generally careless," appears a few sentences down. Though this essay has a somewhat informal tone, I'd reword this phrase to get rid of the word "pretty.")* and tends to not think at full capacity. *(This part of the sentence is awkward; revise.)* Their faces are often red and flushed with the wine. *(Start a new paragraph.)* Also, being a royalist during this period was a dangerous thing to be. Heads were separated from necks at an alarming rate. Being so openly royalist would have been a risky situation. However, because of their attitudes and outlook on life, Cavalier's *(Delete the apostrophe.)* were generally careless with their sentiments and demeanor. They tended to take a "head in the sand" approach to life. They did have very loyal hearts though, and many of them followed Charles II into exile.

The following lines, "When thirsty griefe in Wine we steepe/When Healths and draughts go free," *(Insert the line numbers.)* makes reference *(Change to "make reference," as it refers to "the following lines." Or better yet, revise to say "refer.")* to both drinking and his imprisonment. A general tendency in many people when they experience great grief is to drown their sorrows in liquor. The Cavaliers definitely had reason to grieve. Charles I was on his way to losing his throne and his head, and his son and heir was in exile. Many of his followers were in prison and their lands were confiscated. The word "steep" is commonly associated with the process of making wine, and refers to the extreme soaking of something. If the Cavaliers are steeped in wine, they are pretty drunk. *(Again, reword to lose the "pretty." It's too informal.)*

The ending lines of this stanza sum up the idea that the Cavalier love of wine makes them more free than the "Fishes that tipple in the Deepe" (15). The word "tipple" is a definite allusion to drinking. Fish in the deepest waters are generally free from being bothered or caught, but Lovelace feels that he is freer because of his Cavalier ideals.

Stanza three is royalism at its best. He *(Lovelace?)* starts, in the first line, with a reference to his imprisoned state by comparing himself to "committed linnets", which are caged finches *(This line is a bit wordy; reword to make stronger and more concise.)*. He writes:

> When (like committed linnets) I
> With shriller throat shall sing,
> The sweetness, Mercy, Majesty,
> And glories of my KING;
> When I shall voyce aloud, how Good
> He is, how Great should be; (17–22)

The condition of the linnets parallels his own situation. He is also caged, however, instead of the song of the linnets, he sings about his kind *(Change to "king.")*. His song is also "shriller," meaning louder, piercing, more acute. He wants the world to know of his loyalty and the greatness of his ling *(Change to "king.")*.

The last lines *(of this stanza or of the poem?)* sum again sum up *(Delete the first "sum.")* how his ideals set him free. Although he is caged like a bird, he is still more free and powerful than the "[e]nlarged winds, that curl the flood" (23) because of his love for his king.

The last stanza is a summary of the previous ideals and how they set him free:

> Stone Walls do not a Prison make,
> Nor Iron bars a Cage;
> Mindes innocent and quiet take
> That for an Hermitage. (25–28)

A hermitage is the home of a hermit; a recluse *(A semicolon is not needed here. A comma is fine. Also, include a quick definition on what a hermit/recluse is.)*. Lovelace is saying that for an innocent and peaceful man, a prison can be almost a blessing instead of a punishment. The time spent away from others can be used to think and to contemplate. Besides, they are not really imprisoned as their ideals set them free in mind and spirit.

The last lines *(of the poem?)* make a statement about his view on his values and how they affect him:

> If I have freedome in my Love,
> And in my soule am free,
> Angels alone that soar above,
> Injoy such Liberty. (29–32)

(Indent.) Love is something that cannot be taken away by physical imprisonment. Lovelace is saying that he will always have the freedom to love. If his soul is free, then he cannot really be caged. He has a free and guiltless soul and is assured in his convictions and so his soul will always be free, regardless of the circumstances his body is in *(Reword to avoid the preposition at the end of the sentence.)*. Because only his physical body is caged, but his emotional and spiritual self is free and happy in his feelings and convictions, than only the angels in the heavens enjoy the same liberty that he does, though he is imprisoned. *(This is very wordy. Reword to make more concise. In other words, get to the point! These last several sentences basically state the same thing, so they can be revised.)*

This is a beautiful and uplifting poem about how Lovelace's values and ideals make him feel free even in the most dire of situations. It is a wonderful example of Cavalier poetry that explores the ideals of these poets, one by one, and how each affects the sentiments and attitudes of the Cavaliers *(The phrasing of this sentence is awkward; reword.)*. The imagery of this poem helps to create and maintain the concept of Cavalier ideals that Lovelace so firmly believed in *(Reword to avoid preposition ending.)*.

Version 3: The Final Draft

The third version of the essay is the final, revised copy so you can see how it has transformed from an outline, to a rough draft, to a polished essay ready to turn in.

11 Literary Analysis Essay

The Freedom of Cavalier Ideals

During the early 17th century, Cavalier style ruled the day. The Cavaliers' poetry is full of colorful images and sentiments. The Cavalier ideals of women, wine, and royalism are exalted in every way possible. Richard Lovelace, a poet during this period, wrote a poem while he was in prison entitled, "To Althea, from Prison." This poem is the ultimate Cavalier values poem. Through it, he explores the idea that though his physical body is imprisoned, he can still find freedom through the love of the things he holds most dear, namely, women, wine, and king. Published in 1649, the year Charles I was executed, this poem illustrates how his ideals keep Lovelace's soul free and his spirits high even when he is locked behind stone walls.

The first stanza is devoted to the love of women, in this case Althea. Lovelace starts by personifying his love, describing it as a bird or breath of wind by writing, "When love with unconfined wings/Hovers within my gates" (1–2). Love is not a tangible, animate thing; it cannot hover or fly. However, this is precisely why it can come to him. He is imprisoned, but his love is something that cannot be caged.

In the next few lines, he describes his love, Althea:

> And my divine Althea brings
> To whisper at the Grates;
> When I lie tangled in her hair
> And fettered to her eye, (3–6)

By describing her as "divine," he is exalting womanhood, as he often does in his poems.

He also uses words that describe his imprisonment. To be "tangled" in something generally implies being unable to get free. The word "fettered" is another word for being chained. These are strange words to use when describing his love. They tend to have sinister connotations. However, being "fettered to her eye" could mean that when he looks in her eyes it is impossible to pull himself away, which is a very tender sentiment. The word "fettered" is a good reference to his imprisonment. These images describe both his physical imprisonment and his emotional state that sets him free from the physical.

The last lines of this stanza, "The gods that wanton in the Aire/Know no such Liberty" (7–8), sum up his love for Althea, or women. The word "wanton" certainly has a sexual undertone. Some versions of this poem use the word "birds" instead of "gods." Either word helps to express the idea that even those beings that can play freely in the air are not as free as he is, even though he is in prison. The Cavalier love of women makes them free despite their physical circumstances.

The second stanza is dedicated to the Cavaliers' love of wine. The first two lines, "When flowing Cups run swiftly round/With no allaying Thames," (9–10), personify the cups, suggesting they can run. The Thames referred to is the major river that flows through London. These lines also create the image of overflowing cups of wine being passed around the drunk Cavaliers. In this time period, wine was often watered down to prevent the drinkers from getting too drunk, and the word "allaying" means to reduce or to ease. However, saying that there is "no allaying Thames" suggests that the wine is undiluted.

The next lines, "Our careless heads with roses bound/Our hearts with loyal flames" (11–12), describe the Cavalier's staunch loyalty to the crown. The words "careless heads" could mean several things. A drunken person is often careless and tends to think at less than full capacity. Their faces are often red and flushed with the wine.

Also, being a royalist during this period was a dangerous thing to be. Heads were separated from necks at an alarming rate. Being so openly royalist would have been a risky situation. However, because of their attitudes and outlook on life, Cavaliers were generally careless with their sentiments and demeanor. They tended to take a "head in the sand" approach to life. They did have very loyal hearts though, and many of them followed Charles II into exile.

The following lines, "When thirsty griefe in Wine we steepe/When healths and draughts go free" (13–14), refer to both drinking and his imprisonment. A general tendency in many people when they experience great grief is to drown their sorrows in liquor. The Cavaliers definitely had reason to grieve. Charles I was on his way to losing his throne and his head, and his son and heir was in exile. Many of his followers were in prison and their lands were confiscated. The word "steep" is commonly associated with the process of making wine, and refers to the extreme soaking of something. If the Cavaliers are steeped in wine, they are very drunk.

The ending lines of this stanza sum up the idea that the Cavalier love of wine makes them more free than the "Fishes that tipple in the Deepe" (15). The word "tipple" is a definite allusion to drinking. Fish in the deepest waters are generally free from being bothered or caught, but Lovelace feels that he is freer because of his Cavalier ideals.

Stanza three is royalism at its best. Lovelace begins the first line with a reference to his imprisoned state by comparing himself to caged finches, or "committed linnets." He writes:

> When (like committed linnets) I
> With shriller throat shall sing,
> The sweetness, Mercy, Majesty,
> And glories of my KING;
> When I shall voyce aloud, how Good
> He is, how Great should be; (17–22)

The condition of the linnets parallels his own situation. He is also caged, however, instead of the song of the linnets, he sings about his king. His song is also "shriller," meaning louder, piercing, more acute. He wants the world to know of his loyalty and the greatness of his king.

The last lines of this stanza again sum up how his ideals set him free. Although he is caged like a bird, he is still more free and powerful than the "Enlarged Winds that curle the Flood" (23) because of his love for his king.

The last stanza is a summary of the previous ideals and how they set him free:

> Stone Walls do not a Prison make,
> Nor Iron bars a Cage;
> Mindes innocent and quiet take
> That for an Hermitage; (25-28)

A hermitage is the home of a hermit, a recluse, someone who lives in solitude. Lovelace is saying that for an innocent and peaceful man, a prison can be almost a blessing instead of a punishment. The time spent away from others can be used to think and to contemplate. Besides, they are not really imprisoned as their ideals set them free in mind and spirit.

The last lines of the poem make a statement about his view on his values and how they affect him:

If I have freedome in my Love,

And in my soule am free;

Angels alone that soar above,

Injoy such liberty. (29–32)

Love is something that cannot be taken away by physical imprisonment. Lovelace is saying that he will always have the freedom to love. If his soul is free, then he cannot really be caged. He has a free and guiltless soul and is assured in his convictions. Therefore, his soul will always be free, regardless of the circumstances of his body. Because this is the case, only the angels in the heavens enjoy the same liberty that he does, though he is imprisoned.

This is a beautiful and uplifting poem about how Lovelace's values and ideals make him feel free even in the most dire of situations. It is a wonderful example of Cavalier poetry that explores each of their ideals, illustrating how each affects the sentiments and attitudes of the Cavaliers. The imagery of this poem helps to create and maintain the concept of Cavalier ideals in which Lovelace so firmly believed.

Exercise 11-1

Answer the following questions on the literary analysis essay. (*Answers on page 311.*)

1.   What does a basic literary analysis look at?

_____

_____

_____

_____

_____

_____

2. What are some things you can discuss when you are doing a
    literary analysis?

    _____

    _____

    _____

    _____

    _____

    _____

3. What do you need to include when using examples from the piece
    you are analyzing?

    _____

    _____

    _____

    _____

    _____

    _____

11 Literary Analysis
    Essay

12

Narrative Essay

Lesson 12-1: What Is It?

The narrative essay tells a story. Often, these essays tell of an experience or an event that happened to you or someone else. Just as with any other essay, a narrative essay should have a point to it. For example, if you are writing the essay about how your little brother got lost at the mall, the point of the essay might be to illustrate how you shouldn't wander away from your parents. As always, your essay must be well-organized and flow from paragraph to paragraph.

Narrative essays have an introduction, a body, and a conclusion, just like most essay forms. The introduction should let the reader know what type of narrative the essay illustrates. Is it a cautionary tale? A story that shows an aspect of human nature? Are you giving the reader a moral or lesson? Is it a personal story or describing the events of someone else's life? A personal essay will read more like an actual story, while detailing the events of someone else's life will have a more formal tone.

Think of this just like you would a regular story. You need to set the scene, use a lot of detail, vivid descriptions, and the five senses to help draw the reader into the story. You could even use a bit of dialogue. Narratives are generally written in "first person," which means you can use the word *I*. *Chicken Soup for the Soul* stories are narrative essays.

The story should lead up to the conclusion, which should state the point of the story.

Lesson 12-2: Getting Started

Choose a topic that has meaning for you, something you can either share a personal experience about or share someone else's experience. And remember: Your essay must have a point. Did your grandfather's death make you live your life in a new way? Were you always afraid of heights until you forced yourself to go bungee jumping? Were you a bully at school until you got a taste of your own medicine? Were you inspired to go back to school by watching a friend do the same?

For our example, we'll use the story of a woman who had always been overweight who one day discovered she could take control by taking it one day at a time. Once again, we'll start by making a list. Think about the topic you've chosen. Is it a personal experience? If so, what exactly do you want to highlight about that experience? What is the moral of the story? What do you want to include in the essay? What points do you want to make?

Be sure to answer these questions:
- ▶ Who?
- ▶ What?
- ▶ When?
- ▶ Where?
- ▶ Why?
- ▶ How?

Who is the main character in your narrative? What is his or her problem? When did the story you are telling occur? For example, what time of day or year was it? What day of the week? Where did your story take place? Why are you telling this tale? Why did the situation you are describing occur? Why did the main character make the choice he or she made? And how did the resolution come about? How did he or she solve the problem at hand? How does it end?

Sit down for a minute and just brainstorm ideas, things you want to discuss in the essay. For our example, the woman had always been overweight and then started a paper route. So, if she were making a quick list about this experience and what she wanted to talk about, it might look like this:

- Started a paper route.
- Was overweight.
- Didn't expect the physical part of the route to be hard.
- Ended up being a healthy step in the right direction.

And remember our Who, What, When, Where, Why, and How questions:

- Who?
  - An overweight woman
- What is the issue?
  - She is in pain and doesn't know how to alleviate her problem.
- When?
  - In the winter during the early mornings
- Where?
  - On a paper route
- Why is she telling the story? Or, why did she want to lose weight?
  - To share what she's learned
  - To alleviate her pain and health issues
- How?
  - One step (or one newspaper) at a time

The list doesn't have to be long or profound: just jot down a few notes to get your brain going and to set up your outline. For this type of essay, your outline won't be quite as detailed. You are telling a story. Outline your main points to give yourself a sort of road map as you write, and just tell the story you want to tell.

Lesson 12-3: Elements of the Essay

Once you have your topic chosen and a few basic ideas down, map out a basic outline to help keep your thoughts organized. Again, for our example essay, we have an overweight woman who was too overwhelmed by the amount of weight she had to lose to do anything about it. Then one day, while delivering newspapers, she realizes she can do something if she takes it one day at a time.

Introduction

Our example is an essay that describes an aspect of human nature and gives a moral to the story: anything is possible if you take it one day at a time. For this essay, the introduction introduces the problem at hand, the issue that will be discussed in the essay. The problem is that the author is overweight and has health and body issues because of the extra pounds. In addition, she has found doing anything about this to be difficult *because* of her size. This introduction also gives a hint as to the solution: the body can do extraordinary things.

The Body

The body of the essay will tell the story. It will highlight the situation and the points you want to discuss in a narrative (or conversational) tone, and lead up to your moral, or conclusion. For the example essay, the woman writing it would include things like her weight problem, problems she may have had in the past, starting the paper route and the issues she may have had with it, and the experience she had that led to her change of attitude.

Conclusion

Like any other essay, the conclusion restates the thesis and supporting evidence. In this case, it would present the moral of the story (the thesis) and touch on the issues that were discussed in the body of the essay.

Sample Essays

Look at the following narrative essay that describes the way an overweight woman comes to terms with her issues and discovers a way to follow her goals. The essay begins by introducing the problem and flows into the circumstance that becomes the beginning of a solution for the woman. She learns that she can achieve her goals by likening her situation to delivering newspapers and taking everything one step at a time.

Following is the detailed outline for the essay. Go through it, and then look at the rough draft to see how the essay falls into place. The parts of the essay are labeled in the rough draft with their corresponding numbers from the outline.

The Detailed Outline

I.   Introduction
    A. I'm overweight.
        1. Side effect—back pain
    B. Decided to do something about it
    C. Main concern—exercise
    D. Problems with exercising

II. Body
    A. Started paper route
        1. Porching papers
    B. Noticed a difference
    C. Stepped it up with additional exercise
    D. Started losing weight
    E. Always thought I couldn't do it
    F. Baby steps

III. Conclusion
    A. Moral
        1. Can do anything if you take it slow
    B. Lessons learned
        1. Be proud of the small achievements
        2. Take it one day at a time

12 Narrative Essay

Version 1: The Rough Draft

One Newspaper at a Time

INTRODUCTION

The body is certainly an interesting piece of machinery. It can do things that I would have thought quite impossible. I am what I like to call a recovering foodaholic. **(I A)** In plain English, I am very overweight. **(I A1)** One of the unfortunate side effects of this condition is constant back pain. Sitting, standing, lying down, carrying, lifting…no matter what the activity, my back is always in some state of pain.

(I B) Recently I decided to do something about this. **(I C)** My biggest concern was exercise. How could I possibly move this bulk of mine around when I was already in pain. **(I D)** Stretching, jogging, lifting weights, and all the other activities that I knew would help get the weight off just seemed impossible to do with my back always feeling like it was twisted in a knot.

BODY OF ESSAY

So I started out slow. **(II A)** I got a paper route, which, to be honest, was not a weight-losing strategy at first. **(II A1)** However, after I signed up I found out that I had to porch all of the papers. This may not sound tough to many people, but to a three hundred pound woman the thought of getting in and out of a car and walking up and down 147 driveways just didn't sound fun. And I just knew this would aggravate my back to the point that I wouldn't be able to move at all.

Now here is where it gets interesting. Day one came and I got in and out of my car and I huffed and puffed up one hundred and forty-seven driveways at two in the morning in the frigid cold air and I sweated like I hadn't done in years. I hauled myself home, got in bed, and went back to sleep. **(II B)** When I woke up several hours later, I sat up and realized that not only was my back not throbbing in pain, as I had thought it would, but it actually felt a little bit looser.

Each week I noticed my back pain getting progressively less. **(II C)** Well, I figured that if just walking a little every day could help, maybe adding in a little extra exercise would help even more. I took it easy, a little at a time, doing simple exercises and other activities. And here came another side-effect. **(II D)** I started to loose a little weight. As the weight came off, the back pain lessened.

(II E) I had always thought that I couldn't exercise because I was too large. The pain in my back, neck, legs, and pretty much everywhere else, along with the sheer bulk of me was simply too much to put through any kind of a workout routine. If I did manage to exercise, I just new I would be in agonizing pain the next day. But just the opposite happened. This amazing human body began to function better the more I exercised. Logic had always told me that if I lost weight my back wouldn't hurt so much. After all, three hundred pounds is a lot of weight for one back to carry. But the task of losing that weight just seemed too much to conquer.

(II F) So now, I'm taking baby steps. I have created a mental picture of me, newspaper carrier that I am, with 150 newspapers, each weighing a pound, strapped to my back. Every time I lose a pound, its like I'm throwing away one of those newspapers. Each time I toss a paper, my health is that much better, my back pain is that much less, and I'm one step closer to the healthier, happier person I want to be.

> CONCLUSION

(III A) I try not to look at the whole picture. I don't want to know how much I need to lose, or how much farther I want to go. I take it slow. **(III B1)** I allow myself to be proud of every moment I can sit without leaning over to crack my aching back, proud of every ounce I've lost and every ounce of mobility I've gained. **(III B2)** And I just take each day as it comes, one newspaper at a time.

Version 2: The Edited Draft

The second version of the essay is the edited copy of the rough draft. This version has comments and revision suggestions marked in red. When proofreading your essays, you want to look for technical mistakes, such as spelling and punctuation errors, incorrect grammar, missing words, and awkward sentence structures. But you also want to look for areas where more extensive revision would be helpful. Maybe there is a statement that needs some additional information added, or a transition from one statement to another that could use a little beefing up. All of these things are part of the proofreading and editing process.

12

Narrative Essay

One Newspaper at a Time

The body is certainly an interesting piece of machinery. It can do things that I would have thought quite impossible. I am what I like to call a recovering foodaholic. In plain English, I am very overweight. One of the unfortunate side effects of this condition is constant back pain. Sitting, standing, lying down, carrying, lifting…no matter what the activity, my back is always in some state of pain *(Choose a different word for pain as you repeat this several times in the first two paragraphs.)*.

Recently *(comma)* I decided to do something about this *(Why?)*. My biggest concern was exercise. How could I possibly move this bulk of mine around when I was already in pain. *(Sentence should end in a question mark.)* Stretching, jogging, lifting weights, and all the other activities that I knew would help get the weight off just seemed impossible to do with my back always feeling like it was twisted in a knot.

So I started out slow. I got a paper route, which, to be honest, was not a weight-losing strategy at first. *(You could reword this so it doesn't sound misleading. Revise so it doesn't sound like the reason for the paper route was weight loss.)* However, after I signed up I found out that I had to porch all of the papers *(What does this mean?)*. This may not sound tough to many people, but to a three hundred pound woman the thought of getting in and out of a car and walking up and down 147 driveways just didn't sound fun. And I just knew this would aggravate my back to the point that I wouldn't be able to move at all.

Now here is where it gets interesting. Day one came and I got in and out of my car and I huffed and puffed up one hundred and forty-seven *(You can use numerals for any number over 100, though this is fine if you are doing it for emphasis.)* driveways at two in the morning in the frigid cold air and I sweated like I hadn't done in years. *(This would be a good place to add a few senses or descriptions to make the sensations a little more real. How frigid was the air? Describe it a little.)* I hauled myself home, got in bed, and went back to sleep. When I woke up several hours later, I sat up and realized that not only was my back not throbbing in pain, as I had thought it would, but it actually felt a little bit looser.

Each week I noticed my back pain getting progressively less. Well, I figured that if just walking a little every day could help, maybe adding in a little extra exercise would help even more *(You knew this before, so why is it different now?)*. I took it easy, a little at a time, doing simple exercises and other activities *(like what?)*. And here came another side-effect *(not hyphenated)*. I started to loose *(should be "lose")* a little weight. As the weight came off, the back pain lessened.

I had always thought ~~that~~ *(not needed)* I couldn't exercise because I was too large. The pain in my back, neck, legs, and pretty much everywhere else, along with the sheer bulk of me was simply too much to put through any kind of a workout routine. If I did manage to exercise, I just new *(should be "knew")* I would be in agonizing pain the next day. But just the opposite happened. This amazing human body began to function better the more I exercised. Logic had always told me that if I lost weight my back wouldn't hurt so much. After all, three hundred pounds is a lot of weight for one back to carry. But the task of losing that weight just seemed too much to conquer.

So now, I'm taking baby steps. I have created a mental picture of me, newspaper carrier that I am, with 150 newspapers, each weighing a pound, strapped to my back *(why 150?)*. Every time I lose a pound, its *(needs an apostrophe)* like I'm throwing away one of those newspapers. Each time I toss a paper, my health is that much better, my back pain is that much less, and I'm one step closer to the healthier, happier person I want to be.

I try not to look at the whole picture. I don't want to know how much I need to lose, or how much farther I want to go *(Why?)*. I take it slow. I allow myself to be proud of every moment I can sit without leaning over to crack my aching back, proud of every ounce I've lost and every ounce of mobility I've gained. And I just take each day as it comes, one newspaper at a time.

Version 3: The Final Draft

The third version of the essay is the final, revised copy so you can see how it has transformed from an outline, to a rough draft, to a polished essay ready to turn in.

12 Narrative Essay

One Newspaper at a Time

The body is certainly an interesting piece of machinery. It can do things that I would have thought quite impossible. I am what I like to call a recovering foodaholic. In plain English, I am very overweight. One of the unfortunate side effects of this condition is constant back pain. Sitting, standing, lying down, carrying, lifting…no matter what the activity, my back is always in some state of discomfort.

Recently, I decided to do something about this. Not only did I want to relieve the back pain that carrying around an extra hundred pounds or so creates, I also wanted to head off all the other medical problems I knew were in my future. My biggest concern was exercise. How could I possibly move this bulk of mine around when I was already in pain? Stretching, jogging, lifting weights, and all the other activities that I knew would help get the weight off just seemed impossible to do with my back always feeling like it was twisted in a knot.

Then one day I got a paper route. This was not a weight-losing strategy at first. However, after I signed up I found out that I had to porch all of the papers. Which meant I had to get out of my car (YIKES!!) and physically walk the paper up the driveway and place it on the porch. This may not sound tough to many people, but to a three-hundred-pound woman the thought of getting in and out of a car and walking up and down 147 driveways just didn't sound fun. And I just knew this would aggravate my back to the point that I wouldn't be able to move at all.

Now here is where it gets interesting. Day one came and I got in and out of my car, and I huffed and puffed up one hundred and forty-seven driveways at two in the morning. Moisture froze in my nostrils and, even in the frigid air, I sweated like I hadn't done in years. I hauled myself home, got in bed, ignoring the ink that stained my hands and clothing, and went back to sleep. When I woke up several hours later, I sat up and realized that not only was my back not throbbing in pain, as I had thought it would, but it actually felt a little bit looser.

Each week I noticed my back pain getting progressively less. Well, I figured that if walking a little every day helped as much as it was, maybe adding in a little extra exercise would help even more. I took it easy, a little at a time, doing simple exercises and other activities, like playing with my children instead of popping in yet another movie for them to watch. And here came another side effect. I started to lose a little weight. As the weight came off, the back pain lessened.

I had always thought I couldn't exercise because I was too large. The pain in my back, neck, legs, and pretty much everywhere else, along with the sheer bulk of me was simply too much to put through any kind of a workout routine. If I did manage to exercise, I just knew I would be in agonizing pain the next day. But just the opposite happened. This amazing human body began to function better the more I exercised. Logic had always told me that if I lost weight my back wouldn't hurt so much. After all, three hundred pounds is a lot of weight for one back to carry. But the task of losing that weight just seemed too much to conquer.

So now, I'm taking baby steps. I have created a mental picture of me, newspaper carrier that I am, with 150 newspapers, each weighing a pound, strapped to my back (150 pounds being the amount I'd like to lose). Every time I lose a pound, it's like I'm throwing away one of those newspapers. Each time I toss a paper, my health is that much better, my back pain is that much less, and I'm one step closer to the healthier, happier person I want to be.

I try not to look at the whole picture. I don't want to know how much I need to lose, or how much farther I want to go. If I focus on the fact that I have only delivered ten papers of a 150 paper route, I'm going to want to just crawl in bed and never see the light of day again. So I don't focus on that. I take it slow. I allow myself to be proud of every moment I can sit without leaning over to crack my aching back, proud of every ounce I've lost and every ounce of mobility I've gained. And I just take each day as it comes, one newspaper at a time.

12 Narrative Essay

Exercise 12-1

Answer the following questions about the narrative essay. (*Answers on page 311.*)

1. What does a narrative essay do?

_____

_____

_____

2. What questions should you answer in your essay?

_____

_____

_____

_____

_____

_____

3. What is the purpose of the introduction in this essay?

_____

_____

_____

_____

_____

_____

12 Narrative Essay

13

Research or Term Paper

Lesson 13-1: What Is It?

A research or term paper is a paper in which you present information on a specific topic backed up by other sources. It is similar to an essay. It follows the same steps and has the same basic purpose, but is generally longer and more in-depth than an essay. Depending on your specific paper requirements, your paper could be a simple presentation of facts, or a complex, thorough analysis of your chosen subject.

Just as with other essays, there can be many different types of research papers. Your paper could be analyzing a particular subject, arguing your point of view on a topic, or comparing and contrasting two ideas or subjects. A research paper is simply an expanded form of one of these essays.

For most classes, you know at the beginning of the term if you will have a paper to do or not. At the very least, teachers generally give you a few weeks of advance notice—plenty of time to write a paper. And if you follow these tips, you can actually accomplish this in a nice, leisurely fashion that won't have you scrambling the night before it's due. This chapter will show you how to write a paper by breaking the task down into a six-week process. If you have less than six weeks, don't worry. Most of these steps can be combined and accomplished in much less time.

Lesson 13-2: Week 1—Choose a Topic and Create a Rough Outline

This may seem fairly easy (and it usually is), but sometimes you need to do a little research to decide what you really want to write. So for this week, your only task is to choose a topic. You can get a little head start on next week's task by looking through some sources to make sure there is enough information for you to include in your paper. Then, jot down a rough draft outline.

Say you are going to write a paper on pizza. What kind of information do you want to include? What will you discuss? Maybe you want to write about the history of the food, techniques for making it, different types, and different areas of the globe where this food is popular. So, your rough draft outline could look like this:

I.   Introduction

II.   History

III. Techniques

IV. Types

V.   Where It Is Popular

VI. Conclusion

It's simple and concise, but gives you a direction on which to focus your research, and it will come in handy in a few weeks.

Lesson 13-3: Week 2—Choose Your Sources

For this week, all you need to do is choose your sources—not the information or quotations, just the actual sources. Teachers will often give you a required number of sources, but you should probably find several extra. If you must have five sources, find 10. Many times, the

13 Research or Term Paper

information in several sources can be similar to each other, or you end up not being able to use it. If you have extra sources, you won't have to scramble to find something later. It is always best to have too much, rather than too little.

So how do you find your sources? Here are some good resources:

▶ Indexes. Go to the library, flip to the back of the book, and, if it has your topic listed, put it in your pile. Let's use our pizza example: if the index of the book you are looking at lists pizza, especially if it lists any of the specific aspects of pizza that you outlined, put it in your pile.

You can narrow this down further by seeing how many times your topic is mentioned. Are there 10 pages that mention pizza, or only one? If it only mentions it once, flip to that page and see if it is a good passage or not. If it mentions it several times, chances are there will be a lot of information that will be useful to you (you can check this by exploring the book more thoroughly).

Also, many scholarly books have a bibliography in the back. These can be an excellent source for further information and will give you specific titles to look for.

Don't forget to ask for help! The librarians are there to help you, and most really enjoy the hunt for information. Don't be afraid to ask for help finding sources. It can not only save you a little time in fruitless searches, but it will probably give you a wealth of information in places you might not have thought to look. These people know their stuff, so utilize their knowledge.

▶ Google and other search engines. You can find a lot of really good articles, Websites, and scholarly journals by doing online searches. Be careful of the information you choose online. Make sure the information comes from reputable sources. Though sites like Wikipedia offer a lot of information, this information is supplied by users, meaning anyone who wants to post can put up or add to articles. The information may not be accurate. However, many times the articles on such sites have their own sources lists. I highly recommend double-checking any information you find on sites

13 Research or Term Paper

such as these. The articles with source lists are generally more trustworthy and can give you additional sources in the books and articles they list.

Typing your chosen subject in an online search engine will bring up a lot of different choices. If you specifically search for books (for example, searching for "books on pizza"), the search engine will often pull up a list of books on Amazon, and other books that you may be able to view online without having to purchase. These books frequently let you view the entire book or have a sneak peek at the table of contents or index. If this is the case, you can see if the book is something you could use and jot down the title and author. You can then get or request the book from your local library. If the full book is available online, you could do your research and print the pages you need.

You can do the same type of search for articles or scholarly journal articles. If something on the list looks useful, write down the article information (title, author, journal title, issue, page numbers), and you can request the article from your library. Many times, your local library will be able to e-mail the article directly to you.

▶ Textbooks. Your assigned books for the class can actually be a great source of information. As with the online articles and book indexes, the bibliography can often lead you to more information.

If you searched only a half hour a day for a week, you'd have a nice pile of sources ready and waiting for you, with relatively little effort.

Lesson 13-4: Week 3—Make Notes

Now it's time to use those sources. You can do notes a few different ways, but using index cards seems to be the easiest. They are a very simple way to keep track of your information. However, if you don't want to use these, you can find your own way to keep track of your notes. You can write them in a notebook, type them up, or put them in a spreadsheet as alternatives to writing your notes on index cards.

Grab one of the sources you chose last week, flip to where your information is located, and read. If it is something you can use, make a note on your index card. If you intend on using the full quote, make sure you copy it exactly, with quotation marks, so you know it is a direct quote. If you just want the information but can put it in your own words, then paraphrase the information.

Each card should have only one quote or paraphrase. Be sure to write the source title, author, publisher, publication year, page number, and, if necessary, the URL and date accessed, for each, so you do not accidentally plagiarize your material.

As discussed in Chapter 1, make a note of what kind of information the card is listing. This is where your rough outline really comes in handy. If your paper on pizza will discuss the history of the food, techniques for making it, different types, and different areas of the globe where this food is popular, you'll want to make a note on the card of which category the information falls under. You'll want to get quite a few cards together as you'll need to make sure you have enough information to fulfill the length requirement for your paper.

Lesson 13-5: Week 4—Final Outline

This is where having your information on cards will really be useful. First, organize your cards into the categories you've assigned to them. Next, decide whether or not you will use each card, and put them in the order in which you want to use them. Finally, arrange the information in the note cards into an outline like the one described in Chapter 1.

Lesson 13-6: Week 5—Rough Draft

If you've followed the steps in this chapter, the process of writing the rough draft will be easy. You've already done all the work; you just need to put it on paper. Take your detailed outline and your cards, and string them together with your own words.

13

Research or Term Paper

Write your introduction. Craft a few introductory lines on pizza and be sure to clearly state your thesis: *This paper will discuss the history of the popular food pizza.*

Then on to section one: *The history of pizza is fascinating. Pizza originated in (INFORMATION FROM CARD ONE). It was first made by (INFORMATION FROM CARD TWO). While popular in this and that country, pizza didn't gain popularity in the United States until this year when (INFORMATION FROM CARD THREE).* And so on.

Your rough draft will basically write itself, and you'll have a whole week to do it, though you probably won't need that much time.

Lesson 13-7: Week 6—Final Draft

Now you are ready to finalize your paper. Read through it a couple times, fixing as many errors as you can find. Having someone look over it for you is a good idea. Fresh eyes often pick up mistakes that you, as the author of the piece, might not see. Proofread it, make a few changes here and there, spell-check, double-check your quotes and citations, make sure your Works Cited or Bibliography page is in order...and you are done!

If you had more than six weeks to do your paper, you might be able to turn it in early. A lot of teachers will let you do this and then revise it if necessary for a better grade. Or you can turn it in early, and be able to forget about it and relax the rest of the semester. Or just relax knowing it is done and turn it in when it is due.

If you have less than six weeks, some of these steps can be combined. For instance, you really don't need an entire week to pick a topic and create a rough draft outline. You can do that in one day (or less) and get started on picking your sources. You can make your note cards while choosing your sources. You can also get your final outline together as soon as you are done with your notes, or work on the outline as you gather your notes. Depending on how you combine the tasks, you could get this paper done in much less time, but, most of the time, you will have several weeks to work on your paper. And if you follow these steps, this process will be less stressful, if not downright simple, to accomplish. Good luck!

Sample Papers

The following paper is a longer, more in-depth version of a compare and contrast essay. It explores the character of a vampire slayer and how these characters have evolved through time. The main point of the paper is to show that, just as vampires symbolize a society's fears and taboos, their respective slayers reflect a society's heroes and desired qualities. Bram Stoker's *Dracula* was a required text for this class, so this paper goes into detail with examples from the book. The paper focuses on Van Helsing, the vampire slayer from Stoker's book, and compares him to the modern Buffy the Vampire Slayer.

Following is the detailed outline for the paper. Go through it, and then look at the rough draft to see how the essay falls into place. The parts of the essay are labeled in the rough draft with their corresponding numbers from the outline.

The Detailed Outline

I. Introduction
    A. Opening statements
        1. For as long as there have been vampires, there have been slayers.
        2. When vampires are recreated, so are their slayers.
    B. Thesis: Each vampire slayer is created to represent the needs of the creating culture.
    C. Slayers are diverse, ranging from Van Helsing to Buffy.

II. Interesting evolution
    A. Didn't originate in Transylvania
    B. Vampire hunters are fairly recent inventions.

III. Types of hunters
    A. Half-vampire half-human creatures—*dhampirs*
        1. Offspring of vampire and his human widow
        2. Bruce McClelland quote from Byrne page 1
        3. Natural hunters
    B. Vampires who hunt vampires.
        1. Most are very recent examples.
        2. Nick Knight

        a. Forever Knight

        b. 800 years old

        c. Cop

    3. Angel

        a. Spin-off from Buffy

        b. Is either good Angel or bad Angelus

IV. Stories before Stoker's *Dracula*

    A. No real slayers

    B. Samuel Coleridge's *Christabel*

    C. John Polidori's Lord Ruthven from *The Vampyre*

       1. Quote from story page 85

    D. James Malcolm Rhymer's *Varney the Vampire*

    E. Sheridan Le Fanu's *Carmilla*

       1. Characters of the doctor and Baron Vordenburg are similar to Van Helsing.

       2. They recognize the threat of the vampire.

       3. The doctor warns Laura's father not to leave her alone.

       4. The Baron's research finds Carmilla's resting place.

       5. General Spielsdorf stakes the body and takes the head.

V. Van Helsing

    A. Symbolizes all that was considered good and worthy in Victorian Britain

       1. Yu quote page 154

       2. Second Yu quote page 154

       3. Stoker quote page 243

       4. Stoker quote page 300

       5. Van Helsing is well liked.

       6. Stoker quote page 299

       7. Stoker quote page 305

       8. Ken Gelder quote page 1

       9. Van Helsing is the epitome of the Victorian man.

    B. Van Helsing is also egotistical.

       1. A Victorian audience would have liked these qualities.

       2. A modern audience might find them undesirable or offensive.

       3. Examples—Van Helsing refuses to divulge any information.

        a. Stoker quote page 244–245

        b. Stoker quote page 248–249

        c. Stoker quote page 249

        d. Stoker quote page 250

    4. Motivations

        a. Doesn't want to alarm anyone

        b. He knew he probably wouldn't be believed.

           1) Refuting—could have given them an excuse

        c. Knowledge is power quote

           1) This kept him ahead of everyone else

C. Chauvinistic—Treatment of Mina

    1. Stoker quote page 343 —"dreams"

    2. Stoker quote page 301

    3. Stoker quote page 343—"man's brain"

D. Wrap-up of Van Helsing

    1. His attributes were desirable in Victorian England.

    2. Desire for society to stay the same

    3. White upper-class males were dominant; women stayed home.

    4. Perfect slayer for his time

VI. Transition

A. Societies have changed.

    1. New Woman equals Normal Woman.

    2. Greater equality

B. Vampires have changed.

    1. Made up of different backgrounds, genders, ethnicities

    2. More powers

    3. More seductive and enticing

    4. More human-like

VII. Buffy

A. Created by writer-director Joss Whedon

B. Opposite of Van Helsing

    1. She's young.

    2. Female

    3. Not too smart

    4. Selfish

13 Research or Term Paper

5. Spoiled
6. She becomes a slayer by destiny.
7. Her trials make her into a better person.

VIII. Similarities between Buffy and Van Helsing
    A. Both have backup hunters.
        1. Van Helsing
            a. Seward, Quincy Morris, Jonathan Harker, Arthur, Mina
        2. Buffy
            a. Her Watcher, Giles, Willow, Xander

IX. Differences
    A. Group dynamics
        1. Rhonda Wilcox quote page 212
        2. Buffy doesn't give orders, keep secrets, or dictate actions.
        3. Her group works as a group.
        4. Wilcox quote page 102
        5. Inness quote page 231
    B. Buffy is more open with social commentary.
        1. Deals with regular teenage concerns
        2. Easy for audiences to connect with
    C. Buffy is empowering.
        1. Magoulick quote page 5

X. Conclusion
    A. Rhonda Wilcox quote page 20
    B. Buffy is today's slayer; Van Helsing was Victorian society's slayer.
    C. Every generation has new demons and needs new heroes to fight them.
    D. Van Helsing—perfect for his time
        1. Articulate, older gentleman, intelligent, egotistical, chivalric
    E. Buffy is perfect for modern times.
        1. Appeals to modern women and men
    F. Tomorrow's society will have new monsters and new slayers.

The Rough Draft

From Van Helsing to Buffy: The Evolution of the Vampire Slayer

INTRODUCTION

(I A1) For as long as there have been vampires, they're have been those who have sought to slay them. **(I A2)** Diverse cultures and new generations often recreate the vampire into a creature that best represents a threat particular to the culture in which it is produced. Vampire slayers are also fashioned in such a way. **(I B)** Each vampire slayer is created to represent the needs of the creating culture. **(I C)** These slayers are diverse, ranging from the Victorian Van Helsing to the new age Buffy.

BODY OF ESSAY

(II) The vampire slayer has had an interesting evolution. **(II A)** You might assume that vampire slayers, along with their vampires, originated in Transylvania, or in some other Slavic state. This is, in fact, entirely untrue. To begin with, there were no specific characters such as Van Helsing, who tracked the vampire with a bag full of weapons designed to vanquish it forever. **(II B)** These characters are fairly recent inventions, Van Helsing being the first real hunter of vampires.

(III A) There were, however, tales of half-vampire, half-human creatures, called *dhampir*, or *vampirdzia*. **(III A1)** These were the offspring of a vampire and his human widow. **(III A2)** In his book on this subject, Bruce A. McClelland ironically points out that "in the village context, a widow's pregnancy might have no other logical explanation, for her chastity in widowhood goes without question" (Byrne 1). Therefore it was assumed that her un-dead husband continued to visit her, resulting in half-breed offspring. **(III A3)** As such, they were born with the ability to sense or detect vampires, making them natural hunters.

(III B) They're is also that strange breed of slayer, hunters who are themselves vampires. **(III B1)** There are many examples of such creatures, most from very recent movies or television shows. Two of the most popular are Nicholas Knight and Angel. **(III B2)** Nick Knight, from the television series **(III B2a)** *Forever Knight,* **(III B2b)** is an 800-year-old vampire who **(III B2c)** becomes a police officer, protecting the world from both criminal vampires and those of the human variety.

(III B3a) Angel is a spin-off show from the popular series *Buffy the Vampire Slayer.* Angel is a vampire who has regained his soul through a gypsy curse, and, depending on the circumstances, **(III B3b)** is either the good vampire Angel, helping rid the world of evil, or his evil, soulless, other half, Angelus, a typical blood-sucking vampire.

(IV) In the literary vampire stories preceding Bram Stoker's *Dracula*, **(IV A)** you did not see a real example of a vampire slayer. **(IV B)** In Samuel Taylor Coleridge's "Christabel," the vampire, Geraldine, gets away with her attack on Christabel. **(IV C)** Likewise, John Polidori's Lord Ruthven, from *The Vampyre*, gets away with literal murder, **(IV C1)** marrying Aubrey's sister and then disappearing, having "glutted [his] thirst" with his new bride's blood (Polidori 85). James Malcolm Rhymer's *Varney the Vampire*'s title character requires no slayer as he commits suicide by jumping into a volcano.

(IV E) Sheridan Le Fanu's *Carmilla* differs slightly in that there is a sort of vampire slayer. **(IV E1)** The characters of the doctor and Baron Vordenburg are similar to Van Helsing in **(IV E2)** that they recognize the threat of the vampire. **(IV E3)** The doctor warns Laura's father not to leave her alone, and it was **(IV E4)** the Baron's vast research that uncovered Carmilla's resting place. **(IV E5)** It was General Spielsdorf, however, the bereaved guardian of one of Carmilla's victims, that staked the body and severed the head of Carmilla.

(V) Abraham Van Helsing, is therefore, the first true vampire hunter. *Dracula* can be interpreted many ways. Whether looked at from a feminist, capitalist, racial, or any other point of view, it is obvious that the tale is a commentary on Victorian times. The character of Van Helsing is part of the equation. **(V A)** His character symbolizes all that was considered good and worthy in Victorian Britain. **(V A1)** Van Helsing's "extensive knowledge, supreme rationality, ascetic leanings, and noted willingness to work hard must be with him all along" (Yu 154). He is a great deal like Stoker himself. **(V A2)** Van Helsing "represents the triumph of the Enlightenment, of the transcendental subjectivity" (154).

(V A3) Dr. Seward's description of him in his letter to Arthur illustrates Van Helsing's best qualities:

> I have written to my old friend and master, Professor Van Helsing, of Amsterdam, who knows as much about obscure diseases as any one in the world…He is a seemingly arbitrary man, but this because he knows what he is talking about better than any one else. He is a philosopher and a metaphysician, and one of the most advanced scientists of his day; and he has, I believe, and absolutely open mind. This, with an iron

nerve, a temper of the ice-brook, an indomitable resolution, self-command, and toleration exalted from virtue to blessings, and the kindliest and truest heart that beats…work both in theory and practice [sic], for his views are as wide as his all-embracing sympathy. (Stoker 243)

(V A4) Mina Harker gives a more physical description of this paradigm. She states:

he came towards me; a man of medium weight, strongly built…The poise of the head strikes one at once as indicative of though and power; the head is noble…The face, shows a hard, square chin, a large, resolute mouth…sensitive nostrils…The forehead is broad and fine…Big, dark blue eyes are set widely apart, and are quick and tender or stern with the man's moods. (300)

(V A5) He is obviously, and often instantly, well-liked. **(V A6)** Mina, one of the book's protagonists, states, "I feel from having seen him that he *is* good and kind and of a noble nature" (299). **(V A7)** Her husband, Jonathan, refers to Van Helsing as "this kindly, strong-faced old man" (305). **(V A8)** In his article, "Reading the Vampire," Ken Gelder describes Van Helsing as, "a scientist who mediates between folkish superstitions and enlightened knowledge…[who is] equally at home in these otherwise contradictory spheres. Thus he is both rational and clearheaded" (Gelder 1). All these descriptions tell of a man who seems to have the best of all qualities; strength, intelligence, kindness and sternness, and a "noble nature." **(V A9)** Van Helsing is the epitome of the Victorian man.

(V B) There is much evidence to suggest, however, that as strong, intelligent, and kind as he may be, Van Helsing is also egotistical. **(V B1)** It should be noted that these qualities would not have been viewed as unfavorable by a Victorian audience, except perhaps by that new breed of female, the New Woman. **(V B2)** But a 21st century audience, especially one that includes the modern woman, would see many of Van Helsing's actions as undesirable, if not downright offensive.

(V B3) First, there is Van Helsing's increasingly annoying habit of refusing to divulge any information, to anyone, until the last possible moment. Even upon his first examination of Lucy, Van Helsing must have had some idea of what ailed her. **(V B3a)** Yet Dr. Seward mentions that "Van Helsing made a very careful examination of the patient…He

13 Research or Term Paper

is, I fear, much concerned, but says he must think…As I tell you, he would not say a word more, even when we were alone" (244–45).

Van Helsing later likens his silence to Dr. Seward and his silence with his mental patients. **(V B3b)** He stated, "You tell not your madmen what you do nor why you do it; you tell them not what you think. So you shall keep knowledge in its place where it may rest…I have for myself thoughts at the present. Later I shall unfold to you" (248–49). When Dr. Seward questions this action, Van Helsing launches into a pompous speech about corn and the need for it to grow before it can be harvested. **(V B3c)** He declared, "I have sown my corn, and Nature has her work to do in making it sprout" (249). While it is understandable that he may have needed time in order to formulate a complete plan of action, sharing what knowledge he had could have spared Lucy's life.

It is fairly obvious he had at least a good idea of what was occurring to Lucy. **(V B3d)** Upon finding her one morning, pale and near death, he exclaims, "My God!…this is dreadful. There is no time to be lost. She will die for sheer want of blood to keep the heart's action as it should be. There must be a transfusion of blood at once" (250).

(V B4a) Van Helsing's decision to keep all knowledge to himself could very likely have been motivated by the desire to not alarm those who loved Lucy, as well as the fact that he knew **(V B4b)** he wouldn't be believed if he suddenly proclaimed that Lucy had been attacked by a vampire. **(V B4b1)** However, he could have simply stated that the garlic hanging around the room was for medicinal purposes and must not be touched, as indeed he did the night after Lucy's mother had had it all removed. Lucy's family and servants may have thought it strange to close her up in her room with cloves of garlic everywhere, but his wishes would have been followed.

Why would Van Helsing keep such precious knowledge to himself when sharing it could save lives? **(V B4c)** There is a well-known saying, "Knowledge is power." While it is doubtful that Van Helsing meant any harm, indeed his intentions appear selfless and pristine, it does seem likely that Van Helsing enjoyed the power that his private knowledge brought him. **(V B4c1)** It kept him always a little ahead of the rest.

Van Helsing's secrecy and egotistical behavior has been directed, for the most part, at the men up until this point in the tale. **(V C)** His somewhat arrogant actions soar to new heights with his chivalric, or chauvinistic, treatment of Mina. It is she who feels the full brunt of Van Helsing's prejudiced attitudes. **(V C1)** Though it is her intelligence and hard work that enables the group to track and eventually defeat Dracula, Van Helsing repeatedly insists that she be kept from the group's conversations and activities for fear that "[e]ven if she be not harmed, her heart may fail her in so much and so many horrors; and hereafter she may suffer—both in waking, from her nerves, and in sleep, from her dreams" (343).

(V C2) Upon first meeting Mina, his reply to her statement that she can tell him all about Lucy experiences, is, "Oh, then you have a good memory for facts, for details? It is not always so with young ladies" (301). **(V C3)** Even after Mina has proved her skills time and again, Van Helsing will only admit her intelligence by describing her as having a "man's brain" (343). It appears to be impossible for him to reconcile the idea of an intelligent, strong woman. She must, therefore, have some male qualities to explain her abilities.

(V D1) Van Helsing's attitudes and attributes were very indicative of what Victorian society felt was important. **(V D2)** In an age where industrialization and increased colonization and immigration was changing the empire as it had been, where the New Woman was making her voice heard, there was an increased desire for society to remain as it was. **(V D3)** White, upper- and middle-class males were the dominant members of society and women were expected too stay home and raise their families, putting all of their mental and physical resources to that task. Van Helsing, in his actions and thoughts throughout the book, illustrates this position. **(V D4)** He was the perfect vampire slayer for his generation.

(VI A) But now, societies all over the world have changed. **(VI A1)** The so-called New Woman is no longer new, but "normal." **(VI A2)** Society has changed to allow for greater equality between sexes, ethnicities, and even ages. **(VI B)** Vampires themselves have changed. They are no longer old men who keep a harem of vampire brides in a ruined castle while they feast on the village women. Today's vampires reflect the changes in society. **(VI B1)** They are made up of different genders, backgrounds, and ethnicities. **(VI B2)** They have many more supernatural powers. **(VI B3 and VI B4)** They are more seductive, and often, more human. A new breed of vampire slayer was needed.

(VII) Though there are many, many new tales, each with their own slayer, one stands out. The movie, *Buffy the Vampire Slayer* created the new slayer society needed. **(VII A)** Created by writer-director Joss Whedon, the movie became a popular television series. **(VII B)** Buffy is the opposite of Van Helsing in almost every way. **(VII B1)** She is young, **(VII B2)** female, **(VII B3)** not too bright in the beginning, **(VII B4)** selfish, **(VII B5)** and spoiled. **(VII B6)** She was chosen to be a slayer in a manner similar to the divine right of kings. It was her destiny. **(VII B7)** Through her trials and training she becomes stronger, less selfish, and more intelligent.

(VIII) There are a few similarities between Buffy and Van Helsing, **(VIII A)** the most notable of which is the fact that both slayers had a group of hunters that fought with them. **(VIII A1a)** Van Helsing had Seward, Quincy Morris, Jonathan Harker, Arthur, and at times, Mina.

(VIII A2a) Buffy also has a community of fighters; her Watcher, Giles, and friends Willow, and Xander.

(IX A1) However, in a footnote in her book, *Why Buffy Matters: the Art of Buffy the Vampire Slayer*, Rhonda Wilcox points out that the "interrelationship of the supportive outsider friends in *Buffy* is quite different from the group interaction of those who hunt Stoker's Dracula with, as Auerbach describes it, a 'corporate ethos' and the guidance of the 'overbearing patriarch' Van Helsing" (Wilcox 212). **(IX A2)** Buffy, while technically the slayer, does not order, keep secrets, and dictate actions as Van Helsing did. **(IX A3)** Her group works as a group. **(IX A4)** Wilcox notes that Buffy was successful "because she operates within a group of friends who support but can also question each other" (102). **(IX A5)** Buffy's character, and those similar to her, "have offered new visions of heroism by inflecting the concept of toughness with the notion of flexibility" (Inness 231). She grows in strength and wisdom because of those around her.

While Stoker cleverly wove implications about the New Woman, sexuality, colonization, and other Victorian concerns into his tale, **(IX B)** *Buffy* is much more open about modern society's trials. **(IX B1)** Buffy deals with regular teenage concerns, high school drama, sexual double standards, and parental conflicts, while juggling a secret vampire-slaying career. **(IX B2)** She is easy for audiences to connect with because she is going through the same problems as those who are watching her.

(IX C1) Mary Magoulick, in her article "Frustrating Female Heroism: Mixed Messages in Xena, Nikita, and Buffy," discusses "[c]ritic Frances H. Early [who] likewise argues the positive, feminist merits of *Buffy*, largely because she finds Buffy an empowering, just, conflict-resolving, gracefully acrobatic, ironically distant, morally astute, and patriarchy-rejecting hero in a grand historical tradition of women warriors" (Magoulick 5).

(X A) Rhonda Wilcox, in her book, quotes Nina Auerbach who states, "every age embraces the vampire it needs." She continues that "one might add, the slayer it needs. And though Auerbach's use of the term "age" refers to cultural period, her statement could be extended to apply to a stage of life—in this case, adolescence. Instead of a patriarchal Van Helsing, Buffy provides a sort, slight, teenage girl" (Wilcox 20).

CONCLUSION

(X B) Buffy is the slayer of today's society, as Van Helsing was the slayer of Victorian society. **(X C)** Each generation finds new demons to fight and in so doing, must also find a new hero to fight them. **(X D1)** Though an articulate, older gentleman, intelligent, egotistical, and unfailingly "chivalric" was the perfect slayer for Stoker's generation, **(X E1)** the 21st century needed a slayer who appealed to an audience of women and modern men. Thus was born Buffy. **(X F)** Tomorrow's society will have need of a new slayer for the monsters lurking around new corners.

Works Cited

Byrne, Richard. "Nota Bene." Rev. of *Slayers and Their Vampires: A Cultural History of Killing the Dead*, by Bruce A. McClelland. *Chronicle of Higher Education*. Vol. 53 No. 18 (2007): 13. *EBSCO*. 29 Jan. 2007 <http://library.nu.edu/articles/2472.pdf>.

Gelder, Ken. *Reading the Vampire*. 1994. *Ebrary: the National University Library System*. 1999. 28 Jan. 2007 <http://site.ebrary.com.ezproxy.nu.edu/lib/nuls/Top?channelName=nuls&cpage=1&docID=5004121&f00=text&frm=smp.x&hitsPerPage=10&layout=document&p00=reading+the+vampire&sortBy=score&sortOrder=desc>.

Inness, Sherrie. *Action Chicks: New Images of Tough Women in Popular Culture*. 2004. *Ebrary: the National University Library System*. 1999. 29 Jan. 2007 <http://site.ebrary.com.ezproxy.nu.edu/lib/nuls/Top?layout=search&id=5004121&nosr=1&frm=smp.x&p00=sherrie+inness>.

Le Fanu, Sheridan. "Carmilla." *Three Vampire Tales*. Ed. Anne Williams. Boston: Houghton, 2003.

Magoulick, Mary. "Frustrating Female Heroism: Mixed Messages in Xena, Nikita, and Buffy." *Journal of Popular Culture*. Vol.39, Iss. 5 (2006): 729. *EBSCO*. 28 Jan. 2007 <http://proquest.umi.com/pqdlink?did=1149214191&Fmt=7&clientId=1506&RQT=309&VName=PQD>.

Polidori, John. "The Vampyre." *Three Vampire Tales*. Ed. Anne Williams. Boston: Houghton, 2003.

Stoker, Bram. "Dracula." *Three Vampire Tales*. Ed. Anne Williams. Boston: Houghton, 2003.

Wilcox, Rhonda. *Why Buffy Matters: The Art of Buffy the Vampire Slayer*. 2005. *Ebrary: the National University Library System*. 1999. 29 Jan. 2007 < http://site.ebrary.com.ezproxy.nu.edu/lib/nuls/Top?layout=search&id=5004121&nosr=1&frm=smp.x&p00=why+buffy+matters>.

Yu, Eric Kwan-Wai. "Productive Fear: Labor, Sexuality, and Mimicry in Bram Stoker's Dracula." *Texas Studies in Literature and Language 48.2* (2006) 145-170. Project Muse. 28 Jan. 2007 <http://muse.jhu.edu.ezproxy.nu.edu/journals/texas_studies_in_literature_and_language/v048/48.2yu.html>.

The Edited Draft

The second version of the paper is the edited copy of the rough draft. This version has comments and revision suggestions marked in red. When proofreading your essays and papers, you want to look for technical mistakes, such as spelling and punctuation errors, incorrect grammar, missing words, and awkward sentence structures. But you also want to look for areas where more extensive revision would be helpful. Maybe there is a statement that needs some additional information added, or a transition from one statement to another that could use a little beefing up. All of these things are part of the proofreading and editing process.

13 Research or Term Paper

From Van Helsing to Buffy:
The Evolution of the Vampire Slayer

For as long as there have been vampires, they're *(Change to "there.")* have been those who have sought to slay them. Diverse cultures and new generations often recreate the vampire into a creature that best represents a threat particular to the culture in which it is produced. Vampire slayers are also fashioned in such a way. Each vampire slayer is created to represent the needs of the creating culture. These slayers are diverse, ranging from the Victorian Van Helsing to the new age Buffy.

The vampire slayer has had an interesting evolution. You might assume *(Rewrite this to get rid of the informal "you.")* that vampire slayers, along with their vampires, originated in Transylvania, or in some other Slavic state. This is, in fact, entirely untrue. To begin with, there were no specific characters such as Van Helsing, who tracked the vampire with a bag full of weapons designed to vanquish it forever. These characters are fairly recent inventions, Van Helsing being the first real hunter of vampires.

There were, however, tales of half-vampire, half-human creatures, called *dhampir*, or *vampirdzia*. These were the offspring of a vampire and his human widow. In his book on this subject *(What is the title?)*, Bruce A. McClelland ironically points out that "in the village context, a widow's pregnancy might have no other logical explanation, for her chastity in widowhood goes without question" (Byrne 1). Therefore *(Insert comma.)* it was assumed that her un-dead husband continued to visit her, resulting in half-breed offspring. As such, they were born with the ability to sense or detect vampires, making them natural hunters.

They're *(Change to "there.")* is also that strange breed of slayer, hunters who are themselves vampires. There are many examples of such creatures, most from very recent movies or television shows. Two of the most popular are Nicholas Knight and Angel. Nick Knight, from the television series *Forever Knight*, is an 800-year-old vampire who becomes a police officer, protecting the world from both criminal vampires and those of the human variety.

Angel *(What show is this character from?)* is a spin-off show from the popular series *Buffy the Vampire Slayer*. Angel is a vampire who has regained his soul through a gypsy curse, and, depending on the circumstances, is either the good vampire Angel, helping rid the world of evil, or his evil, soulless, other half, Angelus, a typical blood-sucking vampire.

13
Research or Term
Paper

In the literary vampire stories preceding Bram Stoker's *Dracula*, you *(Use the more formal "one" instead of "you," or reword to make more general, such as "audiences" or "readers.")* did not see a real example of a vampire slayer. In Samuel Taylor Coleridge's "Christabel," the vampire, Geraldine, gets away with her attack on Christabel. *(Who is this?)* Likewise, John Polidori's Lord Ruthven, from *The Vampyre*, gets away *(You used this phrase in the previous sentence. Reword to avoid the repeat.)* with literal murder, marrying Aubrey's sister *(This reference will only be understood by someone who has read the story. This isn't a bad thing—you should know and write for your audience, but it doesn't hurt to be a little more general. Just saying "marrying a woman" gets the point across without introducing a possibly confusing reference.)* and then disappearing, having "glutted [his] thirst" with his new bride's blood (Polidori 85). James Malcolm Rhymer's *Varney the Vampire*'s title character requires no slayer as he commits suicide by jumping into a volcano.

Sheridan Le Fanu's *Carmilla* differs slightly in that there is a sort of vampire slayer. The characters of the doctor and Baron Vordenburg are similar to Van Helsing in that they recognize the threat of the vampire. The doctor warns Laura's father not to leave her alone, and it was the Baron's vast research that uncovered Carmilla's resting place. It was General Spielsdorf, however, the bereaved guardian of one of Carmilla's victims, that *(Use "who" when referring to a person.)* staked the body and severed the head of Carmilla.

Abraham Van Helsing, is therefore, the first true vampire hunter *(The commas should be before and after "therefore.")*. *Dracula* can be interpreted many ways. *(Because it's been a while since you've mentioned that Van Helsing is a character in Dracula, it would be a good idea to restate that here.)* Whether looked at from a feminist, capitalist, racial, or any other point of view, it is obvious that the tale is a commentary on Victorian times. The character of Van Helsing is part of the equation. His character symbolizes all that was considered good and worthy in Victorian Britain. *(Give examples.)* Van Helsing's "extensive knowledge, supreme rationality, ascetic leanings, and noted willingness to work hard must be with him all along" (Yu 154). He is a great deal like Stoker himself. Van Helsing "represents the triumph of the Enlightenment, of the transcendental subjectivity" (154).

Dr. Seward's description of him in his letter to Arthur illustrates Van Helsing's best qualities: *(Though it might be obvious that Dr. Seward and*

Arthur are also characters in the book, and you know your audience knows this, it would lessen any possible confusion to simply state "In the story....")

> I have written to my old friend and master, Professor Van Helsing, of Amsterdam, who knows as much about obscure diseases as any one in the world...He is a seemingly arbitrary man, but this because he knows what he is talking about better than any one else. He is a philosopher and a metaphysician, and one of the most advanced scientists of his day; and he has, I believe, and absolutely open mind. This, with an iron nerve, a temper of the ice-brook, an indomitable resolution, self-command, and toleration exalted from virtue to blessings, and the kindliest and truest heart that beats... work both in theory and practice [sic], for his views are as wide as his all-embracing sympathy. (Stoker 243)

Mina Harker gives a more physical description of this paradigm. She states:

> he came towards me; a man of medium weight, strongly built...The poise of the head strikes one at once as indicative of though and power; the head is noble...The face, shows a hard, square chin, a large, resolute mouth...sensitive nostrils... The forehead is broad and fine...Big, dark blue eyes are set widely apart, and are quick and tender or stern with the man's moods. (300)

He is obviously, and often instantly, well-liked. Mina, one of the book's protagonists, states, "I feel from having seen him that he *is* good and kind and of a noble nature" (299). Her husband, Jonathan, refers to Van Helsing as "this kindly, strong-faced old man" (305). *(Make a new paragraph here to separate the characters' opinions of Van Helsing from the real life Ken Gelder.)* In his article, "Reading the Vampire," Ken Gelder describes Van Helsing as, "a scientist who mediates between folkish superstitions and enlightened knowledge...[who is] equally at home in these otherwise contradictory spheres. Thus he is both rational and clearheaded" (Gelder 1). All these descriptions tell of a man who seems to have the best of all qualities; *(Use a colon here instead of a semicolon.)* strength, intelligence, kindness and sternness, and a "noble nature." Van Helsing is the epitome of the Victorian man.

13 Research or Term Paper

There is much evidence to suggest, however, that as strong, intelligent, and kind as he may be, Van Helsing is also egotistical. It should be noted that these qualities would not have been viewed as unfavorable by a Victorian audience, except perhaps by that new breed of female, the New Woman. But a 21st century audience, especially one that includes the modern woman, would see many of Van Helsing's actions as undesirable, if not downright offensive. *(All three of these sentences are very long and complex. Consider revising to vary the sentence structure.)*

First, there is Van Helsing's increasingly annoying habit of refusing to divulge any information, to anyone, until the last possible moment. Even upon his first examination of Lucy, Van Helsing must have had some idea of what ailed her. Yet Dr. Seward mentions that "Van Helsing made a very careful examination of the patient....He is, I fear, much concerned, but says he must think....As I tell you, he would not say a word more, even when we were alone" (244–45).

Van Helsing later likens his silence to Dr. Seward and his silence with his mental patients *(This sentence is okay, but might sound better if it were more concise and revised to avoid the repeat of "silence.")*. He stated, "You tell not your madmen what you do nor why you do it; you tell them not what you think. So you shall keep knowledge in its place where it may rest....I have for myself thoughts at the present. Later I shall unfold to you" (248–49). When Dr. Seward questions this action, Van Helsing launches into a pompous speech about corn and the need for it to grow before it can be harvested. He declared, "I have sown my corn, and Nature has her work to do in making it sprout" (249). While it is understandable that he may have needed time in order to formulate a complete plan of action, sharing what knowledge he had could have spared Lucy's life.

It is fairly obvious he had at least a good idea of what was occurring to Lucy. Upon finding her one morning, pale and near death, he exclaims, "My God!...this is dreadful. There is no time to be lost. She will die for sheer want of blood to keep the heart's action as it should be. There must be a transfusion of blood at once" (250).

Van Helsing's decision to keep all knowledge to himself could very likely have been motivated by the desire to not alarm those who loved Lucy, as well as *(Insert "by.")* the fact that he knew he wouldn't be believed if he suddenly proclaimed that Lucy had been attacked by a vampire. However, he could have simply stated that the garlic hanging around the room was for medicinal purposes and must not be touched, as indeed he did the night after Lucy's mother had had it all removed. Lucy's family and servants may have thought it strange to close her up in her room with cloves of garlic everywhere, but his wishes would have been followed *(This sentence is technically fine, but it is very long. Consider breaking it up into two or three sentences.)*.

Why would Van Helsing keep such precious knowledge to himself when sharing it could save lives? *(The wording of this sentence is very similar to the wording of the first sentence of the previous paragraph. Consider revising to avoid the repetition.)* There is a well-known saying, "Knowledge is power." *(Who originally said this?)* While it is doubtful that Van Helsing meant any harm, indeed his intentions appear selfless and pristine, it does seem likely that Van Helsing enjoyed the power that his private knowledge brought him. It kept him always a little ahead of the rest.

Van Helsing's secrecy and egotistical behavior has been directed, for the most part, at the men up until this point in the tale. His somewhat arrogant actions soar to new heights with his chivalric, or chauvinistic, *(These are two very different characteristics. Maybe state where the difference comes in—meaning, does it depend on who is looking at it? Would men see it as chivalric and women see it as chauvinistic? Would the Victorian society see it as one while modern society would see it as the other?)* treatment of Mina. It is she who feels the full brunt of Van Helsing's prejudiced attitudes. Though it is her intelligence and hard work that enables the group to track and eventually defeat Dracula, Van Helsing repeatedly insists that she be kept from the group's conversations and activities for fear that "[e]ven if she be not harmed, her heart may fail her in so much and so many horrors; and hereafter she may suffer—both in waking, from her nerves, and in sleep, from her dreams" (343).

Upon first meeting Mina, his reply to her statement that she can tell him all about Lucy *(Change to Lucy's)* experiences, is, "Oh, then you have a good memory for facts, for details? It is not always so with young ladies" (301). Even after Mina has proved her skills time and again, Van Helsing will only admit her intelligence by describing her as having a "man's brain" (343). It appears to be impossible for him to reconcile the idea of an intelligent, strong woman. She must, therefore, have some male qualities to explain her abilities.

13 Research or Term Paper

Van Helsing's attitudes and attributes were very indicative of what Victorian society felt was important. In an age where industrialization and *(Get rid of "and" and use a comma instead.)* increased colonization *(Insert comma.)* and immigration was *(Change to "were.")* changing the empire as it had been, *(Delete "as it had been." It is not needed.)* where the New Woman was making her voice heard, there was an increased desire for society to remain as it was. White, upper- and middle-class males were the dominant members of society and women were expected too *(Change to "to.")* stay home and raise their families, putting all of their mental and physical resources to that task. Van Helsing, in his actions and thoughts throughout the book, illustrates this position. He was the perfect vampire slayer for his generation.

But now *(When is "now?")*, societies all over the world have changed. The so-called New Woman is no longer new, but "normal." Society has changed to allow for greater equality between sexes, ethnicities, and even ages. Vampires themselves have changed. They are no longer old men who keep a harem of vampire brides in a ruined castle while they feast on the village women. Today's vampires reflect the changes in society. They are made up of different genders, backgrounds, and ethnicities. They have many more supernatural powers. They are more seductive, and often, more human. A new breed of vampire slayer was needed *(This closing sentence could be a bit stronger. It should tie the vampires and their slayers together a little more definitively.)*.

Though there are many, many new tales, each with their own slayer, one stands out. The movie, *Buffy the Vampire Slayer* created the new slayer society needed *(When?)*. Created by writer-director Joss Whedon, the movie became a popular television series. Buffy is the opposite of Van Helsing in almost every way. She is young, female, not too bright in the beginning, selfish, and spoiled. She was chosen to be a slayer in a manner similar to the divine right of kings. It was her destiny. Through her trials and training *(Insert comma.)* she becomes stronger, less selfish, and more intelligent *(More intelligent or wiser? The fact that she's learned a few things along the way has no bearing on her basic intelligence.)*.

There are a few similarities between Buffy and Van Helsing, the most notable of which is the fact that both slayers had a group of hunters that fought with them. Van Helsing had Seward, Quincy Morris, Jonathan Harker, Arthur, and at times, Mina.

Buffy also has a community of fighters (This is fine, but because we already know that both Van Helsing and Buffy have helpers, we don't really need this intro. Reword a bit, maybe something like "Buffy's community of fighters includes...."); her Watcher, Giles, and friends Willow, and Xander. However, in a footnote in her book, (This makes it sound like it is Buffy's book. Put the author's name here, instead of after the title.) *Why Buffy Matters: the Art of Buffy the Vampire Slayer,* Rhonda Wilcox points out that the "interrelationship of the supportive outsider friends in *Buffy* is quite different from the group interaction of those who hunt Stoker's Dracula with, as Auerbach describes it, a 'corporate ethos' and the guidance of the 'overbearing patriarch' Van Helsing" (Wilcox 212). (The author's name isn't needed here, because it was introduced before the quote.) Buffy, while technically the slayer, does not order, keep secrets, and dictate actions as Van Helsing did. Her group works as a group. (Maybe substitute the second "group" for "team," so you aren't repeating words.) Wilcox notes that Buffy was successful "because she operates within a group of friends who support but can also question each other" (102). Buffy's character, and those similar to her, "have offered new visions of heroism by inflecting the concept of toughness with the notion of flexibility" (Inness 231). She grows in strength and wisdom because of those around her.

While Stoker cleverly wove implications about the New Woman, sexuality, colonization, and other Victorian concerns into his tale, *Buffy* is much more open *(I'd revise the opening of this sentence to include that Stoker's clever weavings were subtle; it's a more appropriate comparison.)* about modern society's trials. Buffy deals with regular teenage concerns, high school drama, sexual double standards, and parental conflicts, while juggling a secret vampire-slaying career. She is easy for audiences to connect with because she is going through the same problems as those who are watching her.

Mary Magoulick, in her article "Frustrating Female Heroism: Mixed Messages in Xena, Nikita, and Buffy," discusses "[c]ritic Frances H. Early [who] likewise argues the positive, feminist merits of Buffy, largely because she finds Buffy an empowering, just, conflict-resolving, gracefully acrobatic, ironically distant, morally astute, and patriarchy-rejecting hero in a grand historical tradition of women warriors" (Magoulick 5). *(Who is Mary? Maybe add a couple words about who she*

13 Research or Term Paper

is—author, teacher, psychologist? Also, again, her name isn't needed in the citation as she was introduced before the quote, so we know who the quote is from.)

(Indent.) Rhonda Wilcox, in her book, quotes Nina Auerbach who states, "every age embraces the vampire it needs." *(Rearrange a bit so this sentence isn't so broken up with commas. It is fine how it is written, but it doesn't flow very smoothly as the commas cause the reader to frequently pause.)* She continues that "one might add, the slayer it needs. And though Auerbach's use of the term "age" refers to cultural period, her statement could be extended to apply to a stage of life—in this case, adolescence. Instead of a patriarchal Van Helsing, Buffy provides a sort, slight, teenage girl" (Wilcox 20).

Buffy is the slayer of today's society, as Van Helsing was the slayer of Victorian society. Each generation finds new demons to fight and in so doing, must also find a new hero to fight them. Though an articulate, older gentleman, intelligent, egotistical, and unfailingly "chivalric" *(It feels like there are some words missing here. It's worded a bit awkwardly. Revise for clarity and fluidity.)* was the perfect slayer for Stoker's generation, the 21st century needed a slayer who appealed to an audience of women and modern men. Thus was born Buffy. *(Move the first two sentences down here, and move the sentence starting with "While an articulate..." up to the beginning of the paragraph. It is a stronger opening.)* Tomorrow's society will have need of a new slayer for the monsters lurking around new corners.

Works Cited

Byrne, Richard. "Nota Bene." Rev. of *Slayers and Their Vampires: A Cultural History of Killing the Dead*, by Bruce A. McClelland. *Chronicle of Higher Education*. Vol. 53 No. 18 (2007): 13. *EBSCO*. 29 Jan. 2007 <http://library.nu.edu/articles/2472.pdf>.

Gelder, Ken. *Reading the Vampire*. 1994. *Ebrary: the National University Library System*. 1999. 28 Jan. 2007 <http://site.ebrary.com.ezproxy.nu.edu/lib/nuls/Top?channelName=nuls&cpage=1&docID=5004121&f00=text&frm=smp.x&hitsPerPage=10&layout=document&p00=reading+the+vampire&sortBy=score&sortOrder=desc>.

Inness, Sherrie. *Action Chicks: New Images of Tough Women in Popular Culture.* 2004. *Ebrary: the National University Library System.* 1999. 29 Jan. 2007 <http://site.ebrary.com.ezproxy.nu.edu/lib/nuls/Top?layout=search&id=5004121&nosr=1&frm=smp.x&p00=sherrie+inness>.

Le Fanu, Sheridan. "Carmilla." *Three Vampire Tales.* Ed. Anne Williams. Boston: Houghton, 2003.

Magoulick, Mary. "Frustrating Female Heroism: Mixed Messages in Xena, Nikita, and Buffy." *Journal of Popular Culture.* Vol.39, Iss. 5 (2006): 729. *EBSCO.* 28 Jan. 2007 <http://proquest.umi.com/pqdlink?did=1149214191&Fmt=7&clientId=1506&RQT=309&VName=PQD>.

Polidori, John. "The Vampyre." *Three Vampire Tales.* Ed. Anne Williams. Boston: Houghton, 2003.

Stoker, Bram. "Dracula." *Three Vampire Tales.* Ed. Anne Williams. Boston: Houghton, 2003.

Wilcox, Rhonda. *Why Buffy Matters: The Art of Buffy the Vampire Slayer.* 2005. *Ebrary: the National University Library System.* 1999. 29 Jan. 2007 < http://site.ebrary.com.ezproxy.nu.edu/lib/nuls/Top?layout=search&id=5004121&nosr=1&frm=smp.x&p00=why+buffy+matters>.

Yu, Eric Kwan-Wai. "Productive Fear: Labor, Sexuality, and Mimicry in Bram Stoker's Dracula." *Texas Studies in Literature and Language* 48.2 (2006) 145-170. Project Muse. 28 Jan. 2007 <http://muse.jhu.edu.ezproxy.nu.edu/journals/texas_studies_in_literature_and_language/v048/48.2yu.html>.

The Final Draft

The third version of the essay is the final, revised copy so you can see how it has transformed from an outline, to a rough draft, to a polished essay ready to turn in.

From Van Helsing to Buffy:
The Evolution of the Vampire Slayer

For as long as there have been vampires, there have been those who have sought to slay them. Diverse cultures and new generations often recreate the vampire into a creature that best represents a threat particular to the culture in which it is produced. Vampire slayers are also fashioned in such a way. Each vampire slayer is created to represent the needs of the creating culture. These slayers are diverse, ranging from the Victorian Van Helsing to the new age Buffy.

The vampire slayer has had an interesting evolution. Most assume that vampire slayers, along with their vampires, originated in Transylvania, or in some other Slavic state. This is, in fact, entirely untrue. To begin with, there were no specific characters such as Van Helsing, who tracked the vampire with a bag full of weapons designed to vanquish it forever. These characters are fairly recent inventions, Van Helsing being the first real hunter of vampires.

There were, however, tales of half-vampire, half-human creatures, called *dhampir*, or *vampirdzia*. These were the offspring of a vampire and his human widow. In his book *Slayers and Their Vampires: A Cultural History of Killing the Dead*, Bruce A. McClelland ironically points out that "in the village context, a widow's pregnancy might have no other logical explanation, for her chastity in widowhood goes without question" (Byrne 1). Therefore, it was assumed that her un-dead husband continued to visit her, resulting in half-breed offspring. As such, they were born with the ability to sense or detect vampires, making them natural hunters.

There is also that strange breed of slayer, hunters who are themselves vampires. There are many examples of such creatures, most from very recent movies or television shows. Two of the most popular are Nicholas Knight and Angel. Nick Knight, from the television series *Forever Knight*, is an 800-year-old vampire who becomes a police officer, protecting the world from both criminal vampires and those of the human variety.

Angel, the title character from the show of the same name, is a spin-off show from the popular series *Buffy the Vampire Slayer*. Angel is a vampire who has regained his soul through a gypsy curse, and, depending on the circumstances, is either the good vampire Angel, helping rid the world of evil, or his evil, soulless, other half, Angelus, a typical blood-sucking vampire.

In the literary vampire stories preceding Bram Stoker's *Dracula*, there were no real examples of a vampire slayer. In Samuel Taylor Coleridge's "Christabel," the vampire, Geraldine, is able to attack the main character, Christabel. Likewise, John Polidori's Lord Ruthven, from *The Vampyre*, gets away with literal murder, marrying the main character's sister and then disappearing, having "glutted [his] thirst" with his new bride's blood (Polidori 85). James Malcolm Rhymer's *Varney the Vampire*'s title character requires no slayer as he commits suicide by jumping into a volcano.

Sheridan Le Fanu's *Carmilla* differs slightly in that there is a sort of vampire slayer. The characters of the doctor and Baron Vordenburg are similar to Van Helsing in that they recognize the threat of the vampire. The doctor warns Laura's father not to leave her alone, and it was the Baron's vast research that uncovered Carmilla's resting place. It was General Spielsdorf, however, the bereaved guardian of one of Carmilla's victims, who staked the body and severed the head of Carmilla.

Abraham Van Helsing is, therefore, the first true vampire hunter. *Dracula,* the book in which he appears, can be interpreted many ways. Whether looked at from a feminist, capitalist, racial, or any other point of view, it is obvious that the tale is a commentary on Victorian times. The character of Van Helsing is part of the equation. His character symbolizes all that was considered good and worthy in Victorian Britain. He was a white, upper-class male, hard-working and educated—a true gentleman. Van Helsing's "extensive knowledge, supreme rationality, ascetic leanings, and noted willingness to work hard must be with him all along" (Yu 154). He is a great deal like Stoker himself. Van Helsing "represents the triumph of the Enlightenment, of the transcendental subjectivity" (154).

In the story, Dr. Seward's description of him in his letter to Arthur illustrates Van Helsing's best qualities:

> I have written to my old friend and master, Professor Van Helsing, of Amsterdam, who knows as much about obscure diseases as any one in the world....He is a seemingly arbitrary man, but this because he knows what he is talking about better than any one else. He is a philosopher and a metaphysician, and one of the most advanced scientists of his day; and he has, I believe, and absolutely open mind. This, with an iron nerve, a temper of the ice-brook, an indomitable resolution,

13
Research or Term Paper

self-command, and toleration exalted from virtue to blessings, and the kindliest and truest heart that beats...work both
in theory and practice [sic], for his views are as wide as his
all-embracing sympathy. (Stoker 243)

Mina Harker gives a more physical description of this paradigm. She
states:

he came towards me; a man of medium weight, strongly
built.... The poise of the head strikes one at once as indicative
of though and power; the head is noble.... The face, shows a
hard, square chin, a large, resolute mouth...sensitive nostrils....
The forehead is broad and fine.... Big, dark blue eyes are set
widely apart, and are quick and tender or stern with the
man's moods. (300)

He is obviously, and often instantly, well-liked. Mina, one of the
book's protagonists, states, "I feel from having seen him that he *is* good
and kind and of a noble nature" (299). Her husband, Jonathan, refers to
Van Helsing as "this kindly, strong-faced old man" (305).

In his article "Reading the Vampire," Ken Gelder describes Van
Helsing as "a scientist who mediates between folkish superstitions and
enlightened knowledge...[who is] equally at home in these otherwise
contradictory spheres. Thus he is both rational and clearheaded"
(Gelder 1). All these descriptions tell of a man who seems to have the
best of all qualities: strength, intelligence, kindness and sternness, and
a "noble nature." Van Helsing is the epitome of the Victorian man.

There is much evidence to suggest, however, that as strong,
intelligent, and kind as he may be, Van Helsing is also egotistical. It
should be noted that these qualities would not have been viewed as
unfavorable by a Victorian audience, except perhaps by that new breed
of female, the New Woman. But a 21st-century audience, especially one
that includes the modern woman, would see many of Van Helsing's
actions as undesirable, if not downright offensive.

First, there is Van Helsing's increasingly annoying habit of refusing
to divulge any information, to anyone, until the last possible moment.
Even upon his first examination of Lucy, Van Helsing must have had
some idea of what ailed her. Yet Dr. Seward mentions that "Van Helsing
made a very careful examination of the patient.... He is, I fear, much

concerned, but says he must think.... As I tell you, he would not say a word more, even when we were alone" (244–45).

Van Helsing later likens his silence to Dr. Seward's interactions with his mental patients. He states, "You tell not your madmen what you do nor why you do it; you tell them not what you think. So you shall keep knowledge in its place where it may rest....I have for myself thoughts at the present. Later I shall unfold to you" (248–49). When Dr. Seward questions this action, Van Helsing launches into a pompous speech about corn and the need for it to grow before it can be harvested. He declares, "I have sown my corn, and Nature has her work to do in making it sprout" (249). While it is understandable that he may have needed time in order to formulate a complete plan of action, sharing what knowledge he had could have spared Lucy's life.

It is fairly obvious he had at least a good idea of what was occurring to Lucy. Upon finding her one morning, pale and near death, he exclaims, "My God!...this is dreadful. There is no time to be lost. She will die for sheer want of blood to keep the heart's action as it should be. There must be a transfusion of blood at once" (250).

Van Helsing's decision to keep all knowledge to himself could very likely have been motivated by the desire to not alarm those who loved Lucy, as well as by the fact that he knew he wouldn't be believed if he suddenly proclaimed that Lucy had been attacked by a vampire. However, he could have simply stated that the garlic hanging around the room was for medicinal purposes and must not be touched. Lucy's family and servants may have thought it strange to close her up in her room with cloves of garlic everywhere, but his wishes would have been followed.

Why would Van Helsing refuse to share such precious knowledge when doing so could save lives? There is a well-known saying by Sir Francis Bacon, who said, "Knowledge is power." While it is doubtful that Van Helsing meant any harm, indeed his intentions appear selfless and pristine, it does seem likely that Van Helsing enjoyed the power that his private knowledge brought him. It kept him always a little ahead of the rest.

Van Helsing's secrecy and egotistical behavior has been directed, for the most part, at the men up until this point in the tale. His somewhat arrogant actions soar to new heights with his chivalric or, depending on your point of view, chauvinistic treatment of Mina.

13 Research or Term Paper

It is she who feels the full brunt of Van Helsing's prejudiced attitudes. Though it is her intelligence and hard work that enable the group to track and eventually defeat Dracula, Van Helsing repeatedly insists that she be kept from the group's conversations and activities for fear that "[e]ven if she be not harmed, her heart may fail her in so much and so many horrors; and hereafter she may suffer—both in waking, from her nerves, and in sleep, from her dreams" (343).

Upon first meeting Mina, his reply to her statement that she can tell him all about Lucy's experiences, is "Oh, then you have a good memory for facts, for details? It is not always so with young ladies" (301). Even after Mina has proved her skills time and again, Van Helsing will only admit her intelligence by describing her as having a "man's brain" (343). It appears to be impossible for him to reconcile the idea of an intelligent, strong woman. She must, therefore, have some male qualities to explain her abilities.

Van Helsing's attitudes and attributes were very indicative of what Victorian society felt was important. In an age where industrialization, increased colonization, and immigration were changing the empire, where the New Woman was making her voice heard, there was an increased desire for society to remain as it was. White, upper- and middle-class males were the dominant members of society, and women were expected to stay home and raise their families, putting all of their mental and physical resources to that task. Van Helsing, in his actions and thoughts throughout the book, illustrates this position. He was the perfect vampire slayer for his generation.

But in the 21st century, societies all over the world have changed. The so-called New Woman is no longer new, but "normal." Society has changed to allow for greater equality between sexes, ethnicities, and even ages. Vampires themselves have changed. They are no longer old men who keep a harem of vampire brides in a ruined castle while they feast on the village women. Today's vampires reflect the changes in society. They are made up of different genders, backgrounds, and ethnicities. They have many more supernatural powers. They are more seductive and, often, more human. A new breed of vampire calls for a new breed of slayer.

Though there are many, many new tales, each with their own slayer, one stands out. In the early 1990s, the movie *Buffy the Vampire Slayer* created the new slayer society needed. Created by writer-director Joss

Whedon, the movie became a popular television series. Buffy is the opposite of Van Helsing in almost every way. She is young, female, not too bright in the beginning, selfish, and spoiled. She was chosen to be a slayer in a manner similar to the divine right of kings. It was her destiny. Through her trials and training, she becomes stronger, wiser, and less selfish.

There are a few similarities between Buffy and Van Helsing, the most notable of which is the fact that both slayers had a group of hunters that fought with them. Van Helsing had Seward, Quincy Morris, Jonathan Harker, Arthur, and, at times, Mina.

Buffy's community of fighters includes her Watcher, Giles, and friends Willow, and Xander. However, in a footnote in Rhonda Wilcox's book *Why Buffy Matters: The Art of Buffy the Vampire Slayer*, Wilcox points out that the "interrelationship of the supportive outsider friends in *Buffy* is quite different from the group interaction of those who hunt Stoker's Dracula with, as Auerbach describes it, a 'corporate ethos' and the guidance of the 'overbearing patriarch' Van Helsing" (212). Buffy, while technically the slayer, does not order, keep secrets, and dictate actions as Van Helsing did. Her group works as a team. Wilcox notes that Buffy was successful "because she operates within a group of friends who support but can also question each other" (102). Buffy's character, and those similar to her, "have offered new visions of heroism by inflecting the concept of toughness with the notion of flexibility" (Inness 231). She grows in strength and wisdom because of those around her.

While Stoker cleverly wove subtle implications about the New Woman, sexuality, colonization, and other Victorian concerns into his tale, *Buffy* is much more open about modern society's trials. Buffy deals with regular teenage concerns, high school drama, sexual double standards, and parental conflicts, while juggling a secret vampire-slaying career. She is easy for audiences to connect with because she is going through the same problems as those who are watching her.

Author and professor Mary Magoulick, in her article "Frustrating Female Heroism: Mixed Messages in Xena, Nikita, and Buffy," discusses "[c]ritic Frances H. Early [who] likewise argues the positive, feminist merits of *Buffy*, largely because she finds Buffy an empowering, just, conflict-resolving, gracefully acrobatic, ironically distant, morally astute, and patriarchy-rejecting hero in a grand historical tradition of women warriors" (5).

13 Research or Term Paper

Wilcox quotes Nina Auerbach, who states, "Every age embraces the vampire it needs." She continues that "one might add, the slayer it needs. And though Auerbach's use of the term 'age' refers to cultural period, her statement could be extended to apply to a stage of life—in this case, adolescence. Instead of a patriarchal Van Helsing, Buffy provides a sort, slight, teenage girl" (Wilcox 20).

Though an articulate, older, intelligent, egotistical, and unfailingly "chivalric" gentleman was the perfect slayer for Stoker's generation, the 21st century needed a slayer who appealed to an audience of women and modern men. Thus was born Buffy. She is the slayer of today's society, as Van Helsing was the slayer of Victorian society. Each generation finds new demons to fight and, in so doing, must also find a new hero to fight them. Tomorrow's society will have need of a new slayer for the monsters lurking around new corners.

Works Cited

Byrne, Richard. "Nota Bene." Rev. of *Slayers and Their Vampires: A Cultural History of Killing the Dead*, by Bruce A. McClelland. *Chronicle of Higher Education*. Vol. 53 No. 18 (2007): 13. *EBSCO*. 29 Jan. 2007 <http://library.nu.edu/articles/2472.pdf>.

Gelder, Ken. *Reading the Vampire*. 1994. *Ebrary: the National University Library System*. 1999. 28 Jan. 2007 <http://site.ebrary.com.ezproxy.nu.edu/lib/nuls/Top?channelName=nuls&cpage=1&docID=5004121&f00=text&frm=smp.x&hitsPerPage=10&layout=document&p00=reading+the+vampire&sortBy=score&sortOrder=desc>.

Inness, Sherrie. *Action Chicks: New Images of Tough Women in Popular Culture*. 2004. *Ebrary: the National University Library System*. 1999. 29 Jan. 2007. <http://site.ebrary.com.ezproxy.nu.edu/lib/nuls/Top?layout=search&id=5004121&nosr=1&frm=smp.x&p00=sherrie+inness>.

Le Fanu, Sheridan. "Carmilla." *Three Vampire Tales*. Ed. Anne Williams. Boston: Houghton, 2003.

Magoulick, Mary. "Frustrating Female Heroism: Mixed Messages in Xena, Nikita, and Buffy." *Journal of Popular Culture*. Vol.39, Iss. 5 (2006): 729. *EBSCO*. 28 Jan. 2007. <http://proquest.umi.com/pqdlink?did=1149214191&Fmt=7&clientId=1506&RQT=309&VName=PQD>.

Polidori, John. "The Vampyre." *Three Vampire Tales*. Ed. Anne Williams. Boston: Houghton, 2003.

Stoker, Bram. "Dracula." *Three Vampire Tales*. Ed. Anne Williams. Boston: Houghton, 2003.

Wilcox, Rhonda. *Why Buffy Matters: The Art of Buffy the Vampire Slayer*. 2005. *Ebrary: the National University Library System*. 1999. 29 Jan. 2007 < http://site.ebrary.com.ezproxy.nu.edu/lib/nuls/Top?layout =search&id=5004121&nosr=1&frm=smp.x&p00=why+buffy+mat ters>.

Yu, Eric Kwan-Wai. "Productive Fear: Labor, Sexuality, and Mimicry in Bram Stoker's Dracula." *Texas Studies in Literature and Language 48.2* (2006) 145–170. Project Muse. 28 Jan. 2007 <http://muse.jhu. edu.ezproxy.nu.edu/journals/texas_studies_in_literature_and_ language/v048/48.2yu.html>.

13 Research or Term Paper

14

Quick Tips for Researching

Lesson 14-1: Know What You Don't Know

Once you know your topic for your essay or paper, you need to know what exactly it is that you need to research. Do you need to know if toilets were widely used in 1856 for a paper on the history of plumbing? Maybe you need to know what a pistol from 1734 looked like and how it was used.

Make a list, keep a binder, create a spreadsheet, or use note cards. You need to have some way of recording your information. Make of list of things you need to search for and have your note cards handy to record the information you find. Or use a spreadsheet or handwritten notes in a binder—whatever is easiest for you.

Lesson 14-2: Look in a Book, Online Style

When you Google a topic, it almost always pulls up Amazon.com search results for books on the topic. Many times, you can search the index or table of contents of these books on Amazon or sites that sell books. This is very helpful. You can also specifically Google for books on a particular

14
Quick Tips for
Researching

subject. If you need information on paint, Google for "books on paint," or "books on the history of paint." This enables you to find at least some of the books you will need before ever leaving your house.

Once you get several titles that look promising, go to your local library's Website and see if it carries the books in question. Even if your library doesn't have the book, you can usually request it through interlibrary loans without ever having to leave your home.

Lesson 14-3: Look in a Book, the Old-Fashioned Way

Go to the library, flip to the back of the book, and, if it has your topic listed, put it in your "take home" pile. For instance, say you are researching global warming. If the index of the book you are looking at lists global warming, especially if it lists any of the specific aspects of global warming that you outlined, put it in your pile.

Don't forget to check the bibliographies in the back of the books. These can be an excellent source for further information and will give you specific titles to look for.

Your assigned textbooks for a class can actually be a great source of information. As with other books, their bibliographies can often lead you to more information.

Lesson 14-4: Magazines and Journals

Magazines and scholarly and scientific journals are a great place to find information. You can use the Internet to find tons of useful articles without having to spend hours at the library—a great time-saver.

Many scholarly journals will require you to have a subscription or membership, but again, here is where online library tools come in handy. Even if you can't get the full article online, you can usually get enough of an excerpt to see if it will help you. If it is something that you need, but you can't get it online for free, check your local library. Libraries carry many, many scholarly journals and magazines. If they don't have what you are looking for, they should be able to get it. And with journal articles, many times they are able to just e-mail or fax you a copy of the article in question.

Lesson 14-5: Surf the Internet

There are many, many online sites and sources of which you can take advantage. There are many personal Websites and online forums on practically every topic. There are also Websites for groups, societies, companies, and associations for many interests. In almost all of these cases, you can contact the owner of the Website or an expert in a group and ask for information. For example, if you need information on a certain type of flower, you can e-mail a horticulture society and ask for its expert help.

Lesson 14-6: Online Encyclopedias and Information-Gathering Websites

Websites such as Wikipedia and Ask.com are handy, and you can get information quickly, but you need to remember that this information is written by whoever wants to answer the question, so be sure to double-check (if not triple-check) your information. Use these sites for a quick memory refresher or as a starting point. Wikipedia often has sources listed at the end of their articles. These sites can be a useful place to get titles of books and articles to further your own research. Be aware of the articles that do *not* have sources listed. These are the ones that are more likely to contain inaccurate information. Again, any good researcher double-checks the information he finds.

15

Proofreading

Lesson 15-1: Why Bother?

In this day and age, with the wonderful gadgets, technical tools, and word processors we have available, proofreading may seem like an unnecessary step. After all, spell-check finds the misspelled words and can even find things like grammar and punctuation mistakes, right? So why waste time going back over your essay several times when the program has done it for you?

Well, because that program isn't going to catch everything. In fact, it can miss a lot. You could end up with something like *"Eye dew knot kneed two proof reed, w*hen you meant to write *"I do not need to proofread."* All the words in the first sentence are spelled correctly, and if you ran it through a typical spell-checking program it would show up with no mistakes. But it is obviously far from correct!

Or what if you get in a bit of a hurry and forget a word or two? You could end up with a sentence like *"The gorilla learned several methods of and astounded her trainers."* That missing word between "of" and "and" is crucial to make that sentence, and your point, work. Many spell-check programs won't highlight that mistake. These programs also won't tell you if an argument needs more explanation, if you forgot to cite a source, or if you should rearrange a few things.

Proofreading is a crucial part of writing an essay or paper. In fact, not only should you edit your paper yourself, but it is a very good idea to have at least one other person read it as well. Why? Well, our brains are fabulous things that tend to fill in the blanks and mistakes as we read. You know what you meant to write, and many times when you read your essays, your mind reads it the way it's supposed to be, not the way you actually have it written.

Here are a few tips on how to catch those mistakes:

▶ Read aloud. Doing this forces you to slow down and think more about what you are reading. Hearing it aloud can also help find those sentences that are phrased awkwardly or are missing words or punctuation. There are several programs out there that will read your work to you. These can be very handy because, though reading aloud can be greatly helpful, you are still reading your own work. There is still a possibility you may correct mistakes without realizing it. Having someone else read it to you would also work wonderfully.

▶ Read backward. This is very helpful for finding misspelled or incorrect words. Basically you take each sentence and go through it backward, one word at a time. Though a bit time-consuming, it really doesn't take as long as you might think. This is another technique that forces you to slow down and really look at what you've written.

▶ Have someone else proofread. A fresh set of eyes is always a good idea, especially when editing for content. Because you are the author of your essay, you are very close to your work. It's hard to see spots that may be confusing or awkward. Your reader can help find the spots that need work, an argument that might need more clarification or explanation, paragraphs that ramble on and get boring, sentences that don't make sense, and many other problems.

15 Proofreading

Lesson 15-2: Technical Mistakes

Technical mistakes include things like incorrect punctuation, misspelled words, grammar mistakes, and sentence structure. A misplaced comma or a word used in the wrong context can wreak havoc on your carefully thought-out sentences.

Incorrect Punctuation

Incorrect punctuation can change the entire meaning of your sentence. It can emphasize the wrong thing, change the tone of your writing, or make or break your argument. Take a look at these examples:

Let's eat, Mom!

(Correct)

Let's eat Mom!

(Incorrect. The missing punctuation creates a sentence with an entirely different, and very disturbing, meaning.)

"Fire," the frightened child screamed.

(Bland, no tension or fear.)

"Fire!" the frightened child screamed.

(Changes the tone into one conveying urgency and fear.)

A woman, without her man, is nothing.

A woman: without her, man is nothing.

(Both are correct, but the meaning is entirely changed depending on where the punctuation is placed. This is an excellent example used frequently to illustrate the difference punctuation can make.)

Misspelled Words

This can be a tough one. As we saw earlier, misspelled words aren't always caught by a word processor's spell-check program because the words might not be technically misspelled, but are still incorrect for the context in which they are being used. Look at the following poem:

Eye dew knot kneed two proof reed.

Spell check works just fine.

If eye right the wrong thing down,

It gets a bright read line.

Every single one of these words is spelled correctly, but they are certainly not correct for the context.

Now, you can also get the occasional "regular" misspelled word. Spell-checking programs can have their bugs and glitches, and if you write the essay by hand, misspelled words can be a much bigger problem. But for the most part, you'll probably be on the lookout for things like "their" when you should have written "there," or "dog" when you meant "fog."

Sentence Structure

There is a rhythm to reading. Sentence structures and punctuation placement affect how a reader reads a piece of writing. You'll want to take a look at how you have structured your sentences. Again, this is one of those elements that, though it might not be technically incorrect, can affect the reader in a negative way. If your essay is full of sentences that are structured the same way, it can get boring or evoke an undesired response. If you write using a variety of sentence structures, it keeps your readers on their toes.

Take a look at the sentence structures in this paragraph:

The blue clown, thinking it would be funny, threw a pie at my mom. Meanwhile, over at the big top, more mischief was afoot. The donkey, bored with waiting for his turn, sat in the pool by himself. The clown car, with only one clown, circled the center ring. For a Monday, at least for the circus, it was a pretty normal day.

Every sentence in this paragraph is structured the same way. An opening, a middle, an end, separated by two commas. Reading this, especially if there were several more paragraphs full of the same sentence structure, would get tedious for a reader.

Here's another example:

> Vampires are the most popular monsters. They have big teeth and drink lots of blood. They wear black and come out at night. The sun and fire can kill them. They can live to be really old. Some vampires are good and some are not. Some have supernatural powers. They are often called the undead.

This paragraph is full of short, simple sentences. When read aloud, it seems choppy, hurried, and overly simplistic. You might be conveying great information, but when presented like this, the statements lose their "wow factor." Change it up a bit, and you'll have something that can really grab the readers' attention. Here's an example of a paragraph that uses several different sentence structures.

> The new pizza joint in town serves the best pizza around. The ingredients used, including four different kinds of cheese, combine to create incredibly delicious pizzas. The staff is friendly and helpful, even when the store is busy. They also offer free delivery! You can't go wrong choosing Pizza Delight for lunch or dinner.

This paragraph keeps the sentence structures varied and, as a result, it is much more effective.

Does this mean that you have to go through all of your paragraphs and make sure that every sentence in them has a different structure? No. Just be aware of it as you are proofreading your essays so if you come across an instance where this happens, you can rearrange things a bit. This is also a situation where reading aloud can really help. Sentences that have the same structure fall into a certain rhythm that is easy to hear when read aloud. If you find instances of this in your essay, try to reword the sentences to give your paragraphs more variation.

Contractions

Though this probably isn't something that will get you a failing grade, when writing a formal essay, it is best to stay away from contractions. For example, instead of saying, "It's hard to calculate the exact measurements of the moon," write, "It is hard to calculate the exact measurements of the moon."

Here's the good news: you can change the settings of most word processors to catch contractions. Every time you use one, it will highlight the word with a red, squiggly line, and you can go back and change it.

Using "I" and "You"

This is another "rule" that isn't going to send your paper to the flunk pile, but in a formal essay or paper, it is best to stay away from using "I" and "you." For instance, instead of saying "The example I used earlier clearly proves dolphins are intelligent," change it to, "The example used earlier clearly proves dolphins are intelligent." Removing the "I" doesn't change the meaning of the sentence in any way and, in fact, makes it stronger. The "I" makes the statement sound more like an opinion than a fact. Your arguments will be more convincing if you state them as facts.

The same reasoning applies to the use of "you." For example, the sentence "When walking through Central Park, you'll see many kinds of trees," sounds much more formal when worded like, "When walking through Central Park, many kinds of trees are visible." If you get really stuck on rewording, you can replace the "you" with the universal "one": "When walking through Central Park, one can see many kinds of trees."

There are circumstances when it is better to use "I" and "you." If you are writing a narrative essay or an essay that is supposed to be based on your opinion alone or that you want to be more narrative and informal, then "I" and "you" are useful. Some teachers prefer the personal touch on essays and want them very personalized. In that case, use "I" and "you" in your statements. But if your assignment is for a more formal essay, these are good words to watch out for.

Other Common Grammar Mistakes

For grammar, be sure you are following all the rules correctly. Now, there are some instances where incorrect grammar is okay. For example, if you are writing a narrative essay, or a fictional story, especially if you are using a lot of dialogue, then incorrect grammar is actually better. Unfortunately, people don't really speak using correct and proper grammar, so using it incorrectly sounds more natural and "normal." However, in most cases, try and use proper and correct grammar. Here are a few examples of the most common grammar mistakes:

▶ Apostrophes. Be sure you are using apostrophes correctly to show possession or in contractions. Also pay special attention to your/you're, and there/their/they're.

> Its going to be a windy day today. The kitten can't find it's mother.
> (Incorrect)
> It's going to be a windy day today. The kitten can't find its mother.
> (Correct)

▶ Run-on sentences. Makes sure your sentences aren't too long.

> The book I read was pretty good, it would have been better if there was more action, but it was still and entertaining read.
> (Incorrect)
> The book I read was pretty good. It would have been better if there was more action, but it was still an entertaining read.
> (Correct)

▶ Pronoun agreement. This one is tough when writing a formal essay, especially when you are trying to stay away from using "I" and "you." Just remember to keep your plurals and singulars together, and you should be fine.

> Each person at the airport had to remove their shoes.
> (Incorrect)
> All the people at the airport had to remove their shoes.
> (Correct)

▶ Ending a sentence with a preposition. This is one of the rules that you should try to follow as much as possible, but that can occasionally be broken. Avoiding them entirely can sometimes clog your paper with "for which" and "to whoms" that may end up sounding worse than the "technically correct" option.

That's the lady I have to give the paper to.
(Incorrect)

That's the lady to whom I have to give the paper.
(Correct)

"This is the kind of thing up with which I will not put!"
(Technically correct. Quote attributed to Winston Churchill)
"This is the kind of thing I will not put up with!"
(Incorrect, but better sounding)

Lesson 15-3: Editing for Content

Editing your papers for content is extremely important because this is something that your spell-check feature doesn't do. When you are editing for content, you'll want to check for things like:

- ▶ Awkwardly phrased sentences.
- ▶ Arguments or statements that might need more, or less, explanation.
- ▶ Repetitive words or phrases.
- ▶ Correct citations.
- ▶ Transitions between ideas.
- ▶ Flow of thoughts and arguments.
- ▶ Word usage.

Let's take these one at a time.

Awkwardly Phrased Sentences

In terms of punctuation, spelling, and even grammar, a sentence may be perfect. But sometimes the way a sentence is written just doesn't make sense. In such cases, a simple rewording or reordering of the words will give you a better, easier-to-understand sentence.

This sentence is from the "Monkey See, Monkey Do" sample essay from Chapter 3, from the paragraph discussing how primates are just as intelligent as humans and why humans may not want to accept this fact:

> One reason may be because of the fact that the primates are so close to humans that the main thing that separates humans from primates is the humans' intelligence.

Now, technically, there isn't anything wrong with this sentence. But it's clumsy and too wordy. Many people will have to read through this sentence a few times in order to grasp what the author is trying to say. A simple rewording will make this sentence much stronger, highlight the main point of the statement, and make its meaning clear on the first read:

> One reason might be because the main difference between humans and primates is a humans' intelligence.

By removing a few unneeded words and reducing the sentence to its main idea, it has become much clearer, and easier to read and understand.

Awkward phrasing can make your sentences confusing or overly complicated, and can turn a perfectly good argument into something downright silly. For instance:

> For those who use wheelchairs and don't know it, there is a ramp available at the public library.

Well, if you use a wheelchair and don't know it, you probably have bigger problems than worrying about whether or not there is a ramp at your local library. This sentence needs to be rearranged and edited a bit to get the meaning the writer intended:

> For those who don't know, there is a wheelchair ramp available at the public library.

So, be sure to check your essays for awkward phrasing. Mistakes like these can make or break your arguments.

Arguments or Statements That Might Need More, or Less, Explanation

You may present an argument or statement in your essay that is perfectly valid. But depending on how you've presented that statement, you may need to add additional information:

> Please remember to place your vote for vice president in the box along with the person you want for president.

A few more words of explanation are necessary here. At the moment, it sounds as though there is a presidential candidate in the voting box. Adding a few extra words clarifies the meaning of the sentence.

> Please place your vote for vice president in the box along with the name of the person you want for president.

You may also present a statement that has too much explanation. The last thing you want to do is bore your reader to tears with pages full of unnecessary information. It is best to keep your arguments concise and to the point.

Repetitive Words or Phrases

Another thing you want to watch for is repetition. Again, this isn't really a "mistake." But reading the same word or phrase over and over can get boring and irritating, and that really isn't a nice thing to do to the person who is grading your paper. Here is an example:

> The dining table was set with beautiful china. A linen tablecloth stretched the entire length of the table. The cherry wood of the table gleamed in the candlelight. Soon, the diners filtered in, taking their seats at the table as the first course was brought in and set in front of them on the table.

The word *table* was used six times in this description of the table. It's overkill; don't do it. Now, this is an extreme example, but when you get a word that repeats frequently in your paper, it soon begins to stand out. Your readers will find themselves thinking, "Oh, there's that word again," instead of paying attention to the point you are trying to get across.

The good news is that you can do word searches in most word-processing programs. You simply tell it what word you want to find, and it will highlight every instance of that word in your paper. Again, this is another instance where reading aloud will help you to find a problem. If you find a word that you are repeating frequently, do a word search for it and revise your sentences to avoid overuse.

Correct Citations

Citing your sources properly is something that I can't emphasize enough. Failure to do this can result in plagiarism, and, even if it was unintentional, the damage has been done. So, before you turn in your paper, go through every one of your sources and citations and make sure they are done correctly. Here's a checklist for you:

❑ Is there a citation after every quote and paraphrase? If the information didn't come directly from your brain, you need to cite it. When in doubt, cite it. Better safe than sorry. So double-check to be sure all the information you used in your essay or paper is cited.

❑ Are your citations correct? Do they have all the necessary information? Are they formatted correctly for the form of citation you are using?

❑ Is your Works Cited, Bibliography, or References page correct? Are all your sources listed, in their proper order, with all the information they are supposed to have?

Citing your sources and doing it correctly are absolutely vital when writing an essay or paper, so take the time to be sure you've done it right!

Transitions Between Ideas

When you are transitioning between one topic and another, you want the shift to be smooth. If you switch from one train of thought to another with little or no lead-in, it can be confusing and frustrating to readers. You need to give your readers some warning that you are about to change topics and start discussing something new, or they will be expecting a continuation or further development of the previous thought. Introducing new material with no set-up can create enough confusion that readers may have to stop and go back to see if they missed something. Here is an example of a bad transition:

> For the most part, the study was inclusive. No matter the color of kitten, habits and mannerisms seemed to be the same. However, the black kittens were marginally more aware of their surroundings than kittens with lighter coloring.
>
> On February 3, 1989, more than 100 balloons were released over the Hudson River. Those below watched in awe as the multi-colored mass floated above their heads.

There is no transition between the two ideas. The writer takes us from one idea to the next with no warning, and the result is a confusing mess. Let's see how it would work with a good transition:

> For the most part, the study was inclusive. No matter the color of kitten, habits and mannerisms seemed to be the same. However, the black kittens were marginally more aware of their surroundings than kittens with lighter coloring.
>
> In an effort to obtain more data, an experiment was proposed in which small cameras would be attached to balloons that would be released over the nation's largest concentration of wild kittens. The cameras would allow scientists to observe the kittens in their natural habitat with a minimum of human interference. On February 3, 1989, more than 100 balloons were released over the Hudson River. Those below watched in awe as the multi-colored mass floated above their heads.

With just a minor addition, the writing now flows smoothly from one idea to the other, and the two ideas now make sense placed in the same essay.

Flow of Thoughts and Arguments

Just as with the transitions between your ideas, you'll want to be sure your statements and arguments follow a smooth and logical train of thought. If you jump around too much, your reader may not understand the point you are arguing. A good way to transition is to start out with some general information (background, set-up information), move to something more specific, discuss your main point or strongest argument, and then wrap it all up.

For example, if you were discussing the life of Mozart, the most logical way to do so would be to start with his childhood and move through his adulthood toward his death. Discussing his childhood then skipping to his death, then going back to his teen years, and then jumping to the months leading up to his death would be confusing.

Organizing your thoughts, arguments, and information in outline form, before writing your essay, will keep everything nice and orderly, but it's always a good idea to check the flow of your essay during the proofreading stage as well.

Word Usage

When it comes to the words you choose to use, you'll want to pay attention to the things we already discussed, such as repetitive words and incorrect spellings or usage of words. But you should also pay attention to your vocabulary. You may not use the "big" words in everyday speech, but when it comes time for essay writing, break them out! Now, this does not mean using so many huge, obscure words that no one can understand what you are saying. But it might be better to say something like "The conference was everything the participants expected," instead of the very simple, unsophisticated "The meeting was good."

Here are a few good examples of dos and don'ts. Notice that sometimes just changing a word or two makes a huge difference:

Do: Many societies and cultures believe that man and nature originated from the same source.

Don't: Lots of different people think people and other things from nature come from the same place.

Do: Historical fiction is a genre that is set in the past.

Don't: Historical fiction is about stuff that happened a long time ago.

Do: The fire destroyed a large part of the city.

Don't: The fire totaled a huge chunk of the city.

A good rule of thumb is to know your audience. If you are writing a short story for your 5-year-old sister, use simple words and phrases. If you are writing an end-of-the-year term paper going over all the main factors of an era you just spent an entire year studying in your senior history class, you want it to sound intelligent and sophisticated. Keep it appropriate for your grade level, assignment, and audience.

You'll also want to check for things like missing or incorrect words. For example:

Students are collecting donations for their fundraiser. Proceeds will be used to injure flood victims.

This is both missing a word and has an incorrect word. It should read:

Students are collecting donations for their fundraiser. Proceeds will be used to help injured flood victims.

There is a huge difference in the meaning of these two sentences, and it's not a mistake spell-check will catch.

Remember: Though spell-check is a handy feature, it won't catch all the mistakes in your papers, and it won't let you know if something needs to be reworded or revised. Take the time to read through your papers before turning them in. Get someone else to look through them. Read them aloud. The few extra minutes it takes to do this could mean the difference between a passing or failing grade.

For extra help, tips, and practice on basic grammar and English language rules, refer to Maureen Lindner's *Homework Helpers: English Language and Composition*.

16

Citations

Lesson 16-1: Overview

Citations are the established way of giving credit in written works. There are several different ways of citing sources. The ones you will be dealing with the most are MLA, APA, and Chicago/Turabian. If you are writing for a science class, you may be asked to use CSE. Each lesson will go through a few examples of in-text citations and a few of the most common reference-page citations that you will use. Your teachers and professors will probably tell you which style to use in your essays and papers, but if they don't, here is a general list of what style goes with which type of class:

- ▶ MLA: humanities and English (includes courses like art, music, architecture, philosophy, literature, religious studies).
- ▶ APA: social sciences (includes courses like anthropology, economics, history, sociology, psychology, political science).
- ▶ Chicago/Turabian: history.
- ▶ CSE: sciences (such as biology, chemistry, physics, physiology, anatomy).

Lesson 16-2: The Humanities and MLA

The Modern Language Association (MLA) form of citation is the type you will probably use the most, as the majority of your essays will be written for humanities or English courses. Following you will find a few examples of the most common type of citations. For a complete list of every kind of source, you can refer to the *MLA Handbook for Writers of Research Papers*. But, for the most part, the following examples should be sufficient for your needs.

In-Text Citations

When quoting or paraphrasing a source in the text of your paper, you need to note where the information is coming from. For MLA citations, you list the last name of the author and the page number within a set of parentheses after the quote or paraphrase. The punctuation for the sentence comes after the citation. If your source doesn't have an author or editor, use a shortened version of the title. Here are examples of both:

> Van Helsing's "extensive knowledge, supreme rationality, ascetic leanings, and noted willingness to work hard must be with him all along" (Yu 154).

> The pale shade of green that most hospitals use in their décor is thought to "promote calming and healing emotions" ("Color Wheel" 1).

If two citations from the same source follow one another, you just use the page number for the second citation. In general, the use of *Ibid* to denote the same source information is no longer used for MLA citations:

> Van Helsing's "extensive knowledge, supreme rationality, ascetic leanings, and noted willingness to work hard must be with him all along" (Yu 154). He is a great deal like Stoker himself. Van Helsing "represents the triumph of the Enlightenment, of the transcendental subjectivity" (154).

If you introduce the author of your source before the quotation or paraphrase, you only need the page number in the citation:

> In his article on the subject of coins, infamous author Chuck McDuck stated that "no one knows the sweet rush of victory quite like someone who finds a prime collectible in the hidden recesses of a garage sale" (58).

If a quote is longer than four lines, or an excerpt of poetry is longer than three lines, separate it from the rest of the text by double indenting. (A regular indent is generally five spaces, or half an inch, so this puts your quote one inch from the left margin.) You should:

▶ Double-space the long quotation.

▶ Don't add an extra space before or after the quote.

▶ Don't add quotation marks.

▶ Add your citation at the end of the quote as usual, but outside of the punctuation mark.

In explaining why surfspeak is difficult for non-surfers to understand, Trevor Cralle, author of *The Surfin'ary*, states:

> Because surfspeak is so totally dynamic and culture specific…its varied meanings and usages can never be fully conveyed to an outsider who hasn't ridden the big one. This kind of action-based knowledge is intimately understood and masterfully used by those who surf. Outside of the surf context, something gets lost in the translation. (*xi*)

Works Cited Page

MLA uses a Works Cited page. A Works Cited page is different from a Bibliography. A Works Cited page lists only the sources you actually cited in your paper. A Bibliography (used mostly in Chicago/Turabian style for history papers) lists all sources used, referenced, or read, whether they were cited in the book or not.

Until you begin to write longer, more in-depth papers, most of your information will come from books, articles, or online sources.

Here is another place where your research/note cards come in handy. You already have all your information on those cards. In fact, you could have your Works Cited page done before you even start writing your paper. You'll know what sources you'll be using as soon as your outline is finished.

To format your Works Cited page:

▶ Center the words "Works Cited," without using underlining, bold, or italics.

▶ List sources alphabetically by author's last name or the title of the source if there is no author.

▶ List only sources actually cited in the paper, even if you read other sources that were not specifically cited, unless your instructor prefers otherwise.

▶ Use a hanging indent for each source, indenting all lines but the first one.

▶ Italicize the titles of the source. Some instructors prefer underlining, but italicize unless instructed to do otherwise.

▶ Include the medium of the source in each citation, such as print, web, television, lecture, or interview.

▶ Double space.

Griffin, Donald R. *The Question of Animal Awareness.* New York, Rockefeller University Press, 1976. Print.

Hoage, R.J. and Larry Goldman, ed. *Animal Intelligence.* Washington D.C.: Smithsonian Institution Press, 1986. Print.

Walker, Stephen F. *Animal Thought.* Boston: Routledge and K. Paul, 1983. Print.

All citations need to state where the information came from and how someone else can find it. For MLA citations, you'll need to list the author, the title, the publisher, publication date, and media source (print, CD-Rom, web) or the online address where you found the information. Where relevant, also page numbers. For articles, you need to also list the month and year of its publication. If an article doesn't have consecutive page numbers, list the page number followed by a plus sign (56+).

One author:

> Flintstone, Fred. *My Yabba-Dadda Hair Do*. New Rock: Norstone, 1954. Print.

Multiple works by the same author:

> Flintstone, Fred. *My Yabba-Dadda Hair Do*. New Rock: Norstone, 1954. Print.
>
> ———. *Your Friendly Neighborhood Dinosaur*. New Rock: Ballanstone, 1967. Print.

Two authors:

> Flintstone, Fred, and Barney Rubble. *How To Keep Your Dino Running*. New Rock: Norstone, 1954. Print.

Author with an editor:

> Le Fanu, Sheridan. "Carmilla." *Three Vampire Tales*. Ed. Anne Williams. Boston: Houghton, 2003. Print.

Editor:

> Goofball, Ima, ed. *Crazy Things People Say*. New York: Putnam, 2003. Print. (Article in a magazine)
>
> Doe, Jane L., "Amnesia and Other Nuisances." *Brain Dysfunctions Monthly* Sept. 2007: 76+. Print.

For the most part, online sources require the same information as print items. But there are a few extras. In general, you'll need to list:

- ▶ The author or editor.
- ▶ The title of the article, page, and/or site. If the location where you found your info doesn't have a title, you can use something such as "Home Page."
- ▶ Volume, issue, and page number if this info is relevant and available.
- ▶ The sponsor or publisher of the site. You can use "n.p." for "no publisher" if you can't find that information.
- ▶ Date of publication or last update. Use the abbreviation of "n.d." for "no date" if you can't find this information.
- ▶ Your date of access (the date you visited the site).

16 Citations

MLA does not require the URL, but some instructors do. If your instructor wants you to include the URL, list it in angle brackets <URL> at the end of the citation. If it's too long to fit on one line, try to break it up after a slash, but don't add one! Changing anything on the URL will change its usability.

Online journal

Yu, Eric Kwan-Wai. "Productive Fear: Labor, Sexuality, and Mimicry in Bram Stoker's Dracula." *Texas Studies in Literature and Language*. 48.2 (2006): 145–170. Project Muse. Web. 28 Jan. 2007. <http://muse.jhu.edu.ezproxy.nu.edu/journals/texas_studies_in_literature_and_language/v048/48.2yu.html>.

Online magazine article

Bluestein, Greg, and Mark Baker. "Coast Guard Gives BP OK To Try To Stop Oil Leak." *Salon.com*. Salon Media Group, 26 May 2010. Web. 17 July 2010.

Online Book

Flinstone, Fred. *My Yabba-Dabba Hair Do. Funnycartoonbooks.net*. Cartoon Society, 2008. Web. 12 April 2001.

Article or Work on a Website

Dalby, Richard. "All About Jean Plaidy." *Eleanor Alice Hibbert Burford*. Tripod, 1993. Web. 25 May 2010.

Formatting Your MLA Paper

Be sure to check with your instructor in case he or she has special preferences, but in general:

▶ You don't need a title page. Instead, list your name, your instructor's name, the name of your class, and the date in the upper left hand corner of the first page. Leave a few blank lines after it and center your title. If your instructor does want a title page, you can ask for guidelines or create a simple page with the title centered in the middle of the page and your name, teacher's name, class, and date centered at the bottom of the page.

► In the upper right-hand corner of each page, list your last name and the page number (Example: McLean 1).

► Leave 1-inch margins on all sides of the paper.

Lesson 16-3: Social Sciences and APA

The American Psychological Association (APA) form of citation is the one most often used for social science essays and papers. Following you will find a few examples of the most common type of citations. For a complete list of every kind of source, you can refer to the *Publication Manual of the American Psychological Association*. But, for the most part, the following examples should be sufficient for your needs.

In-Text Citations

The in-text citations for the APA style are similar to the MLA in that they are included in parenthesis within the text. For an APA citation, you'll generally list the author's last name, the publication year, and the page number. There are a few different ways of doing this, and the citations are a bit different for direct quotes and paraphrases.

For short quotations, the citation information is included within and just after the sentence containing the quote. The punctuation for the sentence and quote goes after the citation mark.

When the source is introduced within the text, list the publication year near the author's name and the page number (preceded with "p.") after the quotation. Always follow this format even if there are two quotes with the exact same citation information:

> Erickson stated (2001), "Revered as she never was in life, Alexandra was revered now" (p. 334). Erickson (2001) finds it interesting that this is the case, that our "world…has largely forgotten how Alexandra, as empress, was vilified" (p. 334).

If the source is not introduced within the text, list the author's last name, publication year, and page number at the end of the quote:

> She had also, by this time, lived in Russia for nearly half her life, and in that time "had become an ardent Russian patriot" (Erickson, 2001, p. 223).

16 Citations

For long quotes, the citation format is the same, but you must indent the entire quotation five spaces in (half an inch, or one hit of the tab button). Also, the punctuation mark goes after the quotation, before the page number citation:

John T. Alexander (1989), a well-known historian and biographer, addressed Catherine the Great's current reputation when he wrote:

> In the USSR she is presently ignored as an archaic embarrassment or attacked as a despotic foreign adventuress who mouthed enlightened phrases so as to mask tyrannous practices. (p. 330)

If you are paraphrasing information, you still need to cite your source. You do this the same way you would for a direct quote. However, with paraphrases, it isn't necessary to include to page number of your source, just the author's last name and publication year. It is fine if you wish to do this, but not required.

The full citation format:

In 1898, the Empress Dowager stepped aside and the new leader, Emperor Guangxu came to power (Fairbank, 1986, p. 134).

Perfectly acceptable format:

According to Fairbank (1986), there was no real way to enforce the reforms that were put in place.

Reference Page

As stated in the MLA section, APA uses a Reference page, which is similar to a Works Cited page. On this page, you will list all the sources that you actually cited in your paper. To format your Reference page:

▶ Center the word References, without underlining, bold, or italics.

▶ Alphabetize list by author's last name or title if no author is available.

▶ Use a hanging indent for each source, indenting all lines but the first one.

- ▶ List only the author's last name and first and middle initials.

- ▶ List the publication year in parentheses.

- ▶ Only capitalize the first word in the title and subtitle, unless it is the title of a journal, and italicize. Always capitalize proper nouns:

    Caputo, P. (1977). *A rumor of war*. New York: Ballantine.

- ▶ Capitalize all words in journal titles:

    Rubble, B. (2003). Breaking rocks. *Stonecutter Journal*, 23, 36–43.

- ▶ Do not italicize, underline, or place in quotes titles of short works, such as articles that appear in journals or shorter works in anthologies. In the previous example, "Breaking rocks" is the article title, *Stonecutter Journal* is the journal title. Only italicize the longer work, which is, in this case, the journal.

- ▶ Double-space entries.

    Griffin, D. R. (1976). *The question of animal awareness*. New York: Rockefeller University Press.

    Katz, E. (2001). *The film encyclopedia* (4th ed.). New York: Harper.

    Kracauer, S. (1974). *From Caligari to Hitler*. New Jersey: Princeton University Press.

    Rubble, B. (2003). Breaking rocks. *Stonecutter Journal*, 23, 36–43.

For APA citations, list the author, publication year, title, place of publication, and year. Where relevant, also list edition or volume (after the title). For journals and other articles, list volume, issue, and page numbers.

One author:

Flintstone, F. (1954). *My yabba-dabba hair do*. New Rock: Norstone.

Multiple works by the same author:

> Flintstone, F. (1954). *My yabba-dabba hair do*. New Rock: Norstone.

> Flintstone, F. (1958). *Your friendly neighborhood dinosaur*. New Rock: Ballanstone.

For two works from the same author in the same year, alphabetize by title and list them (a), (b), etc.:

> Flintstone, F. (1967a). *Living with dinosaur divas*. San Francisrock: B.C. Publications.

> Flintstone, F. (1967b). *You and your dino*. London: Oxstone University Press.

Two authors:

> Thompson, K., & Bordwell, D. (2003). *Film history: An introduction*. New York: McGraw-Hill.

Author with an editor:

> Stoker, B. (2003). Dracula. *Three Vampire Tales*. (Anne Williams, Ed.). Boston: Houghton.

Editor:

> Williams, A. (Ed.). (2003). *Three vampire tales*. Boston: Houghton.

When citing articles, include:

▶ Author(s).

▶ Publication year. For magazines, include the month, and if it is a weekly periodical, list the day as well. For newspapers, list the exact date.

▶ Title of the article without quotes, italics, or underlining. Only capitalize the first word.

▶ Title of the journal, magazine, or newspaper in which the article appears. Capitalize all words in the title over four letters long and italicize.

▶ Volume number, if relevant.

▶ Issue number in parentheses, if relevant.

▶ Page numbers. For articles where the pages are not consecutive, list all the page numbers.

Article in a magazine:

Schless, R. (2003, June 1). The truth behind sugar substitutes. *Science News, 11*, 46–48, 54, 61.

For the most part, online sources require the same information as print items. Basically, all you are doing is adding a URL or doi (digital object identifier) number to the end of a regular citation. For other online sources, get as much information as possible, including authors, publication date (use "n.d." if no date is available and list access date only if a publication date is unavailable), and include a URL or doi number.

If you are citing a source that could change, such as Wikipedia or any other database that may be periodically updated, be sure to put your retrieval date. Also, when possible, use the doi number. If this number is not available, use the URL. And if the URL is ridiculously long, then use the home page URL.

Online periodicals:

McCloskey, D. L. (1998). Magic fingers work their magic. *Massage Therapy and You, 17*(3), 73-77. doi:10.1378/ssre.2000.0291.

Russ, R. (2001, April). Honey braided pretzels. *Carbs R Us, 12*(2), 23-25. Retrieved May 10, 2003 from http://carbs.org/full/url.

Online book:

Flintstone, F. (1967). *You and your dino*. Retrieved from http://digital.library.urock.edu/full/url.

Note: If the book is only available for purchase, not reading, online, use "Available at" instead of "Retrieved from."

Article or work on a Website:

Stanton, D. (n.d.). *Things I did this summer*. Retrieved January 3, 2008 from http://thingsnoonecaresabout.com/full/url.

Formatting Your APA Paper

Be sure to check with your instructor in case he or she has special preferences, but in general:

▶ A title page with your paper's title centered in the middle of the page with your name, instructor's name, class name, and date centered at the bottom usually suffices.

▶ Include a short version of title and page number in upper right-hand corner on all pages.

▶ Set up 1-inch margins and double spacing through out the paper.

Lesson 16-4: History and Chicago or Turabian Style

The *Chicago Manual* style (CMS) of documenting sources is used most often for history courses. Some humanities instructors also prefer this style, so it is a good idea to be familiar with it. The main difference between this style and MLA and APA is that Chicago style uses footnotes for citations instead of parenthetical in-text notations.

Turabian style is very similar to Chicago style with a few minor differences. If your instructor asks you to use this style of citation, you can refer to the *Manual for Writers of Research Papers, Theses, and Dissertations*. In most cases, though, you'll be fine using Chicago style.

Following, you'll find examples on how to cite sources in your text and in your bibliography. For a more complete list of examples and information, you can refer to *The Chicago Manual of Style, 16th Edition*.

Chicago style uses a Bibliography, not a Works Cited or Reference page, which means you need to cite all sources that you consulted to write your paper, whether you actually included a direct quote or paraphrase in your essay or not.

In-Text Citations

For Chicago style, your in-text citations will be marked with a footnote. The first time you use a source, you will use the full bibliographic information (using commas instead of periods between your information), along with a page number. Afterward, you'll use a shortened version of the information (usually the author's last name, a shortened version of the title, and the page number). If you have two or more consecutive citations from the same source, you use *Ibid*.

For the first citation of a source, you'll need:

▶ Author's name (first, then last).

▶ Title of source (in italics).

▶ Place of publication place, publisher name, and publication year.

▶ Page numbers used in the quote or paraphrase.

▶ Commas between the items.

▶ What it will look like in the text:

In fact, as a child she intensely "disliked noise and crowds and always sought isolation and quiet."[1]

The footnote citation at the bottom of the page:

1. Carolly Erickson, *Alexandra: The Last Tsarina*, (New York: St. Martin's Press, 2001), 1-6.

For subsequent citations for this source, use a shortened version of the info:

4. Erickson, *Alexandra*, 47.

For consecutive citations from the same source, you can use Ibid and the page number. If the page number is also the same, just use Ibid:

4. Erickson, *Alexandra*, 47.
5. Ibid., 68.
6. Ibid.

Set long quotations apart by indenting five spaces (half an inch, or one tab hit). Quotation marks aren't necessary. Include a footnote at the end of the quote. Double-space the quote:

Erickson gives a good description of Alix when she writes:

sunshine and shadow seemed to alternate in Alix's ardent nature,

and she withheld herself warily from anyone she did not know

well, repressing the more vulnerable and appealing side of her

personality and becoming ill at ease.[2]

16 Citations

Bibliography

For Chicago style, you will generally use a Bibliography, unless instructed otherwise. In a Bibliography, you not only list the sources you actually cited in the paper, but all sources you consulted while writing your paper. Did you watch a film on your subject or read an article that was interesting but didn't end up as a quote or paraphrase in your paper? Include it in the Bibliography. Did Book A have the same information as Book B, but Book B said it better so that is the one you quoted? Include both in your Bibliography.

If your instructor prefers a Works Cited or Reference page, you can refer to the MLA or APA sections of this chapter for instructions on how to do those. If you need a Bibliography, keep reading.

To format your Bibliography page:

▶ Center the word "Bibliography," without underlining, bold, or italics.

▶ List entries alphabetically by author's last name or source title.

▶ Separate main elements by periods instead of commas.

▶ Use a hanging indent for each source, indenting all lines but the first one.

▶ List the author's name first (or title if there is no author).

▶ List the title of the source, italicized.

▶ For articles, chapters, or other source-within-a-source items, italicize the longer source, and place the shorter source in quotation marks:

Author last name, first name. "Article Title." *Journal/ Book Title. Publication.*

▶ List the place of publication, publisher name, year of publication.

▶ Double-space entries.

Alexander, John T. *Catherine the Great: Life and Legend.* New York: Oxford University Press, 1989.

Erickson, Carolly. *Alexandra: The Last Tsarina.* New York: St. Martin's
Press, 2001.

Stanton, Jay. "Royal Russians, Rubbles and Religious Rights." *The
Trouble Royals Get Into.* New York: Putnam, 1987.

For Chicago Style citations, list the author, title(s), place of publication, publisher, and year. Where relevant, also list edition or volume
(after the title). For journals and other articles, list volume, issue, and
page numbers.

One author, footnote:

1.   Benjamin Capps, *The Old West: The Indians* (New York: Time
Life Books, 1976), 45.

One author, bibliography:

Capps, Benjamin. *The Old West: The Indians.* New York: Time Life
Books, 1976.

Two authors, footnote:

1.   Wilma Flintstone and Betty Rubble, *Raising a Caveman* (New
Rock: Norstone, 1947) 233–245.

Two authors, bibliography:

Flintstone, Wilma and Betty Rubble. *Raising a Caveman.* New Rock:
Norstone, 1947.

Author with an editor, footnote:

1.   Sheridan Le Fanu, "Carmilla," *Three Vampire Tales,* ed. Anne
Williams (Boston: Houghton, 2003), 38.

Author with an editor, bibliography:

Le Fanu, Sheridan. "Carmilla." *Three Vampire Tales.* Edited by Anne
Williams. Boston: Houghton, 2003.

Editor, footnote:

1.   Richard Poust, ed., *How To Make a Sandwich* (New York:
Ballantine, 1989), 89.

Editor, bibliography:

Poust, Richard, ed. *How To Make a Sandwich.* New York:
Ballantine, 1989.

16 Citations

When citing articles, be sure to:

▶ Use quotations to set the article title apart from the title of the journal, newspaper, anthology, or other longer work.

▶ Capitalize and italicize journal titles.

▶ Place italicized volume numbers after the title, but do not separate them from the title.

▶ List issue numbers using the abbreviation "no." and follow them with the volume number, separated by a comma.

▶ List publication in parentheses.

▶ Place page numbers last, separated from the year by a colon.

Article in a journal, footnote:

1. Mary Magoulick, "Frustrating Female Heroism: Mixed Messages in Xena, Nikita, and Buffy," *Journal of Popular Culture 39*, no. 5 (2006): 729.

Article in a journal, bibliography:

Magoulick, Mary. "Frustrating Female Heroism: Mixed Messages in Xena, Nikita, and Buffy." *Journal of Popular Culture 39*, no. 5 (2006): 729.

For the most part, online sources require the same information as print items, but you also need to include the URL. If page numbers are available, list those. If not, you can add some other information that will help your readers find the information again, such as a heading, page name, paragraph number, or other identifier. In general, you'll want to list as much information as you can. If there is an author and publication date, list them. If not, put whatever other identifying information as you can. You won't generally need to include the date you accessed the material, unless the information is time-sensitive. If it's something like statistic numbers that may change over time, then include your access date.

Online periodicals, footnote:

1. Tim Sullivan, "What Happens When the Dalai Lama Dies," *Salon*, May 29, 2010, http://www.salon.com/wires/world/2010/05/29/D9G0JNEG1_tibet_s_looming_question/index.html

Online periodicals, bibliography:

Sullivan, Tim. "What Happens When the Dalai Lama Dies." *Salon.* May 29, 2010. http://www.salon.com/wires/world/2010/05/29/D9G0JNEG1_tibet_s_looming_question/index.html

Online book, footnote:

1. Ken Gelder, *Reading the Vampire* (New York: Routledge, 1994), 45–51, http://site.ebrary.com.ezproxy.nu.edu.

Online book, bibliography:

Gelder, Ken. *Reading the Vampire*. Routledge, 1994. http://site.ebrary.com.ezproxy.nu.edu/

Article or work on a Website, footnote:

1. Guy Pierce, *Professor Xavier*, http://www.xmenbios.com/full/url.

Article or work on a Website, bibliography:

Pierce, Guy. Professor Xavier. http://www.xmenbios.com/full/url.

Formatting Your Chicago Style Paper

When formatting your paper, be sure to

▶ Double-space, including long quotes.

▶ Use 1 inch margins all the way around.

▶ Center all information on title page. List the paper's title, and drop down a couple lines and enter your name. At the bottom of the page, center the class name, instructor's name, and date.

▶ Number all the pages in the right hand corner, including the title page. Don't show the number on the title page. So, the title page won't have a number on it, but the first page of your paper will be number 2.

16 Citations

▶ Check your instructor's guidelines in case he or she would like more information in the header. Some prefer your name (or just last name) or a shortened version of the title also be listed with the page number in the upper right-hand corner.

▶ For footnotes, single-space each individual note, but double-space between two notes.

Lesson 16-5: The Sciences and CSE

CSE style was formally known as CBE style (Council of Biology Editors). This system, like CMS, has different styles. But the most common is the name-author system, so that is the one discussed here. The CSE system is used for science papers, and the average high school student probably won't need to use this form of citation. However, if you are asked to use this style, you can refer to the manual *Scientific Style and Format: The CSE Manual for Authors, Editors, and Publishers, 7th edition*.

In-Text Citations

For the name-date system, you will list the last name and the publication year of your source after the appropriate information in your papers. If there is more than one author, list both last names and the pub year. If there is no author, list the first couple words of the title followed by ellipsis and the pub year:

Cavemen need to be fed at least three times a day (Flintstone 1963).

Flintstone (1963) stated that cavemen are always hungry and must be fed on a regular basis.

Cavemen's teeth should be attended to daily (Flintstone and Rubble 1963).

The article documented a fascinating study on the relationship between a dinosaur and his keeper (Dinos need love... 1963).

In your sources, be sure to:

▶ Include the author last name and first initial.

▶ List the publication year.

▶ Include the title, with only first word and proper nouns capitalized.

▶ List the publication city and state, and the publisher name.

▶ Include volume and/or issue number if appropriate.

▶ Include page numbers. If the source is a book, list the total pages in the book. If the source is an article, list the page numbers for that article.

▶ Use a hanging indent.

▶ Double-space throughout.

▶ Alphabetize by author last name (or editor or title if there is no author, whichever is listed first in the citation).

Jones M. Word nerds and the people who love them [Internet]. Seattle (WA): Sappy Books; 2001 [cited 2009 Mar. 26]; [about 156 screens]. Available from: http://websitename.com/full/url.

Johnson T. 2003. Why do I have to write essays?. New York (NY): Ballantine; 315 p.

Morrell M. In: Villiers B, editor. 2000. Red valentine teddy bears. New York (NY): Publisher Name; Vol 2: 567 p.

One author:

Johnson T. 2003. Why do I have to write essays?. New York (NY): Ballantine; 315 p.

Two authors:

Flintstone F. Rubble B. 1954. The hidden secrets of dinosaurs. New Rock (NY): Stonehenge; 320 p.

Author with an editor:

Morrell M. In: Villiers B, editor. 2000. Red valentine teddy bears. New York (NY): Publisher Name; Vol 2: 567 p.

16 Citations

Editor:

> In: Williams A, editor. 1998. Three vampire tales. New York (NY): Random House; p. 324.

For articles, list the author, title of the article, journal title, publication year, volume number, issue number if there is one (in parentheses), and the page numbers of the article:

> Smith A. 2002 Jan 13. The frozen yogurt surprise. New Yorker: 32–35.

Article in a journal:

> White S. 2002. The lack of color in milk, Science and Agriculture 32 (4): 65–71.

Online article:

> Arrillaga P. Enraged to engaged: Tea party backers explain why. [news] Salon [serial on the Internet]. 2010 June 19 [cited 2010 Aug. 23]; Available from: http://www.salon.com/wires/us/2010/06/19/D9GEEQ901_us_tea_party_enduring_activism/index.html

Online journal:

> Wong JW, Schwahn AB, Downard KM. 2010. FluTyper—an algorithm for automated typing and subtyping of the influenza virus from high resolution mass spectral data. BMC Bioinformatics [Internet]. [cited June 19, 2010]; 11:266. Available from: http://www.biomedcentral.com/1471-2105/11/266/abstract

Online book (If page numbers are available, use them. If not, list how many screens, paragraphs, pixels or whatever other information you have available):

> Jones M. Word nerds and the people who love them [Internet]. Seattle (WA): Sappy Books; 2001 [cited 2009 Mar. 26]; [about 156 screens]. Available from: http://websitename.com/full/url.

Article or work from a Website:

> Jean Plaidy. Random House Author Bios [Internet]. New York (NY): Random House; c2005. 15 April 1993 [cited June 19, 2010]; [about 2 screens]. Available from: http://www.randomhouse.com/author/results. pperl?authorid=24084.

Formatting Your CSE Paper

When formatting your CSE paper, remember to:

▶ Center everything on the title page, including the title of the paper, your name, the name of your class, and the date.

▶ Number all pages except title page. The first page of the actual paper will be page 2.

▶ Check with your instructor about other information he or she may want in the header. Some prefer a shortened form of the title or your last name by the page number.

▶ Include an abstract. For science papers, you'll often be expected to include an abstract. This is a short summary of what your paper is about.

▶ Insert headings throughout the paper. Set these apart from the rest of the text through the use of different fonts, bold font, or other designation.

▶ Use 1-inch margins all the way around. Check with your instructor for specific guidelines.

▶ Double-space.

16 Citations

17

SAT Essay

Lesson 17-1: What to Expect

The SAT essay is a timed portion of the SAT exam. You are generally given a quote or excerpt of some kind, followed by a question or questions that you will answer with your essay. You are given 25 minutes. That may not seem like much time, but remember that you are not expected to write a 30-page dissertation. You are given a limited amount of space to fill, so you can't write anything too long, even if you want to. A simple, five-paragraph essay will do. It is quality that counts here, not quantity. The graders want to see if you can deliver a clear, intelligent answer when given a specific topic. They want to see you develop your thought process and express your point of view in a smooth, logical manner.

You will also be expected to support your point of view with examples from your studies, readings, or personal experiences. For example, if the question is on whether or not euthanasia (assisted suicide) should be legalized, you could use the example of watching a neighbor die of a slow, painful disease if you are pro, or on the con side, maybe discuss how it could be abused by using Romeo and Juliet as an example. (Don't worry, you don't need to have direct quotes from texts or literature. A general knowledge will suffice.)

There are differing points of view on whether academic examples are better than personal examples. Personal experiences may make the essay more entertaining and relatable, but showcasing your academic knowledge as much as possible is also a good idea. This is an academic test, after all. Whatever you choose, be sure your examples are clear, logical, and, above all, relevant. As long as you discuss something even remotely relevant to the topic, you'll be given at least some credit. If the question is on eco-friendly products and you spend your entire essay discussing how cute Rob Pattinson is in the *Twilight* movies, you won't be getting a passing score.

Something to keep in mind: the graders are reading and scoring your essay very quickly. They aren't going over it multiple times and mulling over your literary genius. So a few well-chosen academic or personal examples should suffice.

Things You Will Be Graded On

No one expects your essay to be perfect. You aren't given enough time to make it perfect. But you will be graded on things like grammar, vocabulary, sentence structure, spelling, punctuation, the content of your essay, and whether or not you answered the question. This does not mean that you will flunk the test if you misspell a word or use a comma in the wrong place. One mistake is not going to sink you. However, an essay full of misspelled or incorrect words, weird and completely incorrect punctuation, and examples that have nothing to do with your argument will hurt you.

So, if at all possible, leave yourself a couple minutes to go back over your essay to check for these things. If you misspelled a word, neatly cross it out and write the correction above it. Things like your essay's length, organization, flow, and examples will be taken care of if you make a quick outline before you begin writing (more on this in Lesson 17-3). If you do that, then all you really need to watch for while writing is the technical stuff like spelling and word usage.

It's a lot to think about when you are trying to quickly churn out a dazzling essay, but if you do several practice runs beforehand, you will get better at editing while you write. If you take a few minutes to write an outline before you begin the essay, you won't be scrambling to come up with what you want to say, and you can pay more attention to the details as you write.

Lesson 17-2: Types of Questions You May See

As stated previously, the prompts for the essays will include some sort of quote or excerpt. This will be followed by a question or two that you will need to answer. Here are two examples similar to those you may see on the test:

1. *It is, in fact, nothing short of a miracle that the modern methods of instruction have not entirely strangled the holy curiosity of inquiry.*

—Albert Einstein

Assignment: Is an educational system based on standardized learning more or less effective than a system that encompasses more creative pursuits? Develop and write an essay answering the question above. Support your point of view with examples from your studies, knowledge, or personal experience.

2. *He has achieved success who has lived well, laughed often and loved much; who has gained the respect of intelligent men and the love of little children; who has filled his niche and accomplished his task; who has left the world better than he found it, whether by an improved poppy, a perfect poem, or a rescued soul; who has never lacked appreciation of earth's beauty or failed to express it; who has always looked for the best in others and given them the best he had; whose life was an inspiration; whose memory a benediction.*

—Bessie Stanley

17 SAT Essay

Assignment: Is the greatest success measured in monetary profits and worldly power or in more personal gains? Develop and write an essay answering the question above. Support your point of view with examples from your studies, knowledge, or personal experience.

Lesson 17-3: The Game Plan

You are only given 25 minutes to write your SAT essay. So being prepared and having a game plan is essential.

Step 1: Be Prepared

Bring everything with you that you'll need, including a watch and several sharp pencils. The watch will let you know how much time you've got before the "pencils down" call. Go through several practice runs before test day. Use the examples in this chapter or go to sites like Majortests.com or Collegeboard.com to find example questions. Set your timer and practice writing the essay. The more you do this, the easier it will be for you to quickly organize your thoughts when it comes time to do it for real.

Practicing writing a timed essay will also help take the pressure off when you sit down to do it for a grade. If you have never written an essay under the pressure of a ticking timer, your nerves may get the best of you. Practice may not make perfect, but it does make you prepared. And being prepared will vastly improve your performance.

Step 2: Outline

With such a short time frame, this may seem like an unnecessary and frivolous step. But nothing could be further from the truth. In fact, I'd say doing an outline is the most important thing you can do for yourself. If you take a few minutes to get your thoughts organized, you'll be able to quickly write your essay. You won't have to take precious time after you've started writing to think about what comes next, because you'll already know. Your essay will be a logically organized, well-thought-out answer instead of a jumbled mess of words.

Take a piece of scratch paper, or use the "scratch paper" area on the test booklet. Take a minute to think about what you want to say and what examples you want to use. Then make a very brief outline. Just jot down a few words for each section to prompt you.

For example, you open your test booklet and see the second example, on page 293 of this book. What do you do?

1. Decide what position you want to take. What is your answer to the question?

2. For our example, we'll argue the position that personal success brings more happiness.

3. Quickly brainstorm examples to support your position. Try to get at least one academic example. You do not need to write these down unless you want to. Just try to think of several examples you could include in your essay that would be good for the essay.
   a. An actor with money, fame, and power recently committed suicide.
   b. King Lear was a king, with money, fame, and power and look how he turned out.
   c. Another academic example
   d. A personal example
   e. Opposing side—Bill Gates seems like a pretty happy guy

4. Decide which type of essay you want to do.

There are lots of different types of essays you can write, and if you have the ability to come up with an intelligent, perfectly flowing compare and contrast essay or enough memorized examples to belt out an entire literary analysis that is relevant to the question asked, by all means go for it.

However, under high-pressure situations such as this, it might be best to stick with a "simpler is better" approach. When it comes to the SAT essay, you generally want to try and aim for the basic essay

17 SAT Essay

format: an introduction, a three-paragraph body, and a conclusion. If you get to the fourth paragraph and find you have an extra few minutes, you can always add another paragraph. For the SAT essay, there are a couple of good ways of presenting your information:

The One-Example Essay

For this essay, you would choose only one of your examples from your brainstorming list, and you will develop it over the course of your essay. So your essay would look something like this:

Paragraph 1:   Introduction

Paragraph 2:   Present example one

Paragraph 3:   Develop that example

Paragraph 4:   Explanation or refute opposing example

Paragraph 5:   Conclusion

This type of essay is a good one to choose if you have a really good academic example that you can fully develop. For our example, we can use King Lear. So our outline might look like this:

Paragraph 1:   Introduction

Paragraph 2:   King Lear had money, fame, and power and thought he could buy happiness and love.

Paragraph 3:   Instead, the daughters who exhibited the qualities he valued rejected him and turned him out, while the daughter who rejected his values was the one that truly loved him.

Paragraph 4:   King Lear learned his lesson.

Paragraph 5:   Conclusion: King Lear was not happy. Therefore, money, fame, and power can't buy happiness.

The Multiple-Example Essay

This type is good to choose if you can think of several good examples you'd like to present or if you can't think of a really good academic example to fully expand. A three-example essay would look something like this:

Paragraph 1: Introduction: Classical literature shows us that money, fame, and power can't buy happiness.

Paragraph 2: Example one: *King Lear*

Paragraph 3: Example two: *The Great Gatsby*

Paragraph 4: Example three or opposing example: The recent example of the actor who seemed to have everything but committed suicide OR Bill Gates seems like a happy guy.

Paragraph 5: Conclusion

Including an opposing argument that you would refute shows that you can see both sides of the argument and gives you further opportunity to show the strength of your argument, by discussing why the opposing side is wrong. You can do this either in the body of the essay or in the conclusion as part of the wrap-up. This doesn't have to be a major production, but just a brief, one-line "Some may argue this, but their argument is incorrect because of this."

Step 3: Write

Once you've thought about what you are going to say and have taken a minute to write down a few notes, you are ready to write your essay. Take a deep breath, refer to your outline to keep yourself on track and organized, and go!

Lesson 17-4: Important Points to Remember
Bring a Watch

This sounds trivial, but it is a great help to be able to look down and see if you've got time to add that extra paragraph or if you need to speed things up a bit.

Answer the Question

Many students focus on the quote or excerpt that is given before the question. This is *not* what you are supposed to do. You are meant to answer the question that is asked after the excerpt. You can use the quote or excerpt as a starting-off point, but it's there more for inspiration. The only wrong answer you can give is one that is irrelevant. An essay that completely ignores the question asked will get a score of zero. So whatever you do, whatever type of essay you choose to write, however many of whatever type of examples you use, be sure they are relevant and answer the question!

Be Neat

If you make a mistake, it's okay to cross it out. In fact, it's better to cross it out than to leave a mistake in the essay. But do it as neatly as possible. Also try to keep your handwriting as clear as possible. This is where practicing ahead of time might be useful. Your graders have a lot of essays to get through in a short amount of time. If your essay is sloppy and hard to read, it's not going to help your grade. After all, your graders can't give you top marks on your awesome essay if they can't read what you are trying to say.

Be Organized

Make sure your essay is organized, flowing smoothly from your introduction, from one example to the next, and into your conclusion. This is why you should take the time to make notes or a rough outline before you begin to write your essay. Keep it simple. Follow the formats discussed in this chapter: introduction, examples, conclusion. Your essay will earn lower marks if your ideas are disjointed and poorly organized. Taking a few minutes beforehand to gather your thoughts can be the difference between full marks or a low score.

Sample Essay

We who lived in concentration camps can remember the men who walked through the huts comforting others, giving away their last piece of bread. They may have been few in number, but they offer sufficient proof that everything can be taken from a man but one thing: the last of human freedoms—to choose one's attitude in any given set of circumstances—to choose one's own way.

—Victor Frankl

Assignment: Do circumstances determine whether or not we have a choice? Develop and write an essay answering the question above. Support your point of view with examples from your studies, knowledge, or personal experience.

Outline

Position: No, we always have some sort of choice so the circumstance does NOT determine whether or not we have a choice.

I.   Intro: Circumstances only determine the consequences of our choices, not whether or not we have them.

II. The Ten Boom sisters in *The Hiding Place* (a book the author of this essay read for a book report in one of her classes)

III. Kate from *Taming of the Shrew*

IV. Personal experience—having surgery

V.   Conclusion: As you can see, attitude and consequences determined the choices, but there are choices in all situations.

Note: This mini-outline probably took a minute or two of thought and another minute or two to write it down. So, in five minutes or less, the author has a clear idea of what she wants to discuss and 20 or more minutes to get it done. Be sure to take the time to organize your thoughts before you write your essay.

Every situation comes with a set of choices. It is the consequence of our choice that determines our fate, not the situation itself. Throughout history there have been examples of historical figures and literary characters who found choices in seemingly hopeless situations, from Cleopatra choosing death over slavery in Rome, to Captain Ahab choosing to spend his life in a fruitless vendetta against a white whale. Even the direst of circumstances offer some sort of choice.

A good example of this can be found in *The Hiding Place*. In this story, the Ten Boom sisters describe with chilling detail the atrocities they were made to suffer as prisoners of a concentration camp. Faced with such a horrible situation, many found themselves devoid of hope. One of the sisters rails against the cruelty of their circumstances. The other sister chooses a different path. When many falter, she remains true to her faith and chooses to be thankful for everything that happened, even for the lice. Those lice end up keeping the guards away, making the lives of the afflicted a little more bearable. She could not choose the situation in which she found herself, but she could choose how she would react.

We can find several such examples in classical literature as well. In *The Taming of the Shrew*, Katrina is forced to marry Petrucio. She has no choice in the situation, but she does have a choice in how she will react. She chooses to behave like a shrew. It is not until her attitude about her circumstance changes that she begins to find happiness. Her situation, being forced into marriage, never changed. It was in the consequences of her behavior that Katrina found her choices.

I have experienced this in my own life as well. A few years ago, I was told I'd need surgery to correct a bone that had set incorrectly. As a minor, I had no choice in whether or not I'd have the procedure done. My parents made that decision for me. But I did have a choice in how I went into the situation. I could have made a bad situation worse with a horrible or fearful attitude. Instead, I chose to make the best of it. Going into surgery with a smile on my face was not easy, but it made a situation I could not change more bearable.

Our lives are filled with unexpected and undesired circumstances, yet we will always have a choice in our actions and attitudes and, as a result, in the consequences of those actions. One of my favorite movie scenes is from *Dangerous Minds*, when the class is discussing the Bob Dylan song, "Tambourine Man." One student makes the observation that if someone shot you, you didn't have a choice in whether or not you died, but you did have a choice in whether or not you'd go down screaming. Circumstances do not determine whether or not we have a choice, because there is always a choice to be made.

18

Taking It One Step Further

Lesson 18-1: Be Economical

E.B. White, the author of *Charlotte's Web*, said that you should "omit needless words" and make "every word tell." Reading can be difficult. The last thing you want to do is make your audience work harder than necessary when reading your material. Inflating your writing with unnecessary words and descriptions won't make you sound more intelligent; it will make your writing tedious. So, how can you be economical in your writing? Be wise with your word choices.

Don't say more than you need to in order to get your point across. Be concise and to the point. Avoid going off on tangents that are only marginally relevant to your topic. Rambling on forever will only create more work for you and bore your reader.

Avoid false verbal limbs. Basically, a false verbal limb is a phrase that crams as many words as possible into a sentence in order to make it sound more important. Politicians are *great* at these. In fact, the next time a politician or CEO of a company that just had a major goof has a press conference, you'll be sure to hear a speech full of them.

For example:

> With respect to the egregious tragedy that occurred on the night of the twentieth in the past week, we at Generic Airlines general headquarters have reached the consensus that prior to beginning the pre-boarding process, the parents of the aforementioned unruly child allowed said child to run about the fuselage of the airplane in question with his canine companion, that was, at the time, infected with the rabies virus of the type species Lyssavirus genus. In view of the fact that many questions remain unanswered and are deserving of serious consideration in order to bring this unfortunate incident to a satisfactory conclusion, we will refrain from making further comment at this particular point in time.

It would be just as acceptable, and make a lot more sense, if they would just say:

> We decided that last week's tragedy started before everyone got on the plane with an unruly child and his rabies-infected dog. Because we don't know all the answers, we won't make any more comments right now.

Bottom line, avoid doing this to your readers. No one should have to work that hard to decipher the meaning of your sentences.

Don't use complex words and phrases when a more simple word will do. A phrase such as "undeniably the most eye-catchingly beautiful person ever" is unnecessary when a simple "attractive" works just as well. Remember: No one wants to have a dictionary in one hand and your work in another. This does not mean you can't use "smarter"-sounding words. But don't go overboard. For example:

> The new kid was the smartest kid in class.
>
> (Simple and informal, but okay.)

> The new student was the most intelligent of his classmates.
>
> (Good. More formal, "bigger" words, but doesn't go overboard.)

> The émigré was by far the most mentally astute of all the peers in his social assemblage.
>
> (Over the top.)

Avoid repeating yourself. Repeating the same thing over and over won't drive your point home; it will drive your reader away. Say it once and move on. Don't say the same thing time and time again. Repetition for repetition's sake is bad. (See, you got my point with the first sentence. No need for the rest of them!)

Lesson 18-2: Keep It Active

Passive writing will happen every now and then, but one passive sentence after another will put your reader to sleep. The good news: Most word-processing programs will highlight passive sentences for you. You just need to keep an eye out for them. Here are a few examples:

> Passive: I was standing on the beach.
> Active: I stood on the beach.
>
> Passive: It is believed to cause cancer.
> Active: Researchers believe it causes cancer.
>
> Passive: Shots are prepared by nurses.
> Active: Nurses prepare shots.

Lesson 18-3: Make It Matter

When writing a an essay, research paper, or even a letter, it's not good enough to just regurgitate facts. There has to be a point to everything you are writing.

Say you send a letter to the editor of your local paper. You write, "In last week's edition of 'What's Happening Now' the name of the local high school was misspelled." The editor might look at that and think, "So what?" Make sure you are including the "so what." For example. "Dear Editor, your spelling error last week will cause many out-of-state alumni to miss the reunion announcement." Ah. Now the editor has a reason to care.

Or say you are writing an essay on the decline of the cat face spider population in a small desert town. So what? Those terrified of spiders would probably sit up and cheer at this news; make them care.

18
Taking It One
Step Further

"The cat face spider, though terrifyingly ugly, is very useful. It helps keep the population of other spiders down. With the decline in the cat face population, the populations of other species of spiders will rise." Okay, *now* they care. They would probably rather have one big, ugly, nasty-looking spider than a whole ton of other species.

Lesson 18-4: Be Gender-Inclusive

The last thing you want to do when writing is to alienate some of your readers. Use neutral terms such as firefighter instead of fireman, or humanity instead of mankind. Additionally, avoid sexist language. Use "he" or "she," alternate between the two with your examples, or just rewrite to avoid gender all together. When using hypothetical examples, case studies, or other situations, make sure the examples include both sexes:

> A doctor practicing medicine in the state of Texas may need to increase his insurance coverage. A surgeon offering her services free of charge for qualifying patients might be able to claim additional tax credits.

> Surgeons offering services free of charge for qualifying patients might be able to claim additional tax credits.

Though you are to be gender-inclusive, only use "they" when referring to plural nouns, and not singular ones:

Do: It may take passengers several hours to get through airport security. They will need to remove their shoes, go through several check points, and have their luggage inspected.

Don't: A teacher in the California school system must make sure they have all their papers in order before applying for their license.

Lesson 18-5: Be Logical

Above all, your paper, letter, article, blog post, or anything else you may write must make sense. You must be consistent. Don't start your paper arguing for one side and then switch to the other midstream. Be sure there aren't any obvious inconsistencies in your arguments.

Don't compare the incomparable. Avoid phrases such as *more perfect* and *less than nothing*. Perfect is as good as it gets, and unless you are discussing math equations, you can't have less than nothing.

Don't mix your metaphors. Metaphors can be powerful and wonderful things, but if you start mixing them, all you have is a confusing mess. Also, be careful when using metaphors. You don't want your work peppered with clichés.

Hit the nail on the head.

(Good, but it's a cliché.)

She was madder than a puppy with a kink in his tail.

(Good.)

If we can hit that bull's eye, then the rest of the dominoes will fall like a house of cards.

(From *Futurama*—funny, but bad on so many levels. Don't mix metaphors like this!)

Lesson 18-6: Know Your Audience

It is very important to know your audience. You need to tailor your work for the readers you are addressing. It wouldn't be appropriate to fill an article for grade schoolers with vulgar language or use overly simplistic vocabulary in a paper for your master's level course.

Keep your language appropriate. If you are writing for a group of young children, use small, simple words and sentences. If you are writing an article for a scientific journal, it's probably safe to flaunt your vocabulary a little more. However, don't fill your work with foreign words, technical jargon, or other such examples unless you are writing for peers or colleagues who will understand to what you are referring.

Define the terms you use, include well-thought-out explanations, and put your quotations in context. Don't assume your readers already know everything you are talking about. However, be sure you don't go too far and over-explain. This is where knowing your audience comes in handy. You want to be sure your readers understand the point you are trying to get across without insulting their intelligence. For example a sentence such as "The United States of America began as a group of colonies, territories that were under the jurisdiction of the British Empire," gives a brief description of the word *colonies*. It defines the term for anyone who might not know it, without diving so far into an explanation that those who do know what it means are irritated.

In general, pay attention to your word choices. If you want to make a simple sentence a little more formal, choose more formal words. If you need to make a very formal paper more understandable and relatable for a younger or less-informed audience, change the vocabulary in the piece to words that everyone understands. Only use as many words as necessary to get your point across. Repeating yourself or adding excess words just to fluff up your work isn't going to do you any good. Keep those sentences active! Be sure they make sense and remember to keep your work appropriate for the audience you are addressing. If you keep in mind these few tips, you'll be able to tailor any piece of writing for any audience.

18 Taking It One Step Further

Exercise 1-1

1. You should record the information, paraphrase, or quote you will be using, plus all relevant publication information, such as the author and title of the source, the publisher and its location, the publication year, the page numbers where the information can be found, and all relevant online information.

2. It is the sentence that will define the focus, or main point, of your paper by making a specific claim or argument that the rest of the paper will support.

3. Make a list, make notes, and make an outline.

Exercise 2-1

1. The main components are introduction, the body of the essay, and the conclusion.

2. The introduction should include some general information about the topic and the thesis statement.

3. The conclusion should include a restatement of the thesis and a summary of the evidence presented.

Exercise 3-1

1. Step 1: Choose a topic; Step 2: Make a pro and con list; Step 3: Research.

2. 1) Introduction, 2) Supporting arguments and evidence, 3) Opposing argument and refuting evidence, 4) Conclusion.

3. The point of this essay is to persuade the reader to agree with your point of view regarding the subject matter of the essay.

Answer Key

Exercise 4-1

1. It analyzes a topic in terms of what caused it and what effects happened as a result.

2. Information can be organized in chronological order, by order of importance, or by category.

3. A chain reaction is when one event triggers a series of effects.

Exercise 5-1

1. It explores and analyzes a work.

2. Sources should include examples from the work itself, evidence from the author, and outside sources that have discussed the work in question.

3. The introduction should include the title and author of the work being analyzed, an introduction to the topic of the paper, your position on the topic, some background information on the work or author, and a summary of the evidence that will be discussed.

Exercise 6-1

1. Method 1 compares all the similarities together, contrasts all the differences together, and forms a conclusion. Method 2 presents all information on one subject, presents all information on the second subject, compares and contrasts, and forms a conclusion.

2. Both women had similar backgrounds, upbringings, arranged marriages, and relationships with their families and the Russian people.

3. Catherine had more problems with the court and her in-laws after her children were born, as opposed to Alexandra, whose problems were never-ending. Also, Catherine was more savvy politically. The greatest difference is in the deaths of the women.

Exercise 7-1

1. It fully defines a topic using more than the dictionary definition.

2. Narrow down the topic.

3. The elements are introduction and thesis, all the aspects of the full definition, and the conclusion.

Exercise 8-1

1. The descriptive essay describes a person, place, object, experience, or event in detail.

2. What am I going to describe? Why do I want to describe it?

3. Fill it with vivid detail and use the five senses.

Exercise 9-1

1. Division and classification essays investigate a topic by dividing it into categories and describing the significance of each.

2. It divides the topic into smaller categories.

3. It takes the divided categories and further separates them into more specialized groups.

Exercise 10-1

1. This essay tries to persuade a reader to the author's point of view by evaluating a work. Book and movie reviews are two examples.

2. Opinions should be presented in a neutral, non-aggressive, and logical tone.

3. Statistics, quotes, articles, charts, and examples from the subject being evaluated.

Exercise 11-1

1. It looks at a theme or element of a particular work and tries to discover the meaning behind it.

2. Discussions can be about imagery, characters, plot, themes, social commentary in the book, settings, time periods, and symbolism.

3. A little background information to help place the examples in context should be included.

Exercise 12-1

1. It tells the story of a person or event.

2. Who, what, when, where, why, and how.

3. It introduces the topic and lets the reader know what type of story he or she will be reading.

Answer Key

Books

The Chicago Manual of Style, 16th ed. (University of Chicago Press, 2010).

Critical Theory Today: A User-Friendly Guide, 2nd Edition. by Lois Tyson (Routledge, 2006)

The CSE Manual for Authors, Editors, and Publishers, 7th Edition. (Council of Science Editors, 2006)

Homework Helpers: English Language and Composition by Maureen Lindner. (Career Press, 2005).

Manual for Writers of Research Papers, Theses, and Dissertations, 7th Edition. (University of Chicago Press, 2007).

MLA Handbook for Writers of Research Papers, 7th Edition. (Modern Language Association of America, 2009).

The Official SAT Study Guide, 4th Edition. (College Board, 2004).

Publication Manual of the American Psychological Association, 6th Edition. (American Psychological Association, 2009).

Websites

APA Website: *www.apa.org*

CMS Website (available through subscription): *www.chicagomanualofstyle.org*

MLA Website: *www.mla.org*

For SAT information and practice: *http://sat.collegeboard.com/practice*

Index

MICHELLE MCLEAN is a freelance writer and the chief editorial consultant for PixelMags, LLC, a company that digitizes magazines and other literature for use on the iPhone, iPad, iPod Touch, and other mobile devices. She earned a bachelor of science degree in history from Weber State University and a master of arts degree with distinction in English from National University. She maintains a blog, Michelle McLean's Writer Ramblings, which appeals to students and writers of all ages, backgrounds, genres, and educational levels who desire to fully understand their assignments. She spends her time writing and teaching beginning writers the ropes. Ms. McLean resides in Pennsylvania with her husband and two children.

About the Author